MW00581986

Leading Lean

Ensuring Success and Developing a Framework for Leadership

Jean Dahl

Beijing · Boston · Farnham · Sebastopol · Tokyo

Leading Lean

by Jean Dahl

Copyright © 2020 Agility1 Consulting, LLC. All rights reserved.

Printed in the United States of America.

Published by O'Reilly Media, Inc., 1005 Gravenstein Highway North, Sebastopol, CA 95472.

O'Reilly books may be purchased for educational, business, or sales promotional use. Online editions are also available for most titles (*http://oreilly.com*). For more information, contact our corporate/institutional sales department: 800-998-9938 or *corporate@oreilly.com*.

Acquisitions Editor: Melissa Duffield	**Indexer:** WordCo Indexing Services, Inc.
Development Editor: Alicia Young	**Interior Designer:** David Futato
Production Editor: Kristen Brown	**Cover Designer:** Karen Montgomery
Copyeditor: O'Reilly Production Services	**Illustrators:** Rebecca Demarest and Rob
Proofreader: Arthur Johnson	Romano

January 2020:   First Edition

Revision History for the First Edition
2019-12-19:   First Release

See *http://oreilly.com/catalog/errata.csp?isbn=9781492046295* for release details.

978-1-492-04629-5

[LSC]

Contents

Foreword. V

Preface. IX

Chapter 1
Overcoming Today's Crisis in Leadership 1

Chapter 2
The Modern Lean Framework™ 21

Chapter 3
Leading Self 37

Chapter 4
Leading Others 57

Chapter 5
Leading Outside In 101

Chapter 6
Leading Enterprise Wide 137

Chapter 7
Leading Innovation 175

Chapter 8
Leading Culture 209

Chapter 9
Becoming a Self-Led Lean Leader 263

Index 297

Foreword

A few years ago, I published my second book, *The Startup Way: How Modern Companies Use Entrepreneurial Management to Transform Culture and Drive Long-Term Growth*. It's both an acknowledgment and an exploration of the many directions Lean Startup has traveled in beyond tech startups and Silicon Valley. Running experiments and processes such as building minimum viable products, following the build-measure-learn cycle, and metered funding have been applied to more kinds of problems than I could ever have envisioned, including in large, long-established companies that are looking to stay vital and relevant in a new world of business. On the surface, these enterprises would seem to have little in common with the other kinds of organizations in which Lean Startup has taken hold—small, newly formed startups, startups that have experienced massive growth, government entities, and nonprofits, to name just a few. But despite their differences in mission and scope, these organizations share a crucial similarity: the people who run them know that adaptability is the key to success in the 21st century.

In other words: leadership.

I've had a lot of conversations with people trying to bring innovation to their companies. These conversations tend to go like this: employees with high-potential new ideas about how to tackle all sorts of issues—from industry-wide reinventions to societal problems or the way their company IT systems work—tell me that they have no way to act on them.

They're trapped in old 20th-century corporate structures upheld by people who, while they no doubt have good intentions, are themselves trapped by a combination of complacency and fear. These leaders are doing what they've always done, even as the stakes of not changing become greater every day. Sometimes they authorize the creation of a separate innovation project or team, but it's never really integrated into the company as a whole and as a result tends to be short-lived. The company culture, and the leaders' roles within it, remain untouched.

These leaders are in denial about both the enormous, rapid changes taking place in the world of work and the importance and influence of their positions. By failing to set an example of openness to change and awareness that responsiveness is crucial, they discourage the very people needed to help their companies evolve, creating stagnation instead of dynamism and, ultimately, the demise of the business.

I've seen it more times than I can count, and so has Jean Dahl, which is why she's written this comprehensive guide to what leaders need to do to truly foster innovation and responsiveness. The process starts, like most transformation, within themselves and their attitudes and actions. From there, it moves outward to take into account the input of their colleagues and communities so that they're prepared to respond equally to disruption or opportunity.

This cultural and structural change is critical. Outdated ways of thinking, in turn, create organizational cultures that are hostile to innovation and responsiveness at the very moment when those qualities matter more than ever. As Jean discusses, the leaders we need now are problem solvers first and foremost, who must be acutely focused on creating and delivering value for the benefit of the ecosystem they exist within.

Let me dwell for a second on what "ecosystem" means. For decades, the only stakeholders companies really needed to worry about were their shareholders. As long as profits were up, business went on as usual. That's no longer true. The world is evolving so quickly that "business as usual" literally no longer exists. Today's usual is tomorrow's obsolete.

It's also no longer enough for companies to have nothing but their bottom line in mind. We know that majorities of people want to work for and buy from companies that are focused not just on profit, but on benefiting the world in which they operate. That includes their employees, their customers, their communities, and even the planet we all share. We also know that companies that think and act this way are just as financially successful as those who don't, so there's no argument for acting any other way. True leaders see clearly the needs of everyone they serve, see when those needs are shifting, and act accordingly.

That's where this book comes in. It gathers together all the information and tools you need to lead both structurally and philosophically, so you can help guide your organization into the next phase of success. The end goal is to create a cycle of continuous innovation in all the processes and products of your company so that it's ready to face whatever changes and challenges come its way. That means paying attention at all times to the information coming in, whether it's from customers, employees, or society at large.

Modern leadership is about providing opportunities and fostering partnerships based on trust. It also requires building a comprehensive strategic plan that takes the need for continuous innovation seriously. This book will show you both why those things are true and how to accomplish them.

—*Eric Ries*
October 2019

Preface

Why *Leading Lean*?

In today's world, change is all around us. Higher and higher levels of volatility, uncertainty, complexity, and ambiguity (VUCA) are the "new normal." Today's leaders must recognize—both within their organizations as well as themselves—the need to continuously evolve in order to stave off extinction and deliver value to their customers.

Leading Lean is a call to action for leaders looking to meet these 21st-century leadership challenges head-on. This book gives you practical methods, tools, and strategies to lead an empowered workforce capable of embracing and achieving fast, flexible decision making. You will learn how to take advantage of the opportunities change brings to ensure long-term success by creating value at every level of your organization.

Chapter 1, *Overcoming Today's Crisis in Leadership*, discusses how embracing agility can empower you to overcome the roadblocks that a 21st century leader faces. Chapter 2, *The Modern Lean Framework™*, introduces you to a framework influenced by the practices and principles of the Toyota Motor Corporation (as well as the work of the Lean luminaries Daniel T. Jones, Jeffery Liker, Eric Reis, Daniel Roos, and James Womack) designed to help you develop and perfect your Lean leadership skills and abilities.

Chapter 3, *Leading Self*, takes a closer look at how leaders can cultivate a healthy mentality for leadership by understanding the skills and abilities necessary to lead one's self, as well as becoming a servant-leader to others. With that foundation, Chapter 4, *Leading Others*, then discusses the necessity for Lean leaders to help continuously develop the people they serve by employing the Toyota Business Practices (TBP) method for problem solving and continuous improvement, as well as offering guidance for on-the-job development (OJD) strategies. It also presents a case study of an organization that undertook implementing Lean principles and methods to turn its business around.

Chapter 5, *Leading Outside In*, addresses the importance of leading a customer-centric company and provides you with tools to build an omnichannel customer experience strategy (OCXS). Chapter 6, *Leading Enterprise Wide*, helps you develop a strategic roadmap that aligns your enterprise with your customer, stakeholder, and company needs, and Chapter 7, *Leading Innovation*, follows that discussion with a look at how to foster innovation and continuous improvement through creating disruptive products/services.

Culture is integral to the success of a Lean organization, which is why Chapter 8, *Leading Culture*, provides you with the Leading Culture dimension of the Modern Lean Framework™, which is a set of beliefs, values, behaviors, and actions that represent the cultural elements of a Lean enterprise that you can adapt to work best for your enterprise. Finally, Chapter 9, *Becoming a Self-Led Lean Leader*, brings all of these principles and practices together with advice on how to move forward as the leader your organization, your workforce, and your stakeholders and customers deserve.

As you read this book, remember that you will experience just as many failures as successes on the journey toward Lean leadership. Acknowledge and view failure as just one more way you now know will *not* work, then adjust, move forward, and try again—and do celebrate your successes! When something goes well, take time to reflect and understand how you achieved that success.

Now, let's get you started on the path toward Lean leadership!

O'Reilly Online Learning

NOTE

For more than 40 years, *O'Reilly Media* has provided technology and business training, knowledge, and insight to help companies succeed.

Our unique network of experts and innovators share their knowledge and expertise through books, articles, conferences, and our online learning platform. O'Reilly's online learning platform gives you on-demand access to live training courses, in-depth learning paths, interactive coding environments, and a vast collection of text and video from O'Reilly and 200+ other publishers. For more information, please visit *http://oreilly.com*.

How to Contact Us

Please address comments and questions concerning this book to the publisher:

O'Reilly Media, Inc.
1005 Gravenstein Highway North
Sebastopol, CA 95472
800-998-9938 (in the United States or Canada)
707-829-0515 (international or local)
707-829-0104 (fax)

We have a web page for this book, where we list errata, examples, and any additional information. You can access this page at *https://oreil.ly/leadingLean*.

Email *bookquestions@oreilly.com* to comment or ask technical questions about this book.

For more information about our books, courses, conferences, and news, see our website at *http://www.oreilly.com*.

Find us on Facebook: *http://facebook.com/oreilly*

Follow us on Twitter: *http://twitter.com/oreillymedia*

Watch us on YouTube: *http://www.youtube.com/oreillymedia*

Acknowledgments

This book would not have been possible without all of the pioneers and continued explorers who have dedicated their careers to advancing the body of knowledge that we today call "Lean." In particular, I'd like to thank Dan Jones, Dan Roos, and Jim Womack, who wrote the groundbreaking book that started it all, *The Machine that Changed the World*, and the Womack and Jones book *Lean Thinking: Banish Waste and Create Wealth in Your Corporation* (Free Press) that defined the principles of Lean thinking. That, in addition to Jeffery Liker's series of books on The Toyota Way, ranging in topics from service excellence, continuous improvement, and Lean leadership; were very influential and impactful in helping me synthesize my thoughts and led me down the path of writing *Leading Lean*. And of course, a special thanks to Eric Ries as series editor and modern day Lean leader who brought Lean into the 21st century by starting a movement that continues to evolve and grow today.

And to all my colleagues who listened to my ideas and offered advice and input. I greatly appreciate you undertaking this journey with me. I thank everyone who took the time to review the book, especially Daniel Jones, Evan

Leybourn, Eric Ries, and Brian Reffell. Your input strengthened the content and helped to produce an outstanding finished product.

I'd also like to acknowledge the impact that Robert Greenleaf's work in the area of servant leadership had in forming the cornerstone of my belief system on self-leadership and serving both myself and others to the best of my servant leader abilities. I believe that in today's 21st century global economy, now more than ever, we need self-led Lean servant leaders who can contribute and move the world forward in the best possible way.

I would also like to thank all of my friends and family who encouraged and supported me during the creation of the book. When O'Reilly Media approached me about writing it, I didn't think I fully understood the level of commitment and effort I was signing up for, in my zeal to contribute to the Lean community. Behind every writer is a village, and I want to say a big thank you to everyone who lives in mine (and for your sacrifices as well). I greatly appreciate all that you do in supporting and encouraging me.

And finally, I would like to thank O'Reilly Media for all of your help in bringing this book into reality. In particular, Laurel Ruma, Melissa Duffield, Alicia Young, and Kristen Brown. You all rock and you made this process so much easier...thank you and write on!

CHAPTER 1

Overcoming Today's Crisis in Leadership

Putting the customer first is at the heart of Lean. Everything a Lean leader does must be driven by the goal of filling your customers' unmet wants, needs, and/or desires. If that's not happening, you're not creating and delivering value. Are you just going through the motions, thinking what you do is value-driven? How do you know whether or not you're moving toward your True North—that is, whether you're accomplishing your vision through mission and purpose and fulfilling your value proposition?

The greatest challenges a Lean leader faces today spring forth from these questions because the meaning of *customers* is very broad in the world of Lean. They can be the employees who create and deliver your products/services, the customers who buy and consume them, and those in your community, your country, and yes, even the world (known as stakeholders) who are impacted by their existence—in other words, the Lean ecosystem that you as a leader call your "world." That means your perspective needs to be far-reaching and not colored only by what is right in front of you.

It also means embracing agility and understanding that you must learn to effectively respond and adjust to change through continuous improvement and evolution. When you stop improving and evolving, the game is over and complacency sets in. Over 40% of all companies today will cease to exist within the next 10 years.[1] Will your company be one that survives and thrives, or will

1 Julie Bort, "Retiring Cisco CEO Delivers Dire Prediction: 40% of Companies Will Be Dead in 10 Years" (*https://oreil.ly/WeiWS*), Business Insider, June 9, 2015.

it be a statistic? The choice is yours to act now to overcome the challenges that face you by "leaning out" your organization to effectively respond to change so that you can survive and thrive in the 21st century.

This chapter focuses on the issues facing Lean leaders and arms you with the appropriate context as you progress through the rest of the book.

Delivering Customer Value: An Enterprise's Ultimate Goal

As Eric Ries states in his book *The Lean Startup* (Crown Publishing Group), "The Lean Startup method [hypothesis-driven product development] builds capital-efficient companies because it allows startups [innovators in general] to recognize that it's time to pivot sooner, creating less waste of time and money."[2] Experimenting with your product/service ideas leads to winning products/services that generate value for your customers, stakeholders, and of course your company.

Therefore, Lean leaders must be keenly focused on winning the hearts and minds of their customers by:

- Delivering products/services your customers deem valuable

- Serving your customers well so your organization maintains a healthy, ongoing relationship with them

- Ensuring the organization stays ahead of your customers' ever-changing unmet wants, needs, and/or desires, as well as competitive market conditions, by taking the time to truly understand what creates and delivers value

However, the digitalization of products/services and of the channels through which they are marketed, sold, and delivered requires a much more holistic enterprise approach. Gone are the days when leaders could hide from their customers. Leaders must be engaged and interact with customers, leading teams that solve both customer and company problems. The product/service development process must be a holistic representation that assembles team members from throughout the entire organization into high-performing teams that understand how to identify and create value and how to then move rapidly toward developing and delivering it.

---

2 Eric Ries, *The Lean Startup: How Today's Entrepreneurs Use Continuous Innovation to Create Radically Successful Businesses* (New York: Crown Business, 2011), 78.

Defining Value

From a customer standpoint, value comes from a product/service of the highest quality that's provided to the market at the right time and at an appropriate price and fulfills some unmet want, need, and/or desire, creating and delivering value when consumed. For both the customer and the company, the value created must be greater than the investment made. Your responsibility as a Lean leader is to ensure this equation is monitored from both a customer and a company perspective and to ensure that waste is not created by allowing investment to exceed value realization. When that happens, the product/service is no longer viable from either party's perspective.

But how is value identified, created, and delivered? For you as a Lean leader, this is a much trickier question to answer. When there are many teams, products/services, and business units, the process of value delivery becomes more and more difficult.

Organizations create and deliver value in two distinct ways:

1. By pushing products/services out to customers, known as an *inside-out approach*, where value is defined from within the organization and customers have little say in the products/services that reach them.

2. From an *outside-in perspective*,[3] where the organization initiates product/service ideation and definition by working with customers and asking them what ideas would be valuable to them. This process pulls customers' requirements through the production system or development process instead of pushing products/services out to the market with very little customer interaction.

The inside-out approach is a more traditional, push-based value creation and delivery system. The outside-in approach is a pull-based system. The flow of value identification starts with the customer and the product management organization working together by pulling ideas and enhancements from the customer through face-to-face discussions, product feedback loops, surveys, focus groups, analytics, etc., and by defining what is most important, relevant, and valuable to them. The team—comprised of product/service management, manufacturing/technology, and operations—evaluates and prioritizes the input, designing the product/service guided by the data collected from customers. The team then develops and delivers the highest-priority features first. When customers make a purchase and then consume/use it, value is created for both the

---

3 George S. Day and Christine Moorman, *Strategy from the Outside In: Profiting from Customer Value* (New York: McGraw-Hill, 2010), 5.

customers and the company in the form of satisfied customer wants, needs, and/or desires and revenue generation or company value. This creates a win/win situation for all involved.

For many companies, allowing the customer to lead and working in holistic product/service teams represent a major shift. However, you must do everything in your power to remain acutely focused on your customers, driving the delivery of customer-centric products/services they find valuable.

Recognizing the Crisis in Leadership Today

The Internet of Things (IoT) has ushered in the age of global, speed-of-light competition. To keep up and stay competitive in a digitally enabled world, leaders must adopt new ways of organizing, executing, and evolving. Allowing these old ways to linger stifles your company's ability to evolve, which directly impacts its ability to remain relevant and competitive in today's global economy. Worse yet, quick fixes that will magically transform your company and bring about new ways of working overnight are simply the stuff of fairy tales.

Unfortunately, leaders of this type openly aspire to mimic what they perceive to be the overnight success stories of companies like Amazon, Google, and Airbnb. Meanwhile, they haven't changed a single thing about themselves or their companies, yet they expect, and even think they deserve, different results. It's unrealistic to think that a giant corporation that has been around for years is going to change everything about itself overnight!

Start-ups like Amazon, Google, Airbnb, Zappos, etc., were all formed in this new age of disruption. They built their value propositions from the perspective of customers, identifying and creating disruption in what had been old and established markets. Amazon unseated companies like Sears and JCPenney, and even eBay—a disruptor that in turn became disrupted to some extent. One advantage that modern companies formed over the last two decades have is that they don't carry all the baggage that established companies do. And their success lies in the way their leaders respond to change. They accept and embrace it, building decentralized organizational structures, operating models, and workforces that are nimble and responsive so that the whole organization can easily shift focus and change direction in a week, two weeks, a month, or a couple of months. This is in stark contrast to more traditional companies that seek to manage variability right out of the system through rigid change control efforts and centralization, which results in an inability to quickly and effectively respond to changing market conditions.

Today, leaders of older, more established companies face intense challenges brought about by trying to stay relevant and competitive in our global economy. They must recognize the sense of urgency and crisis at hand and aggressively lead their organizations in addressing these challenges as quickly as possible. That is the mark of a true Lean leader who rises to the occasion: first acknowledging there is a problem, then facing it head-on in order to continuously evolve to avoid corporate extinction due to an inability to compete on a global level.

Ten 21st-Century Leadership Challenges

Let's take a look at the major challenges you're likely to face and how this book can help you rise to the occasion and overcome them.

Challenge #1: Self-Development for Leaders

Leaders often don't understand they must first develop and lead themselves before they can attempt to lead others. Continuous self-development is the key to being an effective 21st-century leader. You must understand your own multidimensional nature first, which means constantly striving to develop yourself on a social, intellectual, spiritual, physical, and emotional basis. You are constantly evolving whether you realize it or not, and this evolution needs to be conscious and intentional. True leaders know themselves well, first and foremost—they possess self-awareness. They spend time to understand their weaknesses and limitations, and then diligently work to address and overcome them on a continuous basis.

After all, as a Lean leader your goal is the pursuit of perfection. But frankly, such a goal is unattainable, and Lean leaders are savvy enough to understand this fact. However, the pursuit, the unending quest for perfection that is unattainable, still propels them forward. As a result of this quest, you constantly evolve and strengthen your abilities to lead yourself, which then drives your ability to lead others. Who would follow someone whose personal and professional life is a mess? That's not exactly an inspiring or transforming positive experience in the long run for your followers, which is why people choose to follow the leaders they do.

Meeting the challenge:

- Work to understand who you are and what you're about, which all starts by believing in and respecting yourself. Building your self-awareness happens through becoming honest with yourself and making a concerted effort to develop an inner stillness, known as *mindfulness* (Chapter 3). Being in touch with your inner self and understanding what makes you happy and what gives you a feeling of fulfillment and achievement makes you a much better leader in the long run. Knowing where you are and where you want to go is a powerful thing.

- Being driven by a bias toward action and facing challenges head-on is the Lean leader's way (Chapter 3). Persistence, tenacity, and not seeing failure as a world-ending event are traits that people will be drawn to, and they will ask you to help them develop these traits in themselves. Being able to forgive yourself so that you can move on and putting yourself into service for the good of others are marks of a true leader (Chapter 4).

- Tapping into your emotional intelligence to apply reason rather than reacting emotionally to challenging situations shows your followers that you respect and care about them (Chapter 3). People follow leaders they trust and respect, because the feelings are mutual. Being trustworthy comes from being consistent and thoughtful, not from being wild and unpredictable (Chapter 3).

Challenge #2: Outdated Leadership and Management Styles

Command-and-control leadership styles and outdated workforce management strategies do little to develop and support the growth and development of future leaders. The command-and-control leadership styles that have been used for decades in 20th-century companies do not work for a 21st-century workforce engaged with the global economy. Modern leadership styles must be geared toward leading an engaged and connected workforce; you must acknowledge that the world is changing, and your style must develop and evolve as well. Everyone in the organization must commit to its continuous improvement by developing the ability to serve the greater good, to the benefit of its workforce, customers, and stakeholders.

As a leader, you must recognize, acknowledge, and tap into the human capacity to contribute, think, learn, and grow—before you begin to lose the most talented part of your workforce. They WILL leave you in droves in search of a company that offers a connection to a bigger purpose than themselves. Worse yet, cutting staff when bottom-line profits dip is not a sustainable strategy. Every company needs a qualified, well-educated, and trained workforce, regardless of your product/service. The days when people could easily be cut and then replaced when profits were up again are over. People seek stability and a sense of community that feeds the human soul.

A revolving front door is the fastest way to fail, as both valuable talent and knowledge constantly walk through it. Attrition and retention rates matter, and getting a reputation for instability and a fickle management style is the fastest way to push the most talented people away from your doors. After all, who wants to be hired, only to get laid off in six months or a year and have to start a new job hunt all over again? It's an emotionally and intellectually draining experience, not to mention the irreparable harm it may have on an employee's career.

Meeting the challenge:

- Develop an understanding around what it means to lead from a position of service; in other words, become a servant leader that works to contribute to the overall success of the organization by first and foremost serving it and those that follow you (Chapter 4).

- Recognize that the composition of the workforce is changing. According to Daniel Pink in his book *Drive* (Penguin, 2011), this new workforce values autonomy, mastery, and purpose above all else (Chapter 4). They seek out companies whose values and principles match theirs of trust, transparency, being valued and respected, having a voice, and making a difference, which are all motivators in selecting the right company to work for.

- Developing a *kaizen* or continuous improvement mind is a must if you want to inspire and transform those that follow you (Chapter 4).

- Foster and exhibit a tolerance for failure as your staff learns through trial and error (Chapter 4). Making mistakes is part of the learning process. Someone who is not making any mistakes is playing it safe. When workers try something new and it fails, the experience must be viewed as just one more way you know that it doesn't work.

Challenge #3: Customer Centricity and Value Delivery

Leaders must recognize that customer centricity and value delivery are the new driving factors of 21st-century companies. Taking months or years to produce a working product/service is a thing of the past. Organizations have days, weeks, or maybe months to produce something tangible that results in enough value generation to keep them relevant and competitive in our rapidly changing business climate. Those that don't will quickly face disruption by nimbler competitors (which very possibly could be you), obsolescence, and even extinction from the marketplace. It's up to you as a leader to learn how to exploit this cycle to drive the ability to quickly produce and bring to market customer-focused, value-based products/services on an ongoing basis.

Meeting the challenge:

- Focus on identifying and then fulfilling the unmet wants, needs, and/or desires of your customer base first; this means you must identify who your customer is and what they consider to be valuable. Then build a mindful customer experience strategy (CXS) (Chapter 5) to ensure you understand how best to fulfill these unmet wants, needs, and/or desires.

- Understand that value is interpreted differently from the perspective of the customer versus that of the company (Chapter 5).

- Build products/services in increments using iterative product/service development methods (Chapter 7), so that you can harness the ability to release them out to the market with as little investment as possible to gauge customer reaction and acceptance sooner rather than later.

Challenge #4: Prioritizing Profit Above All Else

Some companies are only in the market to make a profit, putting that above everything else. Leaders with an inward focus on what the company wants versus what its customers want must recognize that this is an unsustainable strategy—especially when the lack of acting on this realization means exploiting the environment and damaging the planet to make a profit. This type of behavior can have major repercussions if your actions are uncovered and a backlash ensues, especially if the disaster is proven to have been preventable. Take, for example, the environmental effects in the Gulf of Mexico caused by British Petroleum (BP) in 2010[4] when their deep-water oil well exploded. Even five years later, the area around the spill has not recovered environmentally, socially, and economically. It has drastically affected the wildlife in the area, with dolphins turning up dead from oil poisoning and tar balls still being pushed up onto local beaches. The economy has also suffered: both the fishing and tourism industries have taken a major hit. Shrimping in the bay and recreational use have dropped off. I saw the effects of this spill firsthand when I happened to be in the Tampa area in 2010. The smell of oil was thick in the air, and the closer I got to the water, the stronger the smell and the more nauseated I felt. For BP, all of this translated into enormous lost profits, loss of life (human and wildlife), and a damaged reputation as it struggled to stop the almost three million barrels of Louisiana crude oil from flowing into the gulf. It was the major news story of the day for almost three months, and the big question on everyone's mind was, "Will BP get the spill capped today?" A

---

4 Debbie Elliott, "5 Years after BP Oil Spill, Effects Linger and Recovery Is Slow" (*http://www.npr.org*), NPR, April 20, 2015.

federal judge in Louisiana ruled that it was BP's gross negligence and willful misconduct that caused the spill.[5] Imagine your company being seen so negatively in the public eye for that long, not to mention being accountable for over $28 billion and counting to clean up the spill. Leaders have a responsibility not only to their companies but also to society and the environment, as well as to the people affected by their actions, or lack thereof.

Meeting the challenge:

- Build an awareness of your social, cultural, and environmental beliefs, stances, and actions (Chapter 8).
- Understand the ramifications of producing and developing your products/services and the impact on the environment.

Challenge #5: Cost Reduction Survival Strategies

Outdated ways of operating continue to emphasize cost reduction as a survival strategy. Leaders must recognize that shifting their focus to creating customer-centric products/services that add value for the company as well as the customer is a strategy that prioritizes revenue generation produced from delivering value, not from cutting costs. Many organizations today have stayed afloat by using cost-cutting measures, such as reducing staff, forgoing spending decisions, and keeping a tight rein on R&D (Research & Development). Such strategies cannot continue indefinitely, however, because there comes a point when there is no more "stuff" to cut and when nothing else can be delayed or shifted. The result is the stifling of innovation and development of new products/services, which is a sure way to speed toward corporate extinction.

Meeting the challenge:

- Understand that you must employ an operating model that aligns your product/service lines with an acute focus on revenue generation through value creation and delivery. In this type of model, costs are fixed by maintaining stable production/development teams, while scope fluctuates based on the business value produced by the products/services you build. Remember: variability is something that must be accounted for and not ignored. You must build the ability to respond to change into the system by understanding the importance of breaking the production/development process down into small, manageable chunks (Chapter 7), allowing you to change your mind and direction within an hour, day, week, or month. Working in this manner allows you to restrict your focus to the most

---

5 Ibid.

valuable features/services that can be quickly developed and released out to the market, leaving the lesser value and lower priority features/services to be developed later, or not at all. After all, what good is it to be highly productive at building your products/services, only to find there is no market for them?

- You must closely monitor the revenue your product/service generates so that you can understand how much you have to spend on further production/development efforts. This flips the focus from cost reduction to revenue generation, allowing you to make informed decisions about continuing to invest in, grow, and support a profitable product/service versus stopping or killing those that are underperforming or that have become obsolete (Chapter 6).

Challenge #6: Strategic Misalignment

Strategic misalignment occurs due to lack of detail and transparency around the company's vision, mission, and value proposition. Leaders are responsible for building the company's strategic framework, which should promote holistic, enterprise-wide alignment from the business, financial, technical, and operational perspectives. Leaders who don't spend the time on strategic planning do a disservice to their organizations. Being a management consultant, I cannot begin to tell you how many times I've asked the senior leaders of the organizations I work with for their strategic plan, only to be met with blank stares or excuses about getting that to me tomorrow, when tomorrow never comes. Or worse yet, organizations that adopt Agile product management methods respond with something to the effect of "We're Agile, which means we don't need a set plan, because we are Agile!" This is an excuse and a total distortion of the Agile manifesto.[6] Agile is a mindset, and within a truly Agile organization that understands and embraces agility, planning becomes a big part of a quarterly cycle that repeats itself indefinitely over time. You actually do *more* planning using these methods—you just do it in smaller increments.

When a company has a senior leadership team that's paralyzed by indecision or fear of making a mistake, it doesn't mean decisions don't get made at all. It means that someone else must be brave and courageous enough to make them. In such cases, the responsibility usually falls to tactical or operational managers that possess much less information than senior leadership. After all, the work must continue to flow unimpeded, and people need some sort of direction to get their work done.

---

6 For more information, please reference *www.AgileManifesto.org*.

Meeting the challenge:

- Develop a centralized strategic framework (Chapter 6) in order to keep your workforce engaged and give them the ability to rapidly respond to changing conditions, while still being able to make sound decisions that contribute to the overall vision, mission, and value proposition of the organization.

- Validate the framework with the tactical and operational layers of the organization (Chapter 6) is also crucial because edicts "handed down from the mountain" don't garner buy-in or inspire commitment and support and may also represent strategies that are incomplete. Leaders must ensure they develop strategies that can actually be implemented and maintained by the organization.

Challenge #7: Hierarchies and Silos

Hierarchical structures create silos and promote a disconnected organization. Leaders must recognize the urgency to break down silos within their organizations. They promote destructive Lean patterns of infighting and maintain fiefdoms that build up over time, only benefiting those at the very top. Being customer-centric and value-driven means your operating model must be focused on your enterprise value stream to maximize customer engagement and value delivery.

Meeting the challenge:

- Redesign and replace old hierarchal structures with new operating models that break down functional silos and realign the company's workforce around its product/service lines. This shifts the focus to what you're producing for your customers and to all the activities that revolve around identifying, developing, and releasing your products out to the market, resulting in customer-centric teams organized and aligned to a product's or service's vision, mission, and value proposition (Chapter 7).

- Align your focus as a leader on managing your product/service lines as a business unit, instead of managing vertical functional departments such as R&D, Production, Product Development, Marketing, Finance, etc. Consider everything from ideation to development and all the way to release and support from a horizontal perspective, across all the value-producing activities required to design, develop, release, and support your offering out to the market, known as a *value stream*. By employing this type of operating model, the people closest to the work (as well as your customers) are the ones making the key decisions, using the organization's centralized strategic decision-making (CSDM) framework (Chapter 6) to ensure they are making the best possible decisions throughout the process.

Challenge #8: Traditional Development Practices

Product/service development practices must move away from the slow, traditional methods of the past to become disruptors through innovation. Leaders no longer have months or years to develop and bring products/services to market. Customers expect them to evolve and companies to be able to stay on the edge of innovation to effectively respond to disruption by continuously offering new, innovative, and exciting products/services on a regular basis.

To be able to meet these expectations, *cycle time*—the time it takes a company to identify, develop, and deliver a new product/service to market—must drastically shrink. Companies that spend months or even years developing their products/services run the risk of releasing them too late and experiencing the disappointment of their customer base having absolutely no interest in them at all. The window of opportunity was slammed shut by a competitor that moved quickly to close the gap and fulfill that unmet customer want, need, and/or desire in a timelier manner, capturing the majority of market share. You are then left scratching your head and asking the question, "How did they do that and beat me to market?"

Companies no longer have the luxury of making this type of mistake too many times, because our global economy offers too many alternatives to customers who have become very unforgiving. They can easily leave you and take their dollars elsewhere. Remember, if you're not innovating, you're not evolving, and the end result will not be pretty.

Meeting the challenge:

- Seeing problems as challenges to be overcome is all part of the process by which great companies seek out and achieve innovation. Innovation comes from iteration—that is, by making small steps toward solving a bigger problem. Innovation comes from iteratively working to solve these problems in a team setting. Your workforce is your greatest asset on the road to innovation. Understanding the build/measure/learn loop and its role in problem-solving activities is a must (Chapter 7).

- Foster nimbleness, stress speed to market, and help your organization develop the ability to rapidly respond to changing market conditions in today's globally competitive market (Chapters 5 and 6). Switching to rapid iterative and incremental development methods is no longer just an option; it's a must, and savvy leaders understand these methods are a necessity (Chapter 7). They drastically cut down on cycle times and produce products/services in a timely manner that customers find valuable, because they're designed and developed specifically with customers in mind (Chapter 5). Now *that* is true competitive advantage at its best!

Challenge #9: Technological Advances and Global Competition

Technological advances are causing massive disruption as our world continues to converge, creating more and more global competition and introducing accelerated change around the world. Artificial intelligence (AI), virtual reality (VR), robotics, smart devices, blockchain, and the cloud are just a few of the technological trends that will be disruptive into the foreseeable future. Our world is converging as the Internet of Things (IoT) continues to tie them all together. Companies no longer have the luxury of being concerned only with producing and delivering products to local markets. Leaders must watch how and in which direction the world is changing and must keep a finger on the pulse of technological changes. You must be aware of what's happening within your own R&D departments as well as in your competitors' R&D shops. Disrupt or be disrupted: those are your choices. It's up to you to be forward-thinking enough to understand how to exploit your options, ensuring you remain relevant and competitive.

Meeting the challenge:

- Understand and build systems and processes that exploit and rapidly respond to new technological advances appearing in the market; stay in front of and be responsive to the ever-increasing levels of complexity in our global economy (Chapter 6).

- Recognize that the days when you could rely on brand loyalty are over (Chapter 5); customers can jump ship for the next new "IT" thing or cool new gadget that a competitor halfway around the world can easily introduce, causing complete disruption in your market.

- Recognize that technology is also changing the makeup of our workforce, as companies work to figure out how to integrate both virtual (AI) and robotic workers into the workforce (Chapter 4). This trend has actually been happening for years; however, robots were previously confined to the manufacturing floor. With the maturing of AI, knowledge workers will also experience shifts as technology becomes more and more integrated into white-collar jobs. The age of the "no collar" worker will soon be a reality that 21st-century leaders must face.

Challenge #10: Outmoded Workforce Development Practices

Outmoded workforce development and investment strategies don't embrace diversity, promote advancement, or develop people to their fullest potential, or worse yet, they don't exist at all. Learning and development is a two-fold process. First, we all must take it upon ourselves to continuously evolve our skills and abilities to stay relevant in our rapidly changing world. Second, developing to our fullest potential as leaders is something we cannot do by ourselves. We must rely on others to help us along the way. And, as today's Lean leaders, if what we truly seek is to develop the next generation of leaders, we must put some skin in the game and commit to teaching, coaching, and mentoring them to the best of our abilities.

Meeting the challenge:

- Adjust your attitudes toward investing in your people by offering learning and reskilling opportunities as technology brings waves of change. Workers will look for and gravitate to companies that offer continuing education, training, and reskilling opportunities throughout their careers. To remain relevant and employable, people understand they must continue their learning journey and will periodically, throughout their career, need additional training and reskilling and upskilling, which means retraining and reeducating yourself multiple times throughout your career (Chapter 4). Leaders must proactively develop investment strategies geared toward keeping their workforce fresh and well skilled to address disruption, foster innovation, and remain competitive (Chapter 5).

- Understand that developing Lean leaders is not something that should be left to chance. You must acknowledge that what is needed is a concerted effort to identify, teach, coach, and mentor those who display the potential to become Lean leaders (Chapters 4 and 8). That means instituting a Lean leaders development program designed to build your company's next generation of leaders through a combination of self-development, training, and on-the-job development (OJD) programs (Chapters 8 and 9).

- Build a Lean culture (Chapter 8) that fosters and promotes continuous improvement and agility to be able to effectively respond to our ever-changing world and to the many competitive threats that just might crater your organization. Culture comes from the top and spreads downward. If you want to develop a culture that brings out the best in people, then you need to provide opportunities for them to learn and grow, as well as be a role model they can pattern their own behaviors and leadership styles after. Culture is something that everyone builds, and it takes a village to get it right.

This crisis in industry today is real; if gone unaddressed, we'll see the demise of many companies that refuse to face the facts, and they'll be replaced by competition that's nimbler and more responsive to change. Nothing is constant except change itself, and the world has always favored survival of the fittest. So, as a Lean leader, the question I ask of you is this: "Will you survive and thrive?" Of course, the knee-jerk reaction is to say, "Yes, of course! I have it all under control!" And my next question to you then becomes, "Are you absolutely sure?"

And believe me, it's not that I don't trust you. I've been working with leaders for many years, and I know that facing reality can sometimes be very hard. It often takes an outsider to wake up an organization's leaders and push them to face these challenges head-on. This can be evidenced by the many progressive, innovative leaders who, although highly recruited, leave an organization after only a short period of time, usually less than a year. Change agents who want the organization to face these challenges and affect real change will take getting shot down only so many times before they give up and leave in search of more progressive and innovative companies that are ready and willing to begin the tough work of facing the change curve. As a leader, you must ensure your company doesn't fall by the wayside and vanish from the global economic landscape.

Blockbuster

Blockbuster, established in 1985,[7] was a Dallas, Texas–based provider of home movie and video game rentals, delivered through its retail stores and later through mail order and (toward the end of its existence) subscription-based services. Throughout the 1990s, Blockbuster flourished, opening over 9,000 stores in the US alone.[8] In 2000, it had the opportunity to buy an up-and-coming competitor, Netflix, for $50 million.[9] Blockbuster's leaders made one of the most horrendous decisions in the world of business to date and said, "No thanks!"

By 2010, Netflix had cornered the market, and Blockbuster declared bankruptcy. A 2013 article on CNN.com stated, "If only Blockbuster could rewind back to the 1990s."[10] In their efforts to resist change, Blockbuster's leaders didn't see the opportunity to buy their disruptive competitor that had been dropped right in their laps, and instead of

---

7 Wikipedia, s.v. Blockbuster LLC (*https://en.wikipedia.org/wiki/Blockbuster_LLC*), last modified November 11, 2019, 00:54.

8 Brian Stelter, "Internet Kills the Video Store" (*https://oreil.ly/vLhhU*), New York Times, November 3, 2013.

9 Todd Leopold, "Your Late Fees Are Waived: Blockbuster Closes" (*https://oreil.ly/8j0bL*), CNN.com, November 6, 2013.

10 Ibid.

becoming the competition, they allowed themselves to be overtaken by them. Moral of the story: Resistance to change is a potentially fatal flaw that is a waste of time and could also possibly lead to a company's demise. Leaders must face these challenges head-on to ensure their organizations continue to survive and thrive well into the 21st century.

Why Agility Isn't Easy for Leaders

To ensure leaders don't stunt the growth of themselves or their organizations, both must continue to evolve and change with the times. As a leader, you must embrace, build, and continuously strive to achieve agility. It's defined as the ability to rapidly respond to changing conditions, both internally and externally, to seize and/or maintain competitive advantage that creates and delivers value from a customer, stakeholder, or company perspective. It's the enabler behind any goal or effort to change and evolve, ending in an organization's ability to embrace continuous improvement and evolution so that it remains in existence. Therefore, you must work on developing the organizational "muscles" around the ability to constantly identify, adjust, and respond to both internal and external change, on a local-to-global level.

Agility is about creating a mindset throughout the organization that change is good and that it brings opportunities that may not have existed before. If the company recognizes and correctly responds to these opportunities, it means capturing some benefit in the form of increased revenue, greater profit margins and market share, or the unlocking of a whole new market. The mindset must thrive within the enterprise at the team, product, and portfolio layers and must be championed by strong leaders that support and foster a tolerance for failure, as the organization experiments with agility and builds the capabilities to effectively respond to change.

But agility goes against the techniques taught in scientific management or Tayloristic methods, as they are sometimes called, after their creator, Frederick Taylor. His thoughts, writings, and practices heavily influenced much of the school of management and leadership thinking and practices throughout the 20th century, starting with the dawning of the Industrial Revolution. In the early 1900s, scientific management was taught as the predominant management theory within business schools throughout the world. Taylor, recognized to be the first true management consultant, documented his research findings in a book published in 1911 and entitled *The Principles of Scientific Management*. In it, he laid out his very precise ideas about how to introduce his system and the role of management versus workers into companies:

It is only through enforced standardization of methods, enforced adoption of the best implements and working conditions, and enforced cooperation that this faster work can be assured. And the duty of enforcing the adoption of standards and enforcing this cooperation rests with management alone.[11]

He believed that control, or "enforcement" as he called it, should rest with management and not the workers performing the work. His theories stressed that workers must be taught to follow the rules and obey authority. Coloring outside of the lines was not an option and was highly discouraged. Individualism and creativity were frowned upon on the factory line. Taylor's practices resulted in hierarchical command-and-control organizational and management structures and reward systems that focused on how well managers controlled the whole process, as well as the workforce, without suffering waste or downtime. Everything was standardized, timed, and precise, which worked well in the factories at the time, where work was repetitive and routine. This way of working actually resulted in the United States becoming the world leader in manufacturing during the 20th century.

Command-and-control leadership practices and hierarchical organizational structures flourished all the way up until the early to mid-1980s, as Gen Xers (defined as the generation born between 1961 and 1981) came of age. They were filled with entrepreneurial spirit, individualism, and risk taking and sought more work/life balance than the generations before them. Management thought leaders such as Tom Peters, Warren Bennis, and Stephen Covey wrote about *leadership* instead of management, emphasizing teamwork, collaboration, and a virtually overlooked leadership style known as *servant leadership*.

But leadership thought wasn't the only thing that was changing. In the early to mid-1980s, Microsoft and Apple both released mass-produced personal computers to the general public, changing the face of the workforce forever as the demand for "white collar" workers grew. The demand for people who could program and operate these new computers skyrocketed. With the Gen Xers coming of age and gravitating toward these new thought leaders and machines, it caused a perfect storm, flooding the world with the first wave of innovative disruption. It also saw the ushering in of the dot-com era, kicked off by the founding of Amazon in 1994 and ending in 2003 when Time Warner dropped "AOL" from its title, even though it was AOL that acquired Time Warner.[12]

---

11 Frederick W. Taylor, *The Principles of Scientific Management*. (New York and London: Harper and Brothers, 1919), 83.

12 World History Project, "Dot-Com Bubble timeline" (*https://oreil.ly/6z2Nd*), accessed November 5, 2017.

Now that we are experiencing the second wave of the dot com boom, beginning with the founding of Facebook in 2004, a 2015 study by the Sage Group reported that Gen Xers "dominate the playing field" with respect to founding startups in the United States and Canada, launching the majority (55%) of all new businesses in 2015:[13]

> Small businesses and the entrepreneurial spirit that Gen Xers embody have become one of the most popular institutions in America. There's been a recent shift in customer behavior and Gen Xers will join the "idealist generation" in encouraging the celebration of individual effort and business risk-taking. As a result, Xers will spark a renaissance of entrepreneurship in economic life, even as overall confidence in economic institutions declines. Customers and their needs and wants (including Millennials, those born between 1982 and 2004)[14] will become the North Star for an entirely new generation of entrepreneurs.[15]

Agility is "natural" for many Gen Xers and Millennials, because it stresses the values and principles they believe in, such as risk taking, creativity, autonomy, collaboration, entrepreneurship, and an unwavering focus on the customer. However, there is a mismatch in many companies today, as the old command-and-control structures are not nimble enough to allow them to rapidly respond to our ever-changing world. They struggle to adjust and change with the times, to these new ways of working that require the ability to rapidly respond to both internal and external changes, threats, and opportunities. In today's business climate, waiting days and weeks to run a decision up the hierarchy to upper management is a thing of the past. In the time it takes for a manager to review and understand the problem, develop a solution, and then relay it back down the chain of command, competitive advantage may very well be lost. Nowadays, decisions need to be made in minutes and hours, not days and weeks.

Going back to the Blockbuster example, I had personal exposure to this company's decision-making processes. In the mid-1990s, I was working for a small consulting firm in Dallas, Texas, where Blockbuster was headquartered. I went on a sales call with the senior partner to discuss possibly building a data warehouse and reporting system that would enable faster decision-making capabilities throughout the organization. I very clearly remember sitting in the CEO's

---

13 Sage, *2015 State of the Startup* (*https://oreil.ly/2RXoa*), 2015.

14 Wikipedia, s.v. "Strauss–Howe Generational Theory" (*https://oreil.ly/x7Beo*), last modified November 8, 2019, 21:15.

15 Morley Winograd and Michael Hais, "Why Generation X Is Sparking a Renaissance in Entrepreneurship" (*http://www.beinkandescent.com/articles/942/GenX*), *Be Inkandescent*, accessed April 22, 2013.

office like it was yesterday, as he pulled a huge, three-inch-thick white binder off of his credenza (one of ten, actually), dropped it on his desk with a loud thud, and said (I paraphrase):

> This is how I make decisions about the state of my business. I get these binders every month after the financials run, fifteen days after close. Then, I have to sift through and try to determine what is and isn't important. This stuff is worthless to me (as he slammed it shut) because by the time it reaches me, it's all stale and old news. I need an analytics tool in real time to help me run my business. Can you guys do that for me?

I'll never forget that conversation, because, to the best of my knowledge, they elected not to build that warehouse, or we just didn't win the business. However, either way it was the same result, because not buying Netflix wasn't the only poor decision the management team made. Blockbuster, like many other companies, was struggling to put these old ways aside as the world was changing and shifting underneath them at the dawning of the 21st century. Its leaders knew they needed to change, but the question of how to accomplish that without totally disrupting their business was just too overwhelming, and these new ways of thinking and behaving caused just way too much discomfort.

Leading Lean Is All About Embracing Agility

How do leaders develop a customer-focused digital mindset, engage this new workforce, successfully transform to these new ways of working, and address the crisis in leadership? The answer: by embracing agility. Agility is achieved by embracing Lean values, principles, and methods that offer leaders a way to rapidly respond to both internal and external changing conditions in order to gain or maintain competitive advantage and deliver value to both their customers and stakeholders. In a world of rapidly changing requirements, nimble and lean companies can respond quickly to both threats and opportunities.

In this second wave of disruption, Lean methods offer a better way of working, because they create leaders that are both nimble and responsive and who run their companies in the same manner. First to market is still king, and market share is everything. That has not changed! However, this book will introduce you to a completely new way of leading yourself, others, your customers, the enterprise, innovation, and culture, which, if followed, has the power to completely transform you, those around you, your organization, and potentially even the world. Its focus is on building 21st-century leaders that can quickly identify the opportunities brought on by change and then respond by creating and delivering customer-centric products/services that create value and seize competitive advantage.

Conclusion

Leadership is all about the ability to bring people together to solve the pressing issues at hand, make a fair profit, and work on making our world a better place, whether that means "better" in the creation of a socially responsible product/service or dealing with climate change, pollution, economic well-being, human rights, living conditions, or even world peace. We've lost sight of the fact that a leader's role is not self-serving but about the people that leader serves. It's time to regain our focus by embracing Lean ways of working and leading, to make the world a better place for all of us. As you continue through this book, it is my hope that you'll understand the importance of being "all-in" if you truly aspire to become a Lean leader. If you're not fully committed, those who follow you will sense it and may end up not committing to the change that's necessary. Embracing agility and achieving continuous evolution takes a village, and it's not something leaders can do on their own. In true Lean fashion: Experiment. Learn. Adjust. Repeat! All of these things will be required of you, and there will be just as many failures as successes. Acknowledge and view failure as just one more way you now know will not work. Adjust and move forward and try again, and above all, celebrate each success. Take a moment to reflect and understand how you achieved it before moving on.

Now that you have an understanding of the challenges—and successes—you can face as a Lean leader, let's move on to a more in-depth discussion of how you can face those challenges.

CHAPTER 2

The Modern Lean Framework™

Agility—the ability to respond to changing conditions—is a skill that you must develop so that you can lead from a holistic perspective. The levels of volatility, uncertainty, complexity, and ambiguity (VUCA) are just too high nowadays to lead in any other way.

Lean embraces and fosters agility by instilling a spirit of challenge and the confidence to pursue elusive perfection head-on. It grounds you in the reality that perfection is unobtainable but also drives you forward along the path to continuous improvement. In this chapter, we'll look at the origins of Lean (as defined and developed by the Toyota Motor Corporation) and the Modern Lean Framework™, which will provide you with a road map to follow when developing and perfecting these Lean skills and abilities. This framework will show you how to stave off extinction through continuous evolution and develop the mindset required to embrace and exploit agility.

Staving Off Extinction through Continuous Evolution

Today, leaders spend millions of dollars trying to figure out the "secret sauce" that made the success of start-ups like Amazon and Google look so easy. However, I would bet that if you asked Jeff Bezos, CEO of Amazon, whether he felt like success was easy, he would probably laugh. Amazon was founded in 1994 in Bezos's garage,[1] taking almost ten years to turn a profit.[2] There is no quick or easy fix, and modeling yourself after other companies isn't going to work. *Companies are as unique as people. Trying to copy or duplicate someone else's success without truly understanding how it came about is doomed to failure.*

When failure becomes evident, the blame game ensues. Upper management blames the employees, the employees blame upper management for a lack of leadership, and the management and technology gurus blame the culture. Unfortunately, it's a vicious cycle that will repeat itself over and over again, because nothing changes at the company's core. Leadership and the workforce, either consciously or (more often than not) unconsciously, will sabotage the change effort. This is a lose-lose outcome that will eventually bring about corporate extinction.

All of these considerations have one thing in common: people! Change must be modeled from the top because that's where culture starts. A culture of change assertiveness or change aversion starts with its leaders. Leaders that hold back and take a "wait and see" attitude inspire the same in their followers, especially if there's a revolving door on the C-suite and multiple change efforts have died before ever getting a chance to take hold.

However, the older and more established an organization becomes, the harder it is to ensure it continues to change and evolve. This is where Lean leaders must step in and ensure that the spirit of evolution continues to move the company forward. You must start by addressing the challenges of leadership and acknowledge the sense of urgency that exists to ensure that your company continues to evolve and grow. "Innovate, innovate, innovate to disrupt, disrupt, disrupt!" must be your mantra, because innovation feeds continuous evolution.

---

1 Avery Hartmans, "15 Fascinating Facts You Probably Didn't Know about Amazon" (*https:// oreil.ly/xZHvo*), Business Insider, June 17, 2019.

2 Nick Wingfield, "Amazon Reports Annual Net Profit for the First Time" (*https://oreil.ly/hlndl*), Wall Street Journal, January 28, 2004.

3M: Success Through Continuous Evolution

3M is a company that has continuously evolved for almost 90 years. Focusing on innovation is nothing new for this industry giant. The importance of evolving through innovation and fostering it within the company can be traced back to the 1930s, to a man named Richard Drew.[3] Drew was 22 years old with little formal education, but he possessed an eagerness to learn and an insatiable curiosity. 3M hired him to sell sandpaper to automotive body shop owners. One day when he was out on sales calls, he met with a rather agitated shop owner who was upset about the 3M tape they were using because it was pulling the paint off the two-tone paint jobs they were doing, resulting in a lot of rework. These paint jobs were very popular at the time. However, they were also very labor and cost-intensive because the tape was too strong and would rip the paint from the metal when pulled off, thereby causing the need to use sandpaper to correct the situation and touch up where the paint job had been damaged. Overall, auto body shop owners were eager to meet the demand, but the end product was difficult to attain without a lot of costly rework, which cut into their bottom-line profits.

That day, Drew vowed to find a solution for the body shop owner. For over two years, he worked diligently in his spare time to come up with a tape that would solve the problem. His direct supervisor constantly discouraged Drew because he didn't believe Drew should be spending his time on such an effort. When Drew finally made a breakthrough and invented a tape that wasn't as strong but still achieved the desired results, his supervisor wouldn't pay for the machine to mass-produce the tape because he still felt it was a waste of time. Instead, Drew purchased the parts in increments, just underneath his spending limit, and assembled the machine himself. The result was the invention of Scotch Brand masking tape, which was an overnight success. How many of us have used this product? The product that almost wasn't!

When his boss later found out what Drew had been up to, he rewarded Drew by issuing the following mandate at 3M: "If you have the right person on the right project, and they are absolutely dedicated to finding a solution—leave them alone. Tolerate their initiative and trust them."[4]

As a result of Drew's tenacity and work ethic, 3M provides employees with time (15% of their workday) to explore ideas outside of their regular work assignments. The amazing thing is that this story happened between 1931 and 1933, and even today, 3M gives its employees time to innovate daily—all because of one man who was bold enough to go against the norm.

Do you have an idea that is rolling around in your head? How can you go about making it a reality? Who do you need to convince that it's a great idea? What are you waiting for?

---

3 Zachery Crocket, "The Man Who Invented Scotch Tape" (*https://oreil.ly/4EC1I*), Priceonomics, December 30, 2014.

4 Ibid.

Leading in Our 21st-Century Connected World

The Internet of Things (IoT) has shrunk our world, and the distance between any two people, companies, states, or countries has drastically shrunk as well. You're no longer competing with the business down the street. Your biggest competition may come from halfway around the world—which is why Lean leaders must lead from a position of connectedness. You must be connected to yourself, connected to those around you in your company, connected to your customers, and connected to the wider world.

A highly connected world makes embracing agility an imperative. To be able to holistically respond to the challenges all around you, now more than ever leaders must become situational and adaptive; they must be able to integrate information and perspectives from many disparate sources. Savvy leaders understand that they must work both vertically and horizontally across their organizations, which requires adopting a new mindset. A mindset is the belief system formed through habits and past experiences that have built up over time.

When examining your mindset, ask yourself the following questions:

- Is this the right path or the best possible decision I can make in this situation?
- Am I acting on previous beliefs to handle this new reality or situation?
- Am I seeing the patterns as they exist, or am I relying on old habitual responses?
- Do I need to adjust something to be more effective and responsive?

Understanding the Journey Ahead of You

The journey you're about to embark on can't be completed overnight. As you progress, you'll move through the four stages of competence, a two-factor learning and competency model developed in the 1970s by Noel Burch.[5] These factors are being conscious or aware of (1) what you do or don't know and (2) the skill level or competence that you possess to tackle the situation or problem at hand.

---

5 "The Conscious Competence Ladder" (*https://oreil.ly/Cd3yl*), MindTools.com, accessed September 30, 2018

Phase I: Unconscious Incompetence

In this stage, ignorance is bliss—you don't know what you don't know, and you have no desire to change that. However, since you've undertaken the task of becoming a Lean leader, you're already past this stage! You're moving to the next phase of realizing there is something lacking.

Phase II: Conscious Incompetence

Somehow, possibly through changes in yourself, your environment, your career, etc., your reality has changed, and your awareness that something is lacking has been awoken. Becoming aware of your incompetence brings into focus your inability to respond to change, or maybe you just aren't getting the results that you want to achieve. The search to determine and fill the gaps has begun. After all, you're reading this book—something drove you to pick it up, and you're about to embark on a journey to make the necessary changes to lead from a multidimensional perspective.

Phase III: Conscious Competence

As you examine your leadership style and start to make adjustments, you become more and more aware of how others respond to you and how effective you are in leading them. You use introspection and self-correction as you realize the context in which you operate. You begin to develop an awareness that all events that happen must have context. To rationalize and respond to your customers with a logical mind, you must be able to relate to them and understand what they deem to be valuable. After all, the ultimate goal is to build products/services that they're interested in, by fulfilling their unmet wants, needs, and/or desires. Finally, as you go beyond what you know now and push yourself and others to strive toward perfection by challenging the status quo with a curious and creative mind, you spur innovation.

Phase IV: Unconscious Competence

At some point in your learning curve, you no longer consciously think about how you're going to respond to change. It becomes inherent and ingrained in you. Your response mechanisms now live in your unconscious mind. You've changed your way of being, and now it becomes part of your natural response mechanisms. This is the final stage of competence.

Moving through these four levels of learning allows you to master important skills that can be tapped into and built upon to continue your development. However, not everything can be done through original thought alone. Repetition and rote memory are tools for honing your leadership skills and abilities as well because you can use those patterns as a starting point. Then, based on the situation, you can modify and customize them to advance your learning and mastery, allowing you to fine-tune your ability to observe, analyze, and respond while teaching others along the way. Moreover, as you learn and develop mastery, you will most likely discover new dimensions of the competency you're developing, causing you to drop back down into the lower states. As you break down the process or situation into smaller and smaller parts, you build greater knowledge and competency and move back up through the stages. This is a continuous process of developing your skills and abilities that naturally takes place over time.

Keep in mind that turning the corner from conscious to unconscious competence for any skill requires patience, perseverance, and stamina. The challenges you face as you work to become a Lean leader will most likely steadily increase as you learn to handle harder and more complex situations. True leadership growth happens only when you're challenged. Overcoming these challenges is what pushes you to grow as a leader. As you accept the importance of becoming a Lean leader, you're committing yourself to a lifelong journey of learning, which sparks continuous evolution. Once you begin, there's no turning back, and the status quo becomes change itself.

Let's begin your journey to becoming a Lean leader.

Toyota and the Lean Mindset

The Lean mindset evolved based on the pitfalls and wasteful processes that were in practice in the early 1900s in American manufacturing plants. Henry Ford's dream of making his automobiles so affordable that every American could own one started him on a quest to figure out how to standardize and mass-produce his cars to drive the cost down. Up until that point, cars were made by specialists who assembled them entirely by hand, which was very expensive. Automobiles were luxury items that only the rich could afford. To make cars affordable to everyone, Ford invented the Ford Production System, which was first implemented in his Model T mass production assembly line in 1914. The premise was to break the car-building process down into discrete steps that could be standardized and optimized separately, as compared to one person building the whole thing; this innovation drastically decreased cycle times (the time it takes from start to finish to build a car) and in turn decreased production costs.

In Ford's system, workers got good at only one part of the process, to the point they became experts in just that one step. As a result, the price of cars came way down, and Ford's dream of making them affordable to everyone became a reality. Unfortunately, the quality was low, and they broke down often.

After World War II ended, Kiichiro Toyoda, a successful Japanese businessman, and his head engineer, Taiichi Ohno, brought a Japanese delegation of engineers to the United States to study the now well-known manufacturing marvel that Ford had created in Detroit, Michigan. However, what they found was a system characterized by large amounts of inventory being held on-site, uneven patterns of work that caused large lags, and lots of wait time between steps on the line, which resulted in a lot of rework and poor quality, not to mention dissatisfied employees who performed mundane tasks over and over again as a result of standardized processes. Ford cars were known for poor quality well into the 1970s; many people joked that "Ford" stood for "Fix Or Repair Daily." (My first car in the late 1970s was a Ford Maverick, so I am very familiar with the quality of Ford cars.)

Not impressed with what was going on at Ford, the Toyoda delegation happened into a Piggly Wiggly grocery store. There they observed what would come to be known as a Just-In-Time (JIT) inventory system, whereby only a small amount of inventory (whatever would fit on the shelves) was maintained within the store. There were no large stockpiles laying around as they had observed at Ford, because the grocery store had established a pull system based on customer demand. Reordering and restocking happened only when current inventory levels became low. In this way, the store cut down on its holding costs and only stocked to the level of demand. The result: fresh products that created high customer satisfaction. The whole system was based on pull, or purchasing, from its customers, not on some arbitrary constraint of keeping the manufacturing line moving and workers constantly busy, as was the case in the Ford plants. Idle hands were seen as waste and production lines ran full time, even when the demand was low for the finished product, which resulted in large inventories being held at the plants as well as on dealer lots.

The Toyoda delegation took this knowledge back to Japan and came up with a modified version of Ford's system, which came to be known as the Toyota Production System (TPS). However, the term "Lean" didn't come into existence until the late 1980s, when a research team headed by James Womack, a Ph.D. at MIT's International Motor Vehicle Program, documented "Lean production" methods in use at Toyota in his groundbreaking 1990 book, coauthored by Dan Jones and Dan Roos, *The Machine That Changed the World.*[6] They used the term "lean" to differentiate Toyota from other forms of production systems, such as mass (in the case of Ford) or craft (in use at BMW) systems. Nowadays, Toyota cars are known for their quality and dependability record, ranking third overall (behind Lexus, which is also part of Toyota, and Porsche)

---

6 Daniel T. Jones, Daniel Roos, and James P. Womack, *The Machine That Changed the World: The Story of Lean Production—Toyota's Secret Weapon in the Global Car Wars That Is Revolutionizing World Industry* (New York: Free Press, 2007), loc. 74, Kindle.

in J.D. Power's 2017 Dependability Survey rankings,[7] which is not something that just happens by chance.

Let's take a look at TPS and its pillars and how the Lean mindset and Lean thinking support this approach to business.

The Toyota Production System

TPS is a holistic process that entails five steps that start with the customer:

1. Listen to the customer.
2. Design the product.
3. Coordinate the supply chain.
4. Produce the product from order to delivery.
5. Manage the combined enterprise.[8]

These five fairly simple steps make up the "Lean" way of manufacturing. For Lean manufacturing to work, a company needs to adopt the broad principles of the Lean mindset, which entails truly changing the way you think about your products/services.

The Lean mindset

The Lean mindset emphasizes four important principles:

- Listening to your customers and respecting others
- Removing bottlenecks and waste in the system
- Committing to relentless continuous improvement
- Creating value for the customer and company[9]

Possessing a Lean mindset pushes Lean leaders to create innovative new products/services that create customer-driven value, introducing disruption and pushing others to also continuously improve and evolve to stay relevant. The Lean mindset is a result of practicing a more specific strategy known as Lean thinking.

---

7 "While Lexus and Porsche Rank Highest in Vehicle Dependability, Excellent Long-Term Quality Isn't Exclusive to Luxury Brands, J.D. Power Finds" (*https://oreil.ly/yJTaA*), J.D. Power (press release), February 22, 2017.

8 Ibid., 49.

9 Patrick Van den Bossche, Joe Reifel, Rajiv Shah, Adheer Bahulkar, and Alyssa Pei, *Adopting a Lean Mindset: How Service Industries Are Increasing Profitability* (Chicago: A.T. Kearney, 2008), 2.

Lean thinking

In their groundbreaking book, *Lean Thinking: Banish Waste and Create Wealth in Your Corporation* (Free Press), Jim Womack and Dan T. Jones defined Lean thinking as:

- Exploiting iterative and incremental value creation
- Learning through short feedback loops that encourage ingenuity and passion
- Creating uninterrupted flow through the elimination of waste
- Achieving uncompromised quality
- Emphasizing the use of empirical scientific methods and measurements to gauge progress

Success is measured by releasing a working product/service out to customers at the end of a development cycle. It means empowering people to own the continuous improvement of the system in order to produce innovative products/services that satisfy some unfulfilled customer want, need, and/or desire. It also means committing to directly engaging with those closest to the work to identify and resolve issues as they occur.

Lean thinking is scientific thinking, which means using scientific methods grounded in empirical fact and evidence-based processes to:

1. Observe a problem
2. Form a question around the problem
3. Develop the hypothesis
4. Conduct an experiment
5. Analyze the data to draw conclusions
6. Document the methods and findings and...repeat

It's a process that systematically challenges everything continuously, and it must be performed throughout the entire Lean enterprise.

The Pillars of The Toyota Way

Many of these Lean strategies and approaches can be traced back to the evolution of Toyota. As Akio Toyoda evolved as a leader, so did his company's leadership philosophies and practices. In the early 2000s, Jeffrey Liker studied the underlying philosophy and principles of Toyota's leadership style. He identified five values built on two pillars, known as The Toyota Way,[10] that strongly contribute to the automotive giant's success.

Continuous improvement (CI) pillar

CI is all about facing challenges head-on with courage and creativity. It means being brave enough to push the envelope by developing people and a culture that supports and encourages creativity and an inquisitive mind: teams should continuously ask "why" things are the way they are and "how" can they be improved upon.

There are three core principles associated with this pillar: the spirit of challenge, kaizen, and genchi genbutsu.

The spirit of challenge

Akio Toyoda believed that, regardless of your position within the company,[11] it was everyone's responsibility to face challenges and problems head-on and to do everything within your power to find the root cause and fix it. Taking personal responsibility is deeply rooted in the Toyota Way, no matter where the problem originates. There is no abdicating to others or escalating to superiors within Toyota's culture. Everyone is responsible for overcoming the challenges that occur.

This pillar also pertains to how Toyota faces change. Change represents constant challenges that leaders must address and, as a result, offers learning opportunities. Leaders must take the time to pause and reflect on how they handled the challenge at hand; by folding these learnings back into their problem-solving abilities, they gain the courage and confidence to take on even greater and more challenging problems.

Competition is also viewed as a good thing because it creates a learning opportunity. Overcoming challenges makes Lean leaders stronger and better suited to solving problems as they arise in the future. As Toyota put it in "The Toyota Way 2001," "We accept challenges with a creative spirit and the courage to realize our own dreams without losing drive or energy."[12] Leadership must be developed and honed through experience and by facing and overcoming challenges with the help of your sensei or coach. It's a continuous cycle that moves us from ignorance to greater and greater levels of competency as we practice continuous evolution of ourselves and our leadership abilities.

---

10 Jeffrey K. Liker and Gary L. Convis, *The Toyota Way to Lean Leadership: Achieving and Sustaining Excellence through Leadership Development* (New York: McGraw-Hill, 2011), 35.

11 Ibid., 36.

12 Toyota Motor Corporation, "The Toyota Way 2001" (*https://oreil.ly/Mgc0g*), Toyota Motor Corporation Official Global Website, accessed September 15, 2018.

Kaizen

Kaizen is Japanese for "improvement." Thus a kaizen mind is the vehicle that drives the pursuit of perfection, in the form of iterative and incremental improvements, that over time empowers and encourages everyone to identify improvements, no matter how small—improvements that can benefit the company, teams, or individual performance. It is this relentless pursuit of perfection that drives the company forward, and it's the responsibility of everyone in the organization to pursue better ways of working. Waste is everywhere, no matter how many times the process has undergone improvement.

Genchi genbutsu

Genchi genbutsu means "going to the source," or the source of truth, known as *gemba*. Problems cannot be solved by sitting in your office. To develop a kaizen mind, you must go to the source of a problem and see for yourself what's happening. Only at the source will you be able to obtain the facts, build consensus, and make correct decisions on a timely basis.

Everyone in your enterprise must practice genchi genbutsu. Everyone in the Lean enterprise, no matter their title or position, is expected to go to the source and face challenges head-on to improve the work and pursue perfection in everything the organization does, continuously. Going to the source also helps do away with lengthy discussions on surmising what the problem is, because it's known and understood, based on firsthand knowledge. This cuts down on the time it takes to solve the problem the right way the first time around.

These principles are powerful tools that can bring teams together as they work to solve difficult problems. Working shoulder to shoulder with others is the best way to get to know them and develop a sense of teamwork. People get to know and start to care about not only the company but also one another.

"Respect for people" pillar

Respect for people is the second pillar of The Toyota Way. It means that no matter who you are or what position you hold in an organization, everyone's voice is important and must be heard. Diversity is cherished and sought after—not just diversity in ethnicity, gender, religion, sexual orientation, etc., but also the diversity of ideas, thoughts, and ways of looking at the world. It is Toyota's mission to build a diverse and sustainable workforce that reflects the society at large, as well as Toyota's ever-changing customer base.[13] The two principles under this pillar are teamwork and respect.

---

13 Ibid., 3.

Teamwork

The team is everything within the Lean enterprise; individuals can succeed only within the team, not outside of it. The team benefits from the personal growth of its members, which is all built into the performance incentives and rewards program within Toyota. Contributions to the team are rewarded and incentivized, versus those of the individual, which represent a much smaller component. All leaders must view themselves as members of the team. As such, everyone is responsible for both their personal growth as well as the success of others. Teamwork is grounded in a shared vision and mission, and everyone must understand and work together to achieve it, as well as be allowed to contribute to its success.

Respect

Respect starts with a sincere desire to contribute, from an employee, company, and business partner perspective. Everyone is respected, regardless of who they are, what they do, how much money they make, or the title they hold. Everyone is equal in their potential ability to contribute to the team's pursuit of perfection and to accept personal responsibility for their actions, as well as build mutual trust and understanding with those around them.

Everyone is also respected when it comes to their opinions, perceptions, thoughts, and ideas. No idea is too "out there" that it won't be considered. Pushing yourself to continuously ask "why," in whatever shape or form that takes, is encouraged, as is creative problem solving.

As you can see, a Lean mindset can be developed by learning and applying these principles and values, along with developing and practicing the two pillars of The Toyota Way. It is the conduit to help you face 21st-century leadership challenges head on, because it fosters looking at things in a different way. It gives you the space to be creative and color outside of the lines. It supports you in developing the courage to challenge yourself and others, to innovate and continuously evolve in the pursuit of illusive perfection. The cornerstone of leading Lean is represented in the core values and principles within The Toyota Way. Adopting Lean thinking and developing a kaizen mind results in the development of a Lean leader's mindset, one that addresses the challenges of leading yourself, others, and your customers, within the Lean enterprise and the world we live in, as well as arming you to face and address the disruption that is all around us in today's global business climate.

Leading in the Era of Modern Lean

Lean itself has not remained stagnant over the years and has undergone its own continuous improvement efforts since its inception. Evolving from its humble beginnings in the 1950s in that Piggly Wiggly grocery store in Dearborn, Michigan, when the Toyota delegation came to the United States to study America's state-of-the-art production manufacturing systems.[14] However, they didn't find what they were looking for at Ford or General Motors, because they believed production methods entailed much more than the mechanical processes of standardizing work—they're about harnessing the power of people, as well as process and technology. This belief system was instilled from the start by Sakichi Toyoda, and grounded in his humble core values, which were later thoroughly studied and introduced to the Western world in the 1990s by Dan T. Jones, Dan Roos, and James Womack, as well as Jeffery Liker.

In 2001, Toyota leaders, determined to expand globally, drafted "The Toyota Way," a document that explicitly captured and codified the implicit knowledge that represents the company's beliefs, values, behaviors, and business methods so that Toyota could globally expand its Lean production capabilities.[15] This effort was rewarded in 2007, when Toyota Motor Corporation became the largest auto manufacturer in the world,[16] ushering in what I call the "Era of Modern Lean."

Many books and articles have been written on how to "copy" the Toyota Production System (TPS), and many companies have tried to emulate its success, with very little to show for their efforts. In my opinion, they failed to understand this connection between people, process, and technology. Lean was never intended to be strictly mechanical, focusing only on standardized work as a way of increasing both productivity and quality. However, it has been interpreted as such in many parts of the Western world and turned into a process-oriented initiative that does not capture the hearts and minds of the people that must execute, maintain, and continuously improve upon this system.

Modern Lean is the foundation for the 21st-century Lean enterprise, where all the parts work well separately, as well as together, to form an integrated, optimized system that creates and delivers customer, stakeholder, and company value. This holistic approach embraces the ability to effectively respond to dis-

---

14 Leonardo Group Americas, "How Piggly Wiggly Revolutionized Manufacturing" (*https://oreil.ly/O8BLJ*), Medium. February 4, 2015.

15 Toyota Motor Corporation, "The Toyota Way 2001" (*https://oreil.ly/eT3Fg*), Toyota Motor Corporation Official Website, accessed July 14, 2019.

16 Ibid., Leonardo Group Americas, "Piggly Wiggly."

ruptive change at every level (strategic, tactical, and operational). To truly succeed at embracing Modern Lean, you must understand this connection and work to synthesize all three, to capture and sustain competitive advantage. Without focusing on all of these aspects, you are not firing on all cylinders, nor are you embracing the true spirit of Lean.

The missing ingredient in the discussion, however, is Leadership! Now more than ever, the world desperately needs Lean leaders who can operate within and amongst the six equally important dimensions of the Modern Lean Framework™ (Figure 2-1), to face and conquer the challenges brought on by our rapidly changing 21st-century global economy. To become a Lean leader, you must first focus on developing your own ability to lead so that others will follow you. Then you must be able to put Lean principles into context to lead others across the Lean enterprise, helping them to become leaders as well. The pursuit of illusive perfection drives Lean leaders as they build products/services that deliver value and effectively respond to disruption through constant and calculated innovation. And finally, your culture plays an important part in ensuring all of the dimensions are supported as the Lean enterprise evolves and strives for continuous learning and improvement. It acknowledges the importance of both the parts and the whole and acknowledges the customer is at the center of the Lean enterprise.

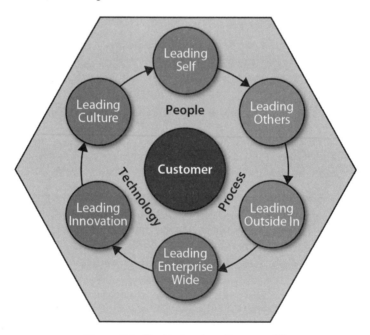

Figure 2-1. *The Modern Lean Framework™*

To become an effective Lean leader, you must build competency on a continuous basis, both within and between each of these dimensions, all while remaining keenly focused on your customer. This framework allows you to evolve your abilities to lead yourself, others, customers, enterprise, and innovation; from a people, process, and technology perspective, within a culture that fosters and supports Lean leaders to stretch and grow together, as a holistic unit. Let's take a brief look at each of these six dimensions and how the rest of the chapters in this book will be dedicated to exploring this framework in greater detail.

Leading Self

The choice to consciously become or be a leader should not be taken lightly and is not an easy one. You must commit to a life of continuous development, learning, and improvement. Chapter 3 will teach you how to develop a sense of emotional intelligence, how to practice mindfulness through reflection and introspection, and how to protect your own time to make yourself a more effective leader.

Leading Others

Leadership is about being of service to others, first and foremost. In Chapter 4 you'll learn how to develop a "servant's heart"—that is, the ability to serve first and foremost—by learning to value the diversity of the people you lead and to respect the individual experiences and points of view of people on your team, and you'll learn how to become an effective problem solver, as well as a mentor and coach. This last tenet is arguably the most important aspect of leading others; as Akio Toyoda, the current president of Toyota Motor Corporation, puts it, "We all need a sensei who will guide us to the next level of achievement. I personally still have many sensei teaching me."[17]

Leading Outside In

As a Lean leader, it's not about what you want; it's about what meets and exceeds your customer's unmet wants, needs, and/or desires. Chapter 5 will teach you how to embrace Lean and systems thinking to define value from a customer perspective, to understand how to identify and build customer experiences that matter by identifying who your customers are and the paths they take to interact with you, and build a meaningful omnichannel customer experience to effectively reach them across all your channels.

---

17 Liker and Convis, *The Toyota Way to Lean Leadership*, loc. 105, Kindle.

Leading Enterprise Wide

Lean enterprises are purpose-driven and outcome-focused, achieved through ensuring there is an overall vision, mission, and value proposition. As you'll learn in Chapter 6, proactively building the centralized strategic decision-making (CSDM) framework and employing Lean enterprise thinking ensures you travel the correct course required to build the right products/services at the right time and for the right reasons to satisfy the "real" unfulfilled wants, needs, and/or desires of your customer base.

Leading Innovation

As many a great football coach or military officer has said, "The best defense is a good offense." So thinking with an innovative mind and going on offense by being the instigator of change (also known as disruption) gives you the advantage of watching your competition react to you. Chapter 7 provides you with strategies on how to adopt a disruptive mind, including how to design and build innovative and disruptive products/services in an iterative and incremental way, as well as fostering innovation through continuous learning.

Leading Culture

Culture is quite possibly the most misunderstood dimension within the framework. Contrary to popular belief, culture is a very visible and malleable thing within the Lean enterprise. Chapter 8 addresses how to identify and resolve issues impacting the creation of a healthy Lean enterprise, as well as how to tie organizational and individual goals together to achieve a sustainable and consistent pace of work that results in tangible and trackable forward progress.

Conclusion

Adopting a Lean mindset and leading from a holistic perspective, represented within the Modern Lean Framework™, is how you will prepare yourself to be a leader in the world of 21st-century Lean enterprise. It will be a journey, and once you embark on it, you will realize it has no end because Lean is a mindset and set of principles that is a way of life. Therefore, it has the power to change your personal and professional life for the better, as well as change those around you, your organization, and even the world, as more and more people respond to the call.

However, let's not get ahead of ourselves. The first step to becoming a Lean leader is to fully understand what it means to lead yourself, so let's start there in the next chapter.

CHAPTER 3

Leading Self

You must be able to lead yourself before you can lead others. The skills, abilities, and competencies discussed in this chapter—self-development, having a bias toward action, meeting challenges head-on, using common sense to inform decision making, and being persistent and tenacious, to name a few—will provide you with the strategies and insight to do just that. As we discuss them, you'll find that many of these skills, abilities, and competencies are quite interrelated and difficult to separate from each other or talk about in isolation. Becoming self-led means being a well-rounded person—someone who is emotionally, physically, intellectually, spiritually, and socially balanced across both their personal and professional dimensions. Let's take a look at how you can develop the expertise to become a leader that people want to follow.

Keep in mind that change doesn't happen overnight. This is a journey that will last a lifetime. And don't beat yourself up or give up when you stray from this path. At any point in time, you can find your way back and continue your journey.

Believing and Trusting in Yourself Through Self-Development

To be a leader that people want to follow, you must offer them the stability and security that comes from truly believing and trusting in yourself. And yes, people are looking for true leaders to believe in and follow, now more than ever.

However, a leader cannot teach what they cannot do. "Do as I say and not as I do" does not apply here. You must develop your skills and abilities before you can teach, develop, mentor, coach, and lead others, which means you must first be able to trust and believe in yourself. To accomplish this, you must dedicate yourself to the lifelong pursuit of perfecting your craft as a leader. Leadership is an art that's situational and adaptive and requires creativity.

The pursuit of perfection is an elusive and ultimately unobtainable goal. However, it's the mechanism that drives you to become a seeker who challenges the status quo. It must become the motivating factor and common thread throughout your life and your leadership journey.

Leaders often experience a "good to great" moment when they're well prepared and are at the right place at the right time. At that moment, they find themselves at the juncture where preparedness meets opportunity. Some call this "luck," but luck has very little to do with it. Continuously practicing and honing your craft through the pursuit of perfection means that when an opportunity presents itself, you are ready to face the challenge head-on. To an outsider looking in, a great leader makes it appear easy to lead well. However, that statement couldn't be further from the truth and actually creates the wrong impression of how difficult it truly is to become an effective leader.

Practicing the craft of leadership is difficult because there are no canned answers; leadership is situational. What worked well in one challenging situation may not work at all in the next one you encounter. You must take that leap of faith and develop the skills and abilities to respond and face each challenge while you continuously develop, improve, and evolve your ability to respond to others in the world around you. Therefore, it is crucial you believe in yourself and your capacity to face the disruptive forces that are all around you, dedicating yourself to always be learning and growing as a leader. "Practice makes perfect!"

And no one can do it for you. Self-development and continuous learning must become a part of your daily routine. Reflection and introspection are two important tools for learning to believe and trust in yourself. It's imperative that you get to know yourself well and that you "check in" every day to figure out how you feel, what you're thinking, and what's on your mind. I've developed the habit of getting up early to take advantage of the stillness the morning offers. Before the hustle and bustle of the day begins, I sit quietly with myself and meditate for at least 15 minutes. I clear my mind and just breathe, taking deep, full breaths from my diaphragm. I push everything but me out of it so that I can concentrate on my body and mind to figure out what is going on inside of me. As I sit quietly, I run through the following checklist:

- How am I feeling in my body today? Can I feel all parts of my body? Does anything hurt (mentally or physically)? Am I feeling any pain anywhere? Asking yourself if you can feel all of your body parts might seem like an odd question. However, keep in mind that we hold our emotions, pain, stress, mental condition, etc., in the cells and tissue that make up our bodies. Acknowledging and dealing with pain is the only way to move through and get rid of it.

- How is my breathing? Smooth? Shallow? Labored?

- What is my emotional state? Happy? Sad? Indifferent?

- Is there anything that's particularly troubling me? Am I finding joy and happiness on my current path?

I've found that practicing daily meditation helps ensure my breathing fills my body with oxygen, which helps me think and act more efficiently. Whether you realize it or not, your mind, body, and soul are all connected and need to be in alignment. Being "in touch" with yourself is very important, because it impacts how you function throughout your day. Emotions, mood, temperament: all come directly from what is going on in your body. And don't kid yourself: if you are in pain or chronically stressed, it will show on the outside.

It took me some time to develop these questions, and I encourage you to give them a try and see how they work for you. Take the time to reflect, and come up with additional questions that help you to understand who you are and how you relate to yourself. Also, make sure to think about the things you've learned and any insights you've gained. I suggest keeping a journal to record your findings so you can refer back to it later—this helps to facilitate awareness of how you respond, both mentally and physically, to different situations and allows you to use those insights in the pursuit of continuous learning and improvement. So use the 15 minutes after you meditate to answer and record your responses, then periodically reflect back on them to ensure you are learning and growing.

I also built an awareness over time of how my body naturally responds to its different states, slowly developing the unconscious competence to effectively deal with and take whatever steps were necessary to correct the things that weren't exactly right within myself so that I could more effectively cope with whatever life might throw at me. Keep in mind this is a process that might take a while, so don't give up on yourself. You're worth taking 30 minutes out of your day to do this type of self check-in. Admittedly, I go through periods where I take really good care of myself, and others when I'm not so conscientious. Make an affirmation that you'll do better tomorrow, and then find your "me" time. Committing to a life of continuous learning, improvement, and evolution is well worth the time and effort. As Ray Kroc (founder and former

CEO of McDonald's) once said, "Always be green and growing, and never ripe and rotting."

Developing a Healthy Mind and Body

Whether you're aware of it or not, your followers are watching you. So if your own life is a mess (either personally or professionally, or even both), why would people want to follow you as a leader? Leading a chaos-filled life doesn't inspire confidence in your followers.

Eliminating Chaos

Figure 3-1 is an illustration of the drama triangle of communication, developed by Stephen Karpman, M.D.,[1] which is a model for explaining social interactions and how we handle conflict. There are three roles when dealing with emotionally charged situations: the victim, the rescuer, and the persecutor. The basic premise of this model is that, if you enter the triangle as a rescuer (which is also indicative of a "hero" or "savior" complex), you will eventually become the persecutor and in the end, the victim, when the person you sought to save turns on you as this drama-filled situation plays out.

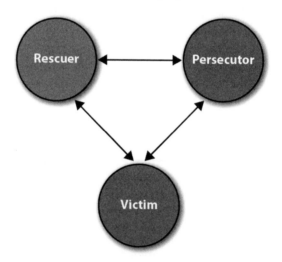

Figure 3-1. *The drama triangle of communication*

Does this sound familiar to you? It did to me. Finding Dr. Karpman's work during my graduate studies was a turning point in my life because I realized I

---

1 Stephen B. Karpman, *A Game Free Life* (San Francisco: Drama Triangle Publications, 2014).

was an adrenaline junkie who thrived on drama and chaos. It left me living on the edge all the time. After this "eureka" moment, I spent a lot of time trying to figure out why I had such a strong need to rush in and play the rescuer or be the "hero." I was not only doing myself a disservice by thriving on always being on the edge of a "flight or fight" response, thus feeding my need to feel the adrenaline rush that those situations created, but I was also enabling the bad behavior of those around me. In the end, my relationships and career suffered, and it was time to take responsibility and figure things out.

If you find yourself in a similar situation, ask yourself:

- Why am I responding in this manner?
- What is it about this situation or person that compels me to want to save them?
- What is motivating me to jump into the triangle?
- How can I break this cycle?

For me, the answers to these questions were life-changing and helped me come down off my adrenaline high. I realized that I didn't believe and trust in myself enough to develop the courage to face reality head-on. I wasn't able to drop all the games I was playing with myself and others. This was a major revelation, and I realized I had just moved from the "ignorance is bliss" phase (unconscious incompetence) into the "boy, this is really self-defeating behavior" phase (conscious incompetence). When you take these steps to develop the competence to break reactionary patterns, you'll be able to handle these types of situations in a much healthier way.

Let me ask you this: Have you ever known someone that leaves you feeling physically, emotionally, or intellectually drained or exhausted to the point that all you want to do is go take a nap after you've spent some time with them? That's a sure sign of a toxic person or one-sided relationship. On the other hand, have you ever spent time with someone and found that, after the interaction, you both felt mutually energized, uplifted, and supported? You can identify a toxic person by checking in with yourself and asking:

- Do I dread seeing, being around, or interacting with this person?
- Does this person pump me up one minute and then put me down the next?
- Am I overlooking or accepting behavior that I wouldn't normally accept in other situations?
- Why do I seek acceptance from this person when deep down I know it will never come?

Now that these questions are top of mind, are you running through your mental Rolodex?

We all have relationships in which the energy ebbs and flows. Sometimes you get more than you give, and vice versa. However, when you end up getting the short end of the stick more often than not in your interactions with a particular person, then it's time to examine how healthy that relationship is for both of you.

As a Lean leader, you will be constantly challenged by those around you to solve their problems for them. I just spoke with someone the other day that wanted me to "save" her by figuring out the answer to a challenging situation she was facing. When I tried to shift the dynamic of the conversation to get her to take responsibility for figuring out the solution, she actually got angry with me and walked away; that was totally her prerogative, and I respected her decision to remove herself. However, it did not change the fact that the situation needed to be addressed and resolved, which was still her responsibility. It just wasn't going to be me who charged in on my white horse and saved her. Those days are long gone for me.

Toyota's leadership development program intentionally places the company's potential leaders in just these types of situations. It is up to them to face the challenge head-on and figure it out. Their sensei or teacher is not going to hand them the answer. Each student must take responsibility for figuring out a solution and then present it to the teacher, so that they can together evaluate its potential to solve the problem. That is the responsibility that leadership brings with it. You are inherently a problem solver, because much of what leadership is comes down to how effectively you face and solve the challenges that cross your path.

Keeping a Healthy Body

When working to develop yourself and to create a healthy mind, it's also important that you assess the health of your body. Many high achievers fall prey to habits that create a self-induced high caused by the endorphins that are naturally released in response to threatening situations. Here are some questions you can ask yourself:

- Does the thought of being still (that is, doing absolutely nothing) scare me to death or create a level of anxiety that's unbearable?

- Do I look for opportunities to "stir things up," in a not very positive way, when things seem to be going well in my life?

- Do I become overly assertive or even aggressive in situations where that type of behavior isn't warranted, necessary, or appropriate? Am I short-tempered, do I have a short fuse, or do I easily "fly off the handle"?

- Do I turn to drugs, sex, alcohol, caffeine, nicotine, etc., to keep my energy level up, keep my "edge," or help me sleep at night? Is the thought of realizing I have an addiction terrifying?

I can openly admit that in my past, when I was honest with myself, I would have answered "Yes" to all of these questions. Again, many high achievers get caught in this cycle; the more successful you become, the more self-induced pressure you put on yourself to maintain that success. It becomes harder and harder to break away from this destructive cycle.

That's where good old-fashioned physical exertion can help. You might already have a physical routine that helps keep you centered, but if you don't, I encourage you to explore physical outlets, like running, dancing, swimming, yoga—whatever appeals to you, and more importantly, whatever you can integrate into your daily life as a habit. The benefits of exercise for mental well-being are well documented, and making exercise a part of your everyday life can help you to work past some of the less desirable mental habits that we sometimes fall into and that can stunt your growth as an effective Lean leader.

Make Time for Yourself

You MUST make time for yourself! "Me time" refreshes your mind and body. Look at your schedule and figure out when you can consistently carve this time out. I've found that mornings are my best chance at me time, though it means making some trade-offs (like not staying out too late with my teams or clients or getting my work done during the day so I'm not working all the time). To find this time, ask yourself:

- What behavior will I need to stop or start to find my me time?
- Am I using the time I have during the day in the most productive way?
- Are there natural lulls in my schedule where I can find time for myself?
- Can I work with my spouse/significant other to ensure we both get regular me time? After all, relationships are two people working at 100% because 50/50 means you're only giving half of yourself to make it work.

Guard your "me time" carefully. It will make you a much calmer and more well-rounded Lean leader, even it turns out to be only a few hours a week. Take it and DO NOT feel guilty about it. Remember, you are worth it!

Understand Your Own Reality

Finally, you must cultivate an awareness of your reality. For me, this meant seeking enlightenment by learning about and practicing Buddhism. Buddhism helps to foster a state of awareness that develops a connection between your mind, body, and soul. It was founded over two and a half millennia ago by Buddha Shakyamuni. He believed that all human suffering was self-imposed and that all pain in life was self-inflicted through negative states of mind and being, such as anger, jealousy, and ignorance. However, he also believed that these states could be overcome by embracing love, compassion, and wisdom to create a positive mind[2] through mindfulness and being aware of who you are and what you are about.

I've found that strong corollaries can be made between Buddhism and The Toyota Way:

- Both are about the lifelong pursuit of self-development, as well as making a commitment to continuous learning in an attempt to strive for perfection —a perfection that's unobtainable because humans are never perfect.

- They both encourage a lifelong quest that drives you to become the best possible person, by focusing on your reality through building an understanding of who you are and how best you can serve yourself, others, and the greater good. They both use techniques that remove confusion and bring about internal stillness, as you clear away the clouds in your mind and those that encase your soul.

- Both stress taking personal responsibility for yourself and the results, or lack thereof, that you achieve in your life. It's up to you and no one else. After all, it's your life and your pursuit of happiness, and no one can achieve enlightenment for you.

In Buddhism, enlightenment is achieved by letting go of those things that you cannot change. Once you realize that fretting over things you can't control results in a lot of wasted time and energy you can never get back, you can begin to focus instead on what's important—that is, the things that are right in front of you, in the here and now. Being present is a wonderful thing because it allows you to experience all that life has to offer in real time. Buddha taught that enlightenment is achieved by developing a stillness of mind that allows you to peacefully live in the present, without all the self-inflicted noise and drama we create for ourselves.

Stillness is achieved through meditation, which, being the overachiever that I am, I thought would be a breeze for me. However, I quickly learned that even sitting still for five minutes was difficult for me. My mind, no matter how hard I tried to focus on my body through deep breathing, would quickly fill and race with ideas, things I needed to do, events of the day, you name it—they

---

2 Bhante Henepola Gunaratana, *Eight Mindful Steps to Happiness: Walking the Buddha's Path* (Somerville, MA: Wisdom Publications, 2001).

were there in my head as I struggled to bring my mind back to focus on my breathing. Over time, though, I found it got easier and easier to sit quietly. First 5 minutes, then 10, then a half hour, and eventually I could sit for as long as I wanted. I ultimately found that about 15 minutes a day works well for me; when I am feeling especially nervous or anxious about a situation in my life, I extend it to about 30 minutes.

I know this might sound odd, but what I discovered was that I actually needed to slow down to move forward. My concentration and overall state of well-being improved, and when I would go for a run, I found myself not replaying the tapes of the day and beating myself up over the things I thought I didn't handle well. I stopped worrying about things I couldn't control, the quality of my relationships improved, and I found I attracted healthier people into my life.

One of the most valuable lessons I learned through all of this was that there's a right way and a wrong way to reflect on the past, and the goal is to "learn forward"—that is, with an eye toward my future, by not dwelling on or repeating the past. *Hansei* is the Japanese word for "reflection." It's the conscious process of looking back at oneself and critically reflecting on:

- What went well?
- What didn't go so well?
- What can I do better or improve upon next time around?

Keeping a journal where you write out your answers to these questions is a great way to learn forward. Writing moves your reflections from your conscious to your unconscious mind. These thoughts are then stored and held there until you encounter a similar issue or situation, and, whether you realize it or not, your mind accesses this information and will apply it the next time around. You can also categorize your journal entries based on the type of dimension, mindful state, and overall outcome so that you can quickly look back and pull those learnings forward into your current circumstances. I've also found it helpful to add a few keywords that will help me quickly recall the essence of the situation so that I can relate it to the problem, issue, or situation at hand. For example, I use the following categories myself and write them in the upper righthand corner of the page for easy reference:

- Dimension: Personal or Professional
- State: Emotional, Intellectual, Physical, and/or Spiritual

- Outcome: Success or Failure
- Keywords (such as leadership, communication, collaboration, strategy, planning, relationships, family, etc.)

Life is a series of patterns that play out over and over again. If you're going to change your responses to these patterns and learn forward, you must be able to examine the past and make changes to affect the outcome the next time around. Reflection and introspection give you the tools to do just that.

Developing a Bias Toward Action

One of the most common traits I've observed in successful leaders is their bias toward action. They don't wait around for someone else to solve their problems. They take it upon themselves to take responsibility for the results they achieve in their lives, both professionally and personally, which is complemented by a strong work ethic and a sense of follow-through. But taking action doesn't necessarily mean rushing to make decisions or trying to quickly handle issues, because without understanding the consequences or thinking through the ramifications of your actions and/or decisions you can end up with an equation for disaster and ultimately experience failure. It means getting off of GO when facing issues or problems and turning your ideas into tangible results that move you and those around you forward. Developing a bias toward action means you're taking on the challenge of developing a new habit, as well as the habitual behaviors to effectively address the problems, situations, and issues you face in your life.

This means eliminating procrastination from your life. I know firsthand what a struggle this can be: I used to play a self-defeating game of procrastinating about stuff that was important to me, both personally and professionally, so that I could rush in and yet again save the day or myself from whatever peril I was encountering (remember that "savior" complex?). But you should not put off important things. Waiting until the last minute might very well backfire on you, resulting in poor work product or bad decisions being made in a rush.

Here are some healthy habits you can adopt to guard against falling into this self-defeating trap:

1. First, understand that you must plan your work and work your plan.
   a. Write down the things that matter to you and that will move you forward.
   b. Identify the decisions that need to be made, the possible expected outcomes, and the obstacles that you might encounter.

c. Then develop a list of next steps that are relevant to the outcome, writing them down and checking them off as you complete each one.

d. Finally, develop a schedule or action plan to accomplish your goal.

2. Then, always keep a finger on the pulse of your reality.

a. Understand early on what is or isn't valid as far as your ideas go, and thoroughly vet them to ensure they are deserving of your time and energy. Being overly optimistic or Pollyannaish about the likelihood of success or overly pessimistic about failure can blind you to the realities of what you're truly trying to accomplish. Stay objective, and don't "fall in love" with your genius. It's a rabbit hole on the scale of *Alice in Wonderland*, and after all, that was just a fairy tale.

b. Keep yourself focused on the here and now and on what you realistically can and cannot achieve. Possessing this type of perspective will keep you grounded.

3. And finally, limit your Work in Process (WIP), and always, always follow through!

a. Understand how much time you can devote to following through on your ideas, which will help you prioritize the most important ones while not wasting time on things that have little or no value when it comes to what you're trying to accomplish.

b. Once you set something in motion, you must see it through. Starting and not finishing is not a pattern that aspiring Lean leaders subscribe to.

c. If you find yourself in a position of being overloaded, prioritize your inflight activities and focus on finishing the high-priority ones first. That is, stop starting and start finishing to get things done and moved off of your plate.

To be an effective self-led leader, you must first be able to take action yourself to get results. You must lead by example and show others that no matter your formal title or role within an organization, there is no task so small that you can't perform it yourself to ensure you get results that move things forward. Possessing a bias toward action will make you a leader that people naturally want to follow.

Facing Challenging Situations Head-On

Life is full of adversity, and going through it thinking that you'll never encounter obstacles is an unrealistic perspective. Many a great leader was born through adversity, because it's in the face of challenging situations that we either rise to the occasion or fail. Yes, we would all love to float through life without facing our challenges. However, that's not a realistic expectation. The difference between those who succeed and those who fail is their attitude toward failure. Practicing the techniques mentioned in the previous section allows you to examine and learn from failure and makes your next attempt even more likely to succeed, as you pull your learnings forward and narrow down the possibilities for how to proceed.

Here are six tips to help you effectively face and deal with the challenges that come into your life:

1. Objectively define the challenge that must be addressed and own all parts of the role you played in it. Playing the "victim" card when it's not warranted is a sure way to lose credibility with the people involved in the situation. You must honestly and openly evaluate the situation to ensure it's worthy of your time and energy. Don't let your pettiness or vanity get in the way of seeing the situation for what it truly is or cause you to make a mountain out of a molehill.

2. Do not allow your emotions to get the best of you. Many challenges may elicit strong emotions that might just overtake you and make things worse. So find a mentor, someone whom you respect and admire, and go over the situation together. Ask your mentor for an objective, third-party opinion. Also, being overly optimistic or pessimistic will taint the way you handle the challenge, so validate your perception of the reality of the situation before taking action.

3. Don't procrastinate. Time doesn't make things better. It only puts the situation farther back in your rearview mirror, and as time passes, you become less and less likely to address it. The problem with procrastinating is that the situation, most likely, will manifest itself in a different form over and over again in your life until you do face it head-on. On the flip side, don't prematurely rush in and try to face it without doing your due diligence. Sometimes cooler heads need to prevail, because a win/win situation is what you're after. Burning bridges or making enemies means that somewhere down the line those actions will come back to haunt or work against you. As Stephen Covey, author of *The 7 Habits of Highly Successful People* (Simon & Schuster) believed, being a leader is about doing the right things. So figure out what those things are, and then take action or do them right, because it's all about how you execute to get the results that benefit everyone involved.

4. Trust in yourself and be confident that you can overcome this challenge. After all, we're all human, and no one has superpowers that are better than yours. Empower yourself using the qualities of integrity, honesty, trust, respect, and belief in yourself to build an attitude of self-empowerment and determination.

5. When you do take action, celebrate the fact that you attempted to face the challenge head-on, no matter the outcome. We don't always get what we want and things don't always turn out as planned. So, regardless of the outcome, pat yourself on the back for having the courage to try: it says a lot about who you're becoming.

6. And finally: welcome adversity, because it builds character and strengthens your resolve. Working through adversity prepares you to take on bigger and bigger challenges as you progress through life. Remember, practice makes perfect, and when you're faced with the biggest challenge of your life, you'll be able to more effectively respond to, resolve, and move through it.

Leveraging Common Sense for Problem Solving and Decision Making

In my opinion, common sense, defined as "sound judgment derived from experience, rather than study,"[3] is the most important skill you can learn as a leader, because people who possess it are seen as reasonable, approachable, reliable, and practical. Developing these qualities in yourself requires practice and takes time. Applying sound judgment means you understand what is and isn't good for you. It means clearly understanding the relationship between cause and effect ("If I do X, it will result in Y.") based on facts versus emotion.

Ask yourself, "What are the ramifications and implications of this course of action or decision for me, my spouse/significant other, colleagues, my community, society, or the planet? Who or what will be positively or adversely affected by my actions or decisions?" Intentionally hurting others for your own gain is both morally and ethically wrong, and it is not on the path to being a self-led Lean leader. Serving others and contributing to the greater good *is* very much a part of being a leader. Not stopping to apply common sense to your decisions can come back to seriously affect you and those around you.

Just the Facts

Making a decision through the use of common sense means making a fact-based decision or coming to a conclusion that can be easily justified using facts. Let's say you're trying to determine whether or not to bring a new product to market; this product is something you've been working on for months, and you're personally invested in ensuring its success. However, while

---

3 Jim Taylor, "Common Sense Is Neither Common nor Sense" (*https://oreil.ly/UZzBg*), *Psychology Today*, July 12, 2011.

conducting focus groups with potential customers, you find the product is appealing to only two in ten customers. Personally and professionally, this is a big blow, because this product could be a career maker for you, if successful. However, the facts clearly show that, as things stand now, if you move ahead, the product will be only marginally successful, which could have majorly adverse effects on your career. So what should you do? Should you ignore the results and move ahead anyway, even though the facts point to the product being a major flop if it's released without any major improvements or changes?

Common sense tells you that you need to go back to the drawing board and fix whatever it is that's unappealing to your potential customers. You must remove your emotions from the decision-making process and concentrate on the facts. Once you let reason fly out the window, you're vulnerable to making poor or bad decisions that cannot be defended when scrutinized, because they were not made from a place of reason or logic. "Just because" doesn't really cut it when your boss calls you into their office and asks why you just threw a couple of million dollars away on a product that appealed to only two in ten people!

A great technique I've found to help with proactive decision making and problem solving is the Lean technique of the 5 Whys. Ask yourself "why" five times, and don't accept your first answer, because it's usually the superficial and most obvious one. The heart of the matter or crux of the problem will reveal itself closer to the fourth or fifth time you ask yourself "why"—for example, "Why did I want to release this product so badly?" or "Why am I ignoring the results of the focus group studies on this product?" Either question would have worked in this situation and would have gotten to the heart of your reasoning. And if you take the 5 Whys and customer feedback into account and then fold those learnings back into the product development process, you might just have yourself a winning product. By the time you get to the fourth or fifth "why," you've removed all emotion from the situation and are running on just the facts. That's when common sense appears and reason prevails.

An Ounce of Common Sense

It's relatively easy to ascertain the degree of common sense someone has by observing their behavior and speech patterns. If they are unable to give a fact-based response or become defensive when you ask them to explain how they arrived at a decision or conclusion, then they're probably not employing common sense or reasoning through the situation. As Frank Lloyd Wright, the renowned American architect, once said, "There is nothing more uncommon than common sense."[4] To apply even an ounce of common sense means you are willing to:

1. *Slow down.* Many poor decisions are made because we feel like we need to rush to a decision. My advice: slow down, take a breath, be still, and think through the situation at hand. Determine what exactly your goal is when solving this problem or coming to a conclusion. A lack of common sense can come from not thoroughly understanding your own goals and from having an unrealistic perception of reality. How does the conclusion you're looking for move you closer to that goal?

2. *Keep your emotions in check to collect all the data.* It's much easier to elicit an emotional response than it is to step back and apply the knowledge and wisdom you've gained through experience to the situation at hand. You should always try to come from a position of reason and logic and commit to turning all your alternatives over in your head. Ask yourself, "Is this the best course of action for all involved? Is this the way I would like to be treated if the tables were turned? Are there multiple solutions that need further examination? Is there a pattern to this problem that I can recognize and apply past knowledge and experience to, in order to improve my options?" And don't forget about that little voice in the back of your head. What is it saying to you about the choice you are about to make? Is it cheering you on or screaming at you not to open your mouth? More times than not, we know a bad choice or decision before we even make it. Settle your emotions, be patient, and let that little voice speak to you before you open your mouth. What you're looking for is to deliver pearls of wisdom, not to taste your own shoe leather.

3. *Get a second opinion.* Sometimes talking things through with someone you respect and trust can be invaluable in coming to the correct decision or conclusion about a situation. As I've said before, finding a mentor or coach you can work with is important to your self-development journey. Getting one sooner rather than later improves your chances of changing your behavior through listening to how someone else might handle the same situation, which might just help you figure out how far off base you are on the common-sense front.

4. *Reflect on your decision and the outcome.* If you don't stop to reflect on the experience, then you've learned nothing in the process and are prone to making the same foolish mistakes over and over again. So remember that

---

4 "Quote by Frank Lloyd Wright" (*https://www.goodreads.com/quotes/tag/intellegence*), Goodreads, accessed February 16, 2019.

common sense is strengthened by reflecting on your experience and then having the self-discipline to learn and adjust.

Tapping into Your Emotional Intelligence

Emotional intelligence (EQ) is a concept introduced in 1995 by psychologist and science journalist Daniel Goleman in his book *Emotional Intelligence*.[5] He defined EQ as the ability to successfully identify and manage one's own emotions, as well as the emotions of others[6] in day-to-day human interactions. People with high EQs are able to either cheer others up or calm them down during emotionally charged situations by focusing on the fact that all people are inherently good, rather than on the negative aspects of human nature. They focus on finding an emotional common ground to build on to form emotionally mature connections with others.

Leaders with higher EQs are more understanding and viewed as more authentic. They possess greater levels of sympathy and empathy. They truly try to see a situation through the other person's eyes, genuinely sharing what they're thinking and feeling in a positive and unthreatening way to work through the emotions and produce positive results for all involved, because they're tuned into the emotional states of others. They also display greater states of compassion, which makes them much more relatable to others. In other words, they're socially aware and understand how their emotions, as well as their emotional well-being, can impact others by reflecting on these interactions.

They also understand that emotions come in short- and long-term versions. The short-term version is the immediate response you feel at the onset of an emotionally charged event. It's your "knee-jerk" reaction. Emotionally immature responses happen to all of us, regardless of our age. Your long-term reaction, after introspection and contemplation, and of course dealing with the fallout from your initial reaction, combine to have a sobering effect once you've calmed down and thought through the situation. Allowing cooler heads to prevail avoids the damage you quite possibly could have done to the relationship through an emotionally charged response. Leaders with high EQ understand that their feelings change over time, and being mature enough to admit when you were wrong or overreacted is a sure sign of emotional intelligence. "I'm sorry" or "My apologies" are the hardest words to say in the

---

5 Daniel Goleman, *Emotional Intelligence: Why It Can Matter More than IQ* (New York: Bantam, 1995).

6 "What Is Emotional Intelligence?" (*https://oreil.ly/C9QSZ*), *Psychology Today*, accessed November 2, 2018.

English language; however, they go a long way toward mending the emotional fallout from a highly charged situation.

To help you work through these types of situations and increase your chances of having a rational conversation with those involved, as well as increasing your EQ, ask yourself the following questions:

- What went well in this situation?
- What didn't go so well?
- How can I improve my responses the next time around?

Yes, these questions are relevant to many situations in which you are trying to learn from what you just experienced. You also need to consider the flip side, where you endeavor to give constructive feedback to others on their own EQ and behavior. This feedback should be given in a genuine, nonthreatening way that's not biting, full of blame, or dripping with sarcasm. Remember, we're all human and pursuing (unobtainable) perfection, so exhibiting patience and an ability to refrain from judgment is what EQ is all about. Supplying positive reinforcement, as well as modeling the behavior in yourself that you are seeking from others, is the fastest way to building a following that sees you as an authentic, genuine, and inspirational Lean leader.

Displaying Persistence and Tenacity

Lean leaders who are tenacious and persistent enough to go after what they want with an unrelenting zeal are exhibiting both self-discipline and self-awareness, as well as being intrinsically motivated. It means that if you try something that doesn't work, you have the willingness and strength to try again because you believe that it can be done and that you'll figure out how you can make it happen and achieve success.

These two characteristics of a self-led Lean leader are crucial to developing a "can do" attitude that allows you to face adversity and the challenges you encounter in your life head-on. These qualities are complementary: you can be very tenacious, but without persistence and the will to overcome the issue or problem, all your efforts could result in very few tangible results. To hone your abilities, skills, and competencies to excel as a Lean leader, you must possess the persistence to hang in there and the tenacity to not accept anything less than what you believe in.

Allowing Yourself to Always Become the Student

Finally, but possibly most importantly, Lean leaders must develop the ability to become a student. Going back to the processes in place at Toyota, all those who aspire to leadership roles are given the same opportunity to take the initiative and study under the tutelage of a sensei. The sensei's responsibility is to provide challenges, structured opportunities, and coaching so that the student has an opportunity to learn by doing. However, it's up to the student to overcome these challenges. The sensei will not offer and may not even know the answer, because there is always more than one way to solve a problem. The point here is that you must grow your leadership abilities through constant and continuous learning throughout your life.

As a self-led Lean leader, you must become a student of human nature and work to develop many of the skills and abilities we've discussed in this chapter. Skills such as facing challenges head-on, developing common sense, and learning to tap into your EQ are not things you're going to learn through formal training or education. They must be developed and honed over time, under the guidance and watchful eye of a mentor, coach, or sensei. It doesn't matter how smart you are or how much you think you have "on the ball"—finding someone who acts as your trusted advisor is crucial to your development as a leader.

When searching for just the right mentor or coach, ask yourself if there is someone whom you admire or respect in your workplace, within your social circle, at your place of worship, or in some other sphere of your life. Do they exhibit the qualities we've discussed throughout this chapter? If the answer is yes, then that person would likely make a great mentor. Don't be afraid to go ask them if they would spend a couple of hours a month mentoring you. We've all been in the position of seeking a mentor at one time or another in our careers, and I've found that most people are more than happy to help when asked.

If you can't identify anyone that can fill this role, then look to a professional leadership coach that can help. Identify a few possibilities and then ask them for references. Talk to the people they have worked with in the past and ask them specific questions pertaining to what you're looking for in a coach. Do your due diligence to ensure you get the right sensei that will help you move forward. But remember that it is ultimately up to *you* to get results from a mentor/mentee relationship.

Understanding the importance of the student/teacher relationship is important from both sides when it comes to trust and respect. As a student, you must be responsible for the effort you put into your development and for the results you produce; whether the outcome results in success or failure, you must own it. That includes reflecting on your performance, understanding the feedback from your teacher, and incorporating those learnings back into the process. In turn, when you act as a teacher, you're responsible for the student's development, because if they fail, you fail as well. The teacher must also reflect on the causes of both success and failure. I take being a teacher and mentor very seriously, and I guard the number of these relationships I have going at any one time because I want to ensure I have the time to devote to each one. It is truly a collaborative learning experience between the teacher and the student, so understanding the responsibility of being both a teacher and a student is essential to the success of the relationship, as well as your continuous learning and development journey.

When you're looking for a mentor, ask them if they can commit the time to work with you. Have a candid conversation about the rules of engagement and set expectations upfront. Doing so creates a win/win situation for both of you. It's also okay if you find that you've outgrown your mentor and need to move on. But don't just disappear on them. Schedule a closure call or meeting and thank them for the time and energy they have put into working with you, and keep them in mind if you come across someone who is also searching for a mentor. Throughout your life, you'll play both roles—mentor and student—and within the relationships you develop, you are never too young or too old to teach others and to learn yourself.

Conclusion

The order of the topics I've covered here is very important. They appear in the order in which you need to work through them and develop the skills and abilities discussed. You will need to make some hard choices, but keep in mind that by working to develop your common sense and hone your problem-solving and decision-making abilities you'll be making well-thought-out choices. By tapping into your EQ, you can make logical and rational choices instead of emotion-filled decisions that aren't in your best interest. Tenacity and persistence play a big part in how successful you are because you'll have developed the "moxie" to stick with it and allow yourself to become both the student and teacher, in the long run learning from your successes, as well as from your failures.

Now that you have the tools and strategies at hand to lead yourself, it's time to move on to the next dimension of Modern Lean: leading others.

CHAPTER 4

Leading Others

Leading through service to others is a major tenet of Lean leadership. In this chapter, we'll explore the complementary relationship between servant leadership and Lean leadership, which means giving yourself over into the service of others. A servant leader fully acknowledges and accepts the responsibility to develop, support, enable, and encourage others on their path to serve and lead. This is a major tenet of Lean leadership philosophy. We'll also look at the two pillars of The Toyota Way—respect for others and continuous improvement—as well as how you can use the Toyota Business Practices (TBP) problem-solving technique in conjunction with on-the-job development (OJD) to develop aspiring leaders.

Defining Servant Leadership for the 21st Century

Servant leadership is focused on empowering and helping others become the best they can possibly be in all facets of their life, from a professional, social, physical, mental, intellectual, and spiritual perspective. The values of The Toyota Way are all brought to life and supported through the practice of servant leadership:

- Continuous improvement through the spirit of challenge and a bias toward action by going to the place where work is performed (the *gemba*) and respecting people by being inclusive
- Taking responsibility
- Acting with humility, dignity, honor, and integrity

The Toyota Way and servant leadership are complementary leadership philosophies: Lean leaders are inherently servant leaders, first and foremost.

Lean servant leaders are acutely focused on serving those they lead, as well as the Lean enterprise, instead of acquiring power or taking control. They attempt to continuously improve the people, processes, and technologies that are all around them. That means putting the needs of others before your own by empowering them and helping them to develop and perform at increasingly greater levels of competency and productivity, as well as improving their overall quality of life.

However, being a Lean servant leader doesn't mean you become an indentured servant. On the contrary, it means your focus is on learning to develop yourself, in addition to enabling those around you, through mentoring, coaching, supporting, and empowerment. Ultimately, what you're trying to create and foster is a collaborative, supportive, empathetic, engaging, and developmental relationship with those you lead—without implying that you're subservient to them. After all, your followers must take responsibility for their development and learning processes as well, which sets them on their path to becoming a Lean servant leader.

Origins of Servant Leadership

Servant leadership is not new. The term was coined by Robert K. Greenleaf (a well-known leadership and management consultant active from the 1950s to 1990) and first published in an essay in 1970.[1] Greenleaf was inspired by reading Hermann Hesse's *The Journey to the East*.[2] In Hesse's story, a band of men on a mythical journey are accompanied by a servant named Leo. Through his incredible presence, Leo becomes the lifeblood of the group. He looks after, entertains, and sustains the men. One day, however, Leo disappears, and the men abandon their journey, because he was such a vital part of it; they no longer believe they can continue on their own. Some years later, the narrator loses his way. As he wanders in the desert without purpose, he's fortunate enough to be taken in by an Order, only to find that Leo, whom he had first known as a servant, is their leader. He is their guiding spirit, a great and noble leader himself.

To Greenleaf, this story exemplifies that "The great leader is seen as a servant first, and that simple fact is the key to his [or her] greatness."[3] Leo's inherent

---

1 Robert K. Greenleaf, "The Servant as Leader" (*https://oreil.ly/WFu60*), Greenleaf Center for Servant Leadership, accessed October 8, 2017.

2 Hermann Hesse, *The Journey to the East* (Important Books, 2013).

3 Greenleaf, "Servant," 2.

desire and ability to serve is what made him a great leader. Leo genuinely enjoyed helping others grow and flourish, both individually and as a team. And in his joy to serve, his leadership abilities sprung forth. In response to the evident servant stature leaders must possess, Greenleaf later went on to say:

> Rather, they will freely respond only to individuals who are chosen as leaders because they are proven and trusted as servants. To the extent that this principle prevails in the future, the only truly viable institutions will be those that are predominantly servant-led. I am mindful of the long road ahead before these trends, which I see so clearly, become a major society-shaping force. We are not there yet. But I see encouraging movement on the horizon.[4]

Characteristics of Servant Leadership

Being a servant leader is defined by how you behave, think, act, and feel. Being of service to others is what motivates you to act. It's a selfless way of life that's based on building a vision that your followers can see and buy into to accomplish a mission that serves the greater good of the company, society, and even the world. Servant leadership can be summarized by three main qualities:

Integrity
Servant leaders lead with integrity, and their reputation for being morally honest and forthright, as well as for being true to their word, is an all-important and defining trait.

Continuous interaction
Servant leaders constantly work with those around them to foster and encourage their development as leaders because they genuinely care about others. Building and sustaining healthy relationships is very important to them, because they possess a strong sense of self-awareness and of the direction they want their lives to go in. Through their actions and behaviors, they lead by example, modeling behaviors they are looking for from their followers.

Diversity
Servant leaders cherish the diversity that life brings and value others' ability to contribute. They recognize that different backgrounds and educational and life experiences provide for a variety of opinions and points of view, adding to the value of their interactions, as well as to the results their teams can accomplish. Diversity is good! It renders more creative solutions.

---

4 Ibid., 3.

Servant leaders see their goals clearly and can communicate them well to others through their actions and words, thereby inspiring, motivating, and transforming others to act. A servant leader's power is informal, gained or generated through influence, inspiration, or expertise in a field or area of knowledge, and achieved through instinctively having a bias toward action when it comes to that vision. As the famous Chinese general Sun Tzu stated in his classic treatise on war, *The Art of War* (written around 500 BC), "A leader leads by example, not by force."[5] The philosopher Lao-Tzu expressed a similar idea in the Tao Te Ching (fourth century BC): "A leader is best when people barely know he exists, when his work is done, his aim fulfilled, they will say: we did it ourselves." That is the mark of a true servant leader.

Why Servant Leaders Are So Important to the Lean Enterprise

Lean servant leaders exist in sharp contrast to managers who possess formal power, which is something bestowed on them through a formal title and/or position within an organization. Managers have the responsibility of setting goals, communicating policies and status, coordinating work both within and among the teams, and providing the resources team members need to get the work done. They are responsible for managing the "work to a specific goal or outcome," acting as the linchpin that connects the team, senior leadership, and the organization.

The world needs both servant leaders and managers. However, you can be a manager without being a servant leader. In contrast, servant leaders often do not possess any formal positional power, even though they can be influential within an organization and make major contributions to its success. The mark of a servant leader who evolves from a manager is measured by their ability to play both roles, allowing the organization to naturally evolve from a controlling, authoritative system to a consultative, service-oriented one in which everyone participates and contributes to achieving its mission, vision, and value proposition. This is a crucial inflection point for the Lean enterprise as it continues to change and evolve under the watchful eyes of its Lean servant leaders.

Lean servant leadership is one of the most effective leadership styles for modern businesses because it is results-driven and also forms a meaningful bond of trust and respect between leaders and their teams, as the constant cycle of development, feedback, and learning happens over and over again. In their willingness to serve, these leaders naturally play the role of teachers, mentors, and coaches who create a safe space in which problem solving through

---

5 Sun Tzu, *The Art of War*, trans. Thomas Cleary (Boulder: First Edition. Shambhala Press, 1988).

listening, observing, experimentation, and learning from mistakes is not only acceptable but encouraged. The most highly skilled parts of our 21st-century workforce respond favorably to this type of leadership style.

These workforce members value inclusion, being challenged, and learning above all else. They are not motivated by a paycheck; instead, it is the intrinsic things that inspire and promote creativity and ingenuity. They refuse to be micromanaged through command-and-control leadership styles, seeking autonomy and a purpose to their life's work. And because of their skills and abilities, if they do not feel supported, empowered, and fulfilled in their current role, throughout their careers they will find it very easy to change employers. It is imperative that 21st century leaders understand this paradigm shift, because this highly skilled part of our workforce will continue to seek out and want to work for leaders who possess Lean servant leadership skills.

As a result, both the face of leadership and followership must change to meet this new 21st-century workplace dynamic. Thus the focus for you as a Lean servant leader must be on winning the loyalty of these highly skilled workers by inspiring, supporting, and developing them to give them everything they need to create and deliver innovative products/services, as well as to feel fulfilled, motivated, and valued by those they serve. Progressive companies understand this shift to support, encourage, and develop Lean servant leaders.

Becoming a Lean Servant Leader

Some people misinterpret the role when they hear the word "servant," thinking that servant leaders are pushovers. On the contrary, being a Lean servant leader is about asking the tough questions and challenging those around you to push themselves to achieve success in whatever they undertake. Your role is to help through good times and difficult ones, offering whatever assistance and support you can to get things moving again.

So how do you go about developing the skills that servant leaders need? Here are a few tips to help you get started.

Develop your True North

Before you can become any type of leader, you first must develop an awareness of the purpose for your life and career. By taking the time to define and develop your convictions around what you intend to accomplish, you build your path forward. Self-reflection and asking for feedback from others are two great tools to define and chart your True North. Spending some time writing down all the things you want to accomplish in your life goes a long way toward identifying and defining your life's purpose. As a Lean leader, you must proactively chart your course before someone else does it for you.

John Goddard (explorer, writer, and founder of the Goddard School) decided at the age of 16 to sit down and write out a lifetime to-do list,[6] similar to the concept of today's bucket list. Throughout his life, he diligently worked to accomplish the things on his list, stating that it gave him purpose and direction, acting as his personal True North. I, too, did the same at about his age, and when I finished it, I folded it up and tucked it away in a scrapbook of pictures and keepsakes from that same year, thinking that would be a good place to keep it safe.

Last year, when I was in the process of packing for a move, the list dropped out of that scrapbook. Immediately, I knew exactly what it was, and for a brief second, I thought to myself, "Do I even want to open it up?" I hadn't looked at it in a very, very long time, but my curiosity got the best of me. I was amazed (actually, "shocked" would be a better word) that when I tallied up what I had accomplished to date in my lifetime, it amounted to about 75% of what I had written down many decades ago. Keep in mind that thoughts are things and writing crystalizes your thoughts, turning them into action. All of those things have been with me, in the back of my mind, as I've progressed through my life. My subconscious mind had taken them in and committed them to memory. And yes, becoming an author was on that list.

So as you work to chart out your True North, ask yourself:

- Do you know what you want to accomplish?
- Are you proud of what you have accomplished in your life to date?
- If someone asked you to state your life's purpose or value proposition, how would you answer them?

Lean servant leaders help others to discover their True North. Ask those you mentor or coach to spend some time thinking about and writing down their lifetime to-do lists. If they have such a list already, ask them how you can help them accomplish these things. I think you'll be amazed at the drive and purpose such a list creates in both you and your followers. Checking things off your list can be very motivating and can drive your desire to achieve greater and more complicated things in your life.

Drop the "Lone Ranger" act

As a Lean servant leader, you must give up the notion that you're the only one that has to have all the answers or solve all the problems. As the old saying goes, "There is no 'I' in 'team'!" The next time you feel compelled to jump on that white horse of yours, stop and ask yourself, "Who should I ask to help me

---

6 Goddard's list can be found at *https://www.johngoddard.info/life_list.htm.*

with this problem?" After all, even the Lone Ranger had help. Who are your "go-to" people that care about supporting and developing you as you move through life? Figure that out, and then pull them in, challenging them to find new and more creative ways to solve the problems you face together, as a team.

See the potential in everyone

Lean servant leaders are thoughtful enough to take the time to understand what motivates others. They don't carelessly jump to conclusions about things, such as why someone is underperforming. Poor performance may not have anything to do with work but may instead be caused by something bleeding over from someone's personal life. Next time you're confronted with an employee performance issue, initiate a candid conversation around the issue at hand. Work with the person to find a solution that solves the problem so that once again they can contribute as a valuable member of the team. Lean servant leaders don't give up on people; they see the potential we all have to achieve great things. They extend the effort to help us to overcome the obstacles on our way to success.

I once knew a woman who was a stellar employee. Over time, however, she began calling in sick a lot, and when she was at work, her mind seemed to be elsewhere. She eventually started spending more and more time away from work. I called her into my office to speak candidly with her about her recent downward performance trend, and in the course of the conversation, she disclosed to me that she was experiencing some serious personal issues. I had not expected that our conversation would take that kind of turn. I asked her what steps she was contemplating, and she said she very much wanted to address and resolve these issues, but she felt she did not have the support network to remove herself from this dysfunctional situation that was severely affecting both her personal and professional life. As we talked through her issues, I gave her the name and number of a friend of mine who could possibly help, leaving it up to her to take the first step.

A month later, her performance had drastically improved, and she told me she had reached out to the resource I had suggested and made some major changes in her life for the better. By simply asking her what was wrong and how I could help, she felt like someone cared, and it gave her the strength to make the necessary changes in her life and stick with the decision to move forward. Over the next six months, her performance continued to improve. Of course, not every employee will have such a drastic reason for performance issues (hopefully). But the takeaway here is that you never know what's happening with someone until you ask.

Seek out and provide whatever is needed

Figure out what your team needs and then supply the right resources, whether that means adding skill sets or more people, removing impediments, or providing materials, tools, or realistic, constructive feedback to ensure they feel empowered and can be successful.

Get out of your office. Lean servant leaders don't hide away from their people. They practice genchi genbutsu—the art of going and seeing for yourself what's going on at the gemba (the place where the work is being performed). That doesn't mean calling a meeting and herding everyone into a conference room. It means going to where your people are and spending time with them.

Look at problems as opportunities for improvement

Repeat after me: "Problems are good! Problems are good!" You must look at problems as opportunities to practice continuous improvement. Anyone that takes the attitude that there are no problems (also known as waste or *muda* in Lean) in their work area is kidding themselves. There is always room for improvement and making things better. Thinking that things are perfect ensures a culture of apathy in which problems fester and start to affect the quality of your work, causing people to become frustrated regarding their inability to effectively make positive change. Ignoring problems and thereby allowing them to grow and intensify is the fastest way to lose your best and brightest employees, because they will go in search of more honest and empathic companies and leaders who seek out their creativity and passion for improvement.

As a Lean servant leader, looking for and solving problems with your people should be the activity to which you devote most of your time and energy. Again, practice genchi genbutsu at the gemba, talk to your team, understand the problems they face, and work with them to solve those problems as a team. Then work to continuously improve on the solutions you put in place by challenging them to focus on the removal of muda (waste) at the gemba.

Develop an inquisitive mind in yourself and others

Many times, getting to the root cause of a problem requires digging. Accepting the first answer usually puts the focus on a symptom rather than the actual cause. You must challenge yourself and others to go beyond their normal thinking patterns by asking probing questions. Challenging people and exhibiting vulnerability in the problem-solving process is the way you grow both yourself and your people. Both the teacher and student end up learning something in the process.

Build a tolerance for failure

Your attitude toward mistakes and how you handle failure is also a determinant as to whether or not you are a true Lean servant leader. Mistakes must be looked at as just one more way we now know something doesn't work. Mistakes aren't life-ending events. Mistakes and failings offer valuable experiences that we can learn from and incorporate back into the process. If you're not taking risks, you're not learning and moving forward. Remember, the goal is to break the problem down into small, manageable chunks. And if you fail in one attempt to solve a problem, it doesn't mean the end of the world as you know it. It just means you haven't found the solution to the problem and must try again until a viable solution is found. For instance, did you know that Thomas Edison made one thousand unsuccessful attempts at inventing the light bulb? One thousand attempts! Failing was not part of his plan, and when a reporter asked him, "How did it feel to fail one thousand times?" Edison replied, "I didn't fail one thousand times. The light bulb was an invention with one thousand steps."[7]

Encourage independent thinking

Identify the gap or problem that needs to be solved and make sure your team has the resources to solve it, and then stand back and let them have at it. Just because they might not solve the problem the way you would doesn't mean their solution is wrong. If they get stuck, be available to help. Ask them challenging questions about the direction they've taken to solve the problem, but encourage them to think independently.

During problem solving, encourage the importance of building consensus for the possible solution among all the stakeholders involved, before the solution is implemented. Building consensus uncovers additional ideas that might offer better solutions to the problem or identify possible unconsidered risks. Consensus ensures the people who must implement the solution thoroughly understand the effects it may have on their work. In this way, everyone feels like they've been given the opportunity to voice and address any concerns they might have about the most viable solution, validating that it's the most optimal solution at the time.

Leave your ego and pride at the door

This one might be the hardest to accomplish, because successful leaders are generally full of self-confidence, willpower, and determination. However, as I've said before, being a Lean leader is not about you! It's about helping those

---

7 A. U. Shastri, reply to "How many times did Thomas Alva Edison fail exactly?" (*https://oreil.ly/ 52Vae*), Quora, August 9, 2014.

you serve to develop *their* self-confidence, willpower, and determination to succeed.

You must share, not hoard, your power to set your people up for success. You can't intentionally let them fail so that you can ride in and save them. That type of behavior is self-serving and only boosts your ego. However, if what you are trying to build is an army of Lean servant leaders who lead by example, with respect, integrity, honesty, and dignity, and who live to serve and develop others, then you must leave your own ego and pride at the door. Instead, take pride in developing and supporting others as you and they both evolve to higher and higher levels of Lean servant leadership.

Respecting Others on the Road to Continuous Improvement

For those who aspire to practice Lean servant leadership, it all starts with the two pillars of The Toyota Way, which are (1) a profound respect for people and (2) a commitment to continuous improvement, known as kaizen.

Giving Context to Respecting Others

The easiest way to understand why respect is so important is to think about a time when you felt disrespected. Whether it was expressed through a person's words or behavior, I bet the message came through loud and clear. How did that make you feel? How did you react? Probably with anger or disbelief for having been treated in this manner. It probably left you asking, "So what did I do to them to deserve this type of treatment?"

More times than not, the answer is "Nothing!" When people behave disrespectfully toward you, the underlying reason usually says more about them than it does about you. Disrespect often comes from an apathetic mind, which usually develops when people feel like no one cares for or respects them—so they treat others in this manner. Unfortunately, feeling that you've been disrespected enables disrespectful behavior, and you can either consciously or unconsciously return that disrespect to them, which can become a vicious circle in any relationship.

However, remember the old adage "You get what you give!" Being mindful and mature about your reactions and remaining respectful, acting with honor and humility, will get you much further than throwing attitude and returning the disrespect. When I run across someone like this, my first instinct is to be as respectful to them as I possibly can, because as a Lean leader you must model the behavior you're looking for, as hard as that might be. When you treat people in the manner you want to be treated, it introduces a whole new dynamic to your interactions with them.

I've also found that smiling and being vulnerable helps as well. I smile and give an opening statement that asks for the person's help; this goes a long way toward getting a conversation started off on the right foot. It takes the other person out of their head and current situation to focus on you and the situation at hand. Most people are more than willing to help others. As humans, we are inherently wired that way; it's part of our nature to respond to vulnerability in a protective manner, instead of immediately putting up walls that cause miscommunication and mistrust. So the next time you are in a situation like this, give this technique a try. You might be amazed at the response you get.

Thinking with a Kaizen Mind

Contrary to popular Western beliefs and practices, kaizen is not an event or something you do occasionally. It's a way of life and a philosophy that is practiced every day, at all levels, throughout the entire Lean enterprise. Its goal is the continuous improvement and optimization of not only the parts (such as individuals, teams, processes, services, and technology) but the entire system. It's acutely focused on the removal of needless waste (muda) through the implementation of small, continuous improvements, aimed toward increasing productivity, quality, safety, and customer and employee satisfaction; improving delivery times; and lowering costs.

To develop a kaizen mind means you realize the importance of eliminating waste by committing to continuous, long-term improvement in the form of proactive, measured change. Yes, there is that word again: change! Kaizen is about spotting the necessary changes that need to be made to keep you, your followers, and the organization moving forward. Change is handled better when it's acknowledged and dealt with in small, incremental steps, which is what kaizen is all about. Unfortunately, most change efforts fail due to the change being initiated and implemented as a massive, last-ditch effort to correct something that should have been addressed incrementally over time. If kaizen is happening, there's no need for large-scale, disruptive change. Lean servant leaders realize that change is inevitable, and they don't blindly ignore it. The need for continuous change must always live in the forefront of your conscious mind.

Kaizen is driven by a respect for people from both your customers' and employees' perspective, because it's all about making the lives of those that buy or produce your products better and more rewarding. That means reducing the waste that's all around you, from an emotional, mental, and physical perspective. When everyone in your organization is constantly seeking out waste and systematically removing it, then you've developed a kaizen culture in which continuous improvement becomes a way of life.

Acknowledging Your Responsibility to Develop Others

As a Lean servant leader, you have two main goals. First, you're responsible for developing yourself and other potential leaders from both a job performance and a skill-set perspective, helping them to hone their leadership abilities. Second, you must continuously identify opportunities that enable yourself and others to stretch and grow by challenging the status quo and never accepting or becoming complacent in your quest for perfection. It's just as important to vertically develop your skills and abilities within your area of expertise as it is to horizontally develop them across the organization, pushing yourself to be able to perform continuous improvement both within and outside of your comfort zone or area of expertise. In doing so, you put yourself in situations that remove you from the role of an expert, forcing you to learn to develop and draw upon your leadership skills, such as motivating people, inspiring by building your vision, influencing through consensus building, team development, listening, and coaching, to name a few. When you're no longer the "expert," you have no choice but to lead through your soft skills.

Also, a crucial responsibility of a Lean servant leader is to ensure that your "students" take responsibility for their self-development. However, as a leader, you remain accountable for their results. I know that sounds a little one-sided, but if you aspire to lead others, you must take full responsibility for developing your people as well. After all, you probably received assistance at some point in your career from someone who helped you to develop your abilities to lead. However, it's unrealistic to think you will be able to devote major chunks of your time to everyone. So you must choose wisely and take the time to identify and then develop those individuals who show the most potential to effectively lead and work as a team. Here are some tips on how to accomplish that:

- Closely observe those who follow you, making mental notes concerning who shows the potential for leadership versus those who don't have any aspirations or interest in leading at all (which is okay as well). However, don't make the mistake of thinking they don't want to be developed. Different people have different career goals. Some may aspire to become an expert in their field, showing absolutely no interest in becoming a leader. You must recognize there are many ways to help someone develop, such as by freely sharing your expertise, which is good for both the individual and the company.

- For your direct reports, set aside regular time to work on and discuss their development. You need to ensure they are on track and are getting what they need to continue their development. I suggest you also set aside four to six hours a month to mentor and coach those whom you don't directly manage or lead. Allot time on a first-come, first-serve basis. I find mentoring and coaching others to be personally rewarding, and I've had many mentors, coaches, and teachers throughout my career, even though I wasn't in a position to help them at that time. I am a firm believer in the "pay it forward" process of helping others.

- Set clear expectations for those you lead so that both you and your students can measure progress and be accountable for their self-development. One of the things I do is to give my students a challenge they must complete before our next formal touchpoint. With my formal relationships, I expect the students to come prepared to discuss how they have attempted to solve the challenge given to them. With my informal relationships, I leave it up to the students to schedule the next meeting, after they've attempted to solve the challenge given to them. In this manner, I can easily ascertain who is willing to put the actual time and effort into their development so that we're both using our time as wisely as possible. Also, using this technique puts the responsibility of self-development squarely on the shoulders of the students, who can take it as fast or slow as their schedule and time constraints permit.

- Know that you're going to be held accountable by your followers. This is a radical departure from the way many companies operate today. Ultimately, if a company is failing, who else should be held accountable for that end result other than the leadership team? However, more and more it seems that Western leaders have perfected the art of becoming "Teflon"—that is, not being accountable or taking responsibility for a lack of results. Everything just slides right off them. Followers must hold their leaders accountable, ensuring that Teflon leaders are not acceptable in a Lean culture. Leaders must share responsibility and accountability with their followers, as well as with other leaders, to ensure that the company continues to grow and evolve.

Learning to Serve While Developing Others

Becoming a Lean leader means being in a continuous loop that places you in the role of student, as well as teacher, over and over again throughout your career. And being a Lean servant leader requires developing a kaizen mindset so that you can help others in their development as well. This two-step process can be achieved with the help of the following Lean techniques:

Toyota Business Practices (TBP)
   The most powerful tool for developing a kaizen mind is a problem-solving technique known as the Toyota Business Practices, or TBP. It's based on the Plan/Do/Check/Act (PDCA) cycle, which has evolved over the years and was modified by the Japanese for their production purposes. Its focus

is on helping you develop and hone your problem-solving capabilities through a systematic and repeatable continuous improvement process.

On-the-job development (OJD)

Once you've mastered TBP at the individual and team leader levels, you're ready to move to the second step, which is assisting others in the development of their leadership skills, using another Lean technique known as on-the-job development, or OJD. OJD puts you in the role of sensei (coach or mentor) by working to develop potential leaders as they move through their TBP experiences. In this second step, your goal as sensei is to help others develop their abilities to both serve and lead.

However, before you move on to OJD, you need to understand another underlying tenet of the TBP, which is the PDCA cycle.

Kaizen and the PDCA Cycle

The PDCA cycle (shown in Figure 4-1) can be used to solve just about any problem or issue a leader, team, or company encounters. PDCA follows the scientific method[8] that dates as far back as Galileo and is the standardized process scientists have used for centuries to uncover the best possible solution to a problem. The process itself is quite simple. First, you build the hypothesis, stating both the true and false or "null" states. Then you identify all the possible conclusions or outcomes. Next, you conduct experiments or studies to test the hypothesis, observing the results along the way. You continue to test over and over again, incorporating your learnings back into the hypothesis until it's proven to be either true or false.

The PDCA cycle consists of the following four steps:

- Step 1. Plan: Define a problem and hypothesize possible causes and solutions.
- Step 2. Do: Implement the solutions.
- Step 3. Check: Evaluate the results.
- Step 4. Act: Return to step 1 if the results are unsatisfactory, or standardize the solution if the results are satisfactory.[9]

---

8 Ronald D. Moen, "Foundation and History of the PDSA Cycle" (*https://oreil.ly/Z5b-t*), W. Edward Demings Institute, accessed December 17, 2018).

9 Ronald D. Moen and Clifford L. Norman, "Circling Back: Clearing Up Myths About the Deming Cycle and Seeing How It Keeps Evolving" (*http://www.apiweb.org/circling-back.pdf*), *Quality Progress*, November 2010, 4.

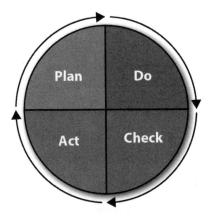

Figure 4-1. *The PDCA circle*

The Evolution of PDCA and TBP

In 1985, Dr. Kaoru Ishikawa, the father of the Total Quality Control (TQC) movement and author of the book *What Is Total Quality Control? The Japanese Way* (Prentice Hall), extended the Japanese PDCA cycle to include additional planning steps, adding goals and targets and developing methods for reaching those goals in the Plan steps[10] so that the organization can identify, solve, and standardize what has been learned. Dr. Ishikawa's PDCA cycle consists of the following six steps:

- Step 1. Plan: Determine goals and targets.
- Step 2. Plan: Determine methods of reaching goals.
- Step 3. Do: Engage in education and training.
- Step 4. Do: Implement work.
- Step 5. Check: Check the effects of implementation.
- Step 6. Act: Take appropriate action.

Toyota leaders then extended Ishikawa's PDCA cycle to include two additional steps: in Step 1: Plan, they added "clarify the problem," and in Step 2 they added "break down the problem," to shift the emphasis to the customer, ensuring the problem is worth working on to gain consensus. They also deleted step 3 and added step 4: "perform root cause analysis," ensuring the root cause of the problem being solved is well understood. This revised PDCA cycle became known as the Toyota Business Practices (TBP) method and has been

---

10 Toyota Institute, *How to Teach the TBP Steps* (Nagoya: Toyota Motor Corporation, 2006), 9.

implemented throughout Toyota as their overall problem-solving method. Figure 4-2 depicts the eight steps of the modern PDCA cycle, as implemented at Toyota, as well as the corresponding Toyota values that come alive through the implementation of the steps. For Toyota, TBP is not just a problem-solving method; it's a way of bringing to life their values, expressed within the Toyota Way, through concerted and intentional effort.

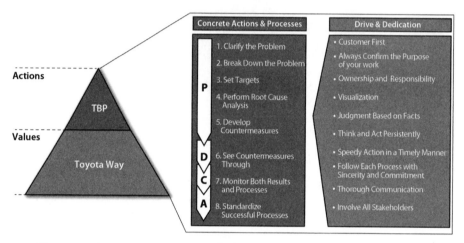

Figure 4-2. *Toyota Business Practices (TBP) and Toyota values (source: Toyota Motor Corporation)*

Learning to Serve through TBP

You must first learn to serve your team through performing transformative kaizen projects and using the TBP problem-solving technique. Its focus is on the further development of both your leadership skills and your kaizen mind and Modern Lean capabilities. TBP is a consistent method that can be applied over and over again to develop leaders, both individually (by tackling a problem on your own) and in a team setting (where you either lead or follow under the watchful eye of your sensei or coach).

If you're new to TBP and a coach cannot be found within your organization, consultants can act as coaches to teach you the techniques of TBP. However, in the long run, you and your team must own the solutions you create through TBP. It's up to you to continuously improve the solution, which is how real and lasting change occurs and is sustained over time.

Keep in mind that your sensei is not there to supply answers. On the contrary, they are there to challenge and stretch you and/or the team. The sensei uses observation, questioning, and probing to ensure mastery of each step before you can move to the next one. TBP is also a means by which leaders can develop both vertically (within their areas of expertise) and horizontally (across the enterprise), because you don't necessarily need to be an expert to contribute to the problem-solving process. For example, if you're an expert in the field of human resources, you may well be able to contribute to a problem-solving effort in engineering with the kaizen team.

Now that you have an understanding of some of the core principles underlying the practice of leading and developing others through Lean servant leadership, let's take a look at some of these principles in action.

Case Study: The Eight Steps of TBP in Action

The New Horizons car dealership in Portsmouth, North Carolina, was in trouble. The latest service ticket processing errors report from the customer service department of their automotive manufacturing supplier showed that the error ratio had hit an all-time high of 75%—5% higher than the previous month—and the company's net promoter score had dropped to –20. To make matters worse, the owner, Jim Collins, had just received an email from the manufacturer stating that if New Horizons didn't get the situation under control, they would take serious corrective measures.

Jim showed the report to his manager, Jannie. However, she was not an expert on running a service department this large. So Jim decided to call in Jannie's long-time colleague, Nancy Peterson, whom Jannie had actually recommended to help them with the issues in the service department.

Upon arriving at the dealership the next day, Nancy immediately saw there was no one at the receptionist's desk. Service agents and technicians were milling around, ignoring her—not a single person showed any indication of ending their conversation to help what very well could have been a customer waiting on the service department floor.

As she continued to stand there unassisted, as if she was invisible, she glanced through the service bay windows to see four men standing around the service bay desk. There wasn't a single car in the bay, which struck her as odd because it was Monday morning, and the service departments she had managed in the past were usually packed with customers dropping off their cars. It was usually one of the busiest days of the week for a service department.

Nancy brought these concerns to Jim and Jannie when she finally sat down with them. Over the next couple of days, she spent a lot of time at the gemba within the service department. She observed the employees performing work in the service agent area, service bay, and garage. She listened to the receptionist take service request intake calls and watched the service agents' interactions with customers, as well as with each other as they went about their daily duties. Nancy also dealt with a lot of irate customers both in person and over the phone. Most of them were upset over unauthorized service items that had mysteriously appeared on their service tickets, while others were upset about the work they had requested that wasn't performed at all.

It quickly became clear to Nancy that she needed to discuss the whole service ticket issue with Jim. A lot of New Horizons' issues were originating from how the service agents initiated service requests, and Nancy wanted to learn more about the dealership's business practices. In a conversation with Jim, she asked him whether it was the policy of the dealership to add unauthorized repair and/or maintenance items to a service ticket, without informing the customer.

Jim was aghast and said of course that was not the policy—he was taken aback when Nancy reported that very thing was happening a lot. This type of behavior was not only unethical but also illegal. At that point, Jim and Nancy realized they needed to perform a complete overhaul of the Service Ticket Intake process. Nancy suggested using TBP to help get the department back on track; she proposed assembling a small kaizen team of staff members for three to four hours a day over the next couple of weeks to work with her to solve this problem. Since she had worked with Jannie before and knew she understood TBP, Nancy wanted her to lead the team.

Jim then confided to Nancy that the auto manufacturer had put him on probation; if he didn't make some real headway on this problem over the next six months, they were going to revoke his dealership license. Nancy offered to have him join the team. However, Jim declined, admitting that he knew very little about the service department. Selling cars was his area of expertise and what he was very good at. He also wanted to avoid the appearance that the team was on a witch hunt with the staff, which Nancy understood and respected.

That night, before she left for the evening, Nancy sent out an email to Jannie, Rick, and Randy asking them to meet her in the break room tomorrow at 8:00 a.m. The first two were service agents, while Randy was a service technician. She explained in her email that they were going to embark on a problem-solving exercise around the service ticket error rate in an effort to identify and correct any problems they uncovered, and Jannie would act as team lead. She also added that their involvement was completely voluntary, and if they chose not to participate, there would be no repercussions.

Finally, she composed an email for Jim to send out to the entire staff, explaining the reason that Nancy and her team would be asking for their assistance over the next several weeks to figure out the root cause and begin to work on bringing the error rate down. Nancy viewed this as a very important step in the process. Communication is key to ensuring everyone understands what's going on so that they can help with the problem-solving activities. Lean methods are based on the belief that the people closest to the work are best suited to solve the problems and improve upon the process. That means they must be the ones that identify and then solve the issue to ensure the actions taken are sustained and maintained over time.

The next morning, Nancy was at the dealership bright and early. She was excited to embark on this journey and to help Jim get the dealership's problems solved. And, whether Jim realized it or not, they were all about to embark on a Lean journey that would set the dealership on a perpetual course of continuous improvement.

When she arrived in the break room, Rick, Randy, and Jannie were waiting for her, as well as a fourth person—Donna. Donna handled New Horizons' loaner car program, and Jannie thought she'd be a great addition to the team. Nancy agreed, and they dug right into the discussion. Nancy started by providing an overview of the eight steps of the TBP problem-solving method, depicted in Figure 4-3. Her plan was to use a just-in-time method to give the team more in-depth coaching as they approached each step in the process. For now, a simple overview was enough.

8 STEPS	PROCESSES
Step 1. (Plan) Clarify the Problem	1. Clarify the "ultimate goal" of your responsibilities & work 2. Clarify the "ideal situation" of your work 3. Clarify the "current situation" of your work 4. Visualize the gap between the "current situation" and the "ideal situation"
Step 2. (Plan) Break Down the Problem	1. Break down the problem 2. Select the problem to pursue 3. Specify the point of cause by checking the process through genchi genbutsu
Step 3. (Plan) Set Targets	1. Make the commitment 2. Set measurable, concrete, and challenging targets
Step 4. (Plan) Perform Root Cause Analysis	1. Consider causes by imagining the actual situation where the problem occurs 2. Based on facts gathered through genchi genbutsu, keep asking "Why?" 3. Specify the root cause
Step 5. (Plan) Develop Counter-measures	1. Consider as many potential countermeasures as possible 2. Narrow down the countermeasures to the most practical and effective ones 3. Build consensus with others 4. Create a clear and detailed action plan
Step 6. (Do) See Counter-measures Through	1. Quickly and as a team, implement countermeasures 2. Share progress by following the correct reporting, informing, and consulting communication procedures 3. Never give up, and proceed to the next step quickly
Step 7. (Check) Monitor Both Results and Processes	1. Evaluate the overall results and the processes used, then share the evaluation with involved members 2. Evaluate from three key viewpoints: customer's, Toyota's, and your own 3. Understand the factors behind the success or failure
Step 8. (Act) Standardize Successful Processes	1. Standardize the successful processes 2. Share the new precedent through yokotenkai 3. Start the next round of kaizen

Figure 4-3. *The eight steps of the Toyota Business Practices problem-solving method (source: Toyota Motor Corporation)*

Step 1: Clarify the Problem (Plan)

Nancy explained that the team must start this process with the end state in mind by thinking about the "art of the possible." As the team began to discuss the issues, they came to the realization that they were close enough to the work being performed to understand that there was a problem with how the department handled service tickets. Nancy referenced the 75% error processing rate, which represented a 65% increase over the last year. The auto manufacturer supplying the dealership with vehicles had set an acceptable error rate of 10%, and they tracked this statistic over time, because customer satisfaction was a priority. Nancy stressed that this error rate needed to become a metric the dealership tracked and paid attention to as well, because it was a measure of how the dealership provides value to its customers. "I don't know if you've noticed," she said, "but this dealership isn't exactly brimming with business in the service department."

"Wow, we suck," Randy chimed in. "That's awful!"

"Yes, that is why Jim has brought Nancy in," Jannie added, "She's dealt with other dealerships that have had similar problems. I know, because I've worked with her before and have seen this process work. I'm 120% behind this effort, because we need to get much better for our customers, the dealership, and of course for ourselves as well. This situation is really unacceptable!"

"Thanks Jannie, I appreciate your vote of confidence, and of course your support," Nancy responded with a big smile. "So let's get back to clarifying the problem." Nancy kept the team on task and returned to clarifying the problem. She asked, "If you were to look out into the future, what would be the ideal state?" She reminded them that by starting with their ultimate goal and ideal situation, they could remove themselves from what was familiar and get away from preconceived notions concerning how they thought things ought to work. This is "the art of the possible"—envisioning the process functioning in an unencumbered, perfect future state. The gap between this state and the current reality was what the team needed to work on and solve for.

The team spent the next hour or so discussing the problem, the current and ideal situations, and the ultimate goal, identifying and diagramming them in Figure 4-4.

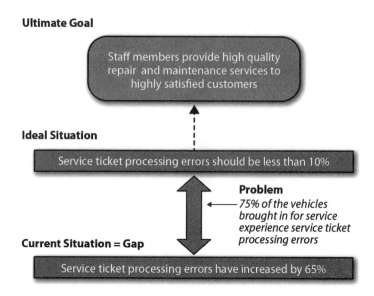

Ultimate Goal

Staff members provide high quality repair and maintenance services to highly satisfied customers

Ideal Situation

Service ticket processing errors should be less than 10%

Problem
75% of the vehicles brought in for service experience service ticket processing errors

Current Situation = Gap

Service ticket processing errors have increased by 65%

Figure 4-4. *Step 1: Clarify the problem (Plan)*

Step 2: Break Down the Problem (Plan)

After completing step 1, Nancy prepared the team for step 2, arguably the most difficult of the eight steps: breaking down the larger problem into multiple smaller, more specific problems that are mutually exclusive and collectively exhaustive so that they can be tackled individually in small steps.

Nancy asked the group to form two subteams for this step: Jannie with Randy and Rick with Donna. Each subteam picked a service agent to sit with for the rest of the morning to observe how the Service Request Intake process worked. They would discuss their observations the following day.

The next day, the team was eager to talk about what they'd learned—in fact, to Nancy's surprise and delight, they reported they had stayed after work the previous night and worked on breaking down the problem. Jannie had even worked up a graphic (Figure 4-5) on a large whiteboard in the break room to illustrate the insights they had gained from spending time at the gemba.

Jannie reported that the team rotated through the agents every hour during the day, allowing them to gain insights from everyone. Breaking the main problem down, the team identified four subproblems; they then prioritized the subproblems, talking through each one's level of urgency, importance, and potential for expansion, by asking the following questions:

- Does it need to be solved now?
- What would be the consequences of forgoing work on it?
- What is its overall contribution to improving the situation?
- What will happen if we continue to ignore it?

The team's analysis verified that the Service Request Intake process was the biggest issue, since all the problems seemed to originate from there and were compounded downstream from that area. Randy noted he thought the Point of Service process was second, because a lot of tickets were not entered into the system, and half the time, the staff could not read the service agent's handwriting. Getting service agents to come back to the garage to clarify a ticket was like pulling teeth. Donna noted that the loaner department experienced similar issues with scheduling. New Horizons needed better communication and coordination between the areas within the service department to ensure they were working as a team.

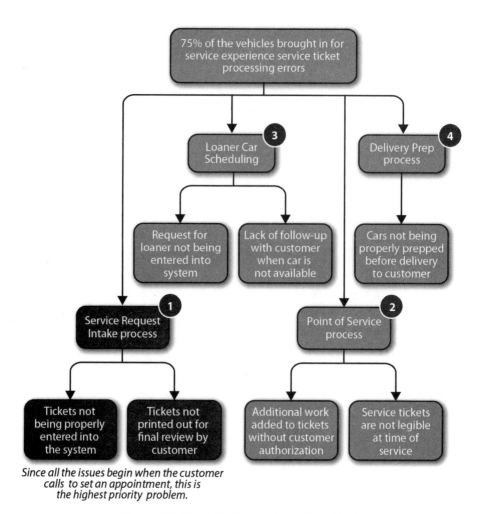

75% of the vehicles brought in for service experience service ticket processing errors

3 Loaner Car Scheduling

4 Delivery Prep process

Request for loaner not being entered into system

Lack of follow-up with customer when car is not available

Cars not being properly prepped before delivery to customer

1 Service Request Intake process

2 Point of Service process

Tickets not being properly entered into the system

Tickets not printed out for final review by customer

Additional work added to tickets without customer authorization

Service tickets are not legible at time of service

Since all the issues begin when the customer calls to set an appointment, this is the highest priority problem.

Figure 4-5. *Step 2: Break down the problem (Plan)*

Turning the whiteboard around to display another diagram, Jannie revealed the team had also documented the Service Request Intake process (Figure 4-6). The graphic showed a combined representation of what all of the service agents were currently doing. The team came to the consensus that the point of cause was when the ticket was initiated, which could either be using the service ticket system or by hand, since there was no standard set requirement. About 75% of the service agents preferred to skip using the system, because writing the tickets out by hand was faster and easier. A few had also said that because they were relatively new, they had not received any training on the system, and with the demands of their job, it was easier to write them out by hand than to enter them into the system.

The team also found that customer calls were randomly routed to the next available service agent. If agents were not on the phone, the automated system rang their desk phone until someone picked up. That might mean a customer could be rerouted up to seven times, and if no one picked up, the call then went to the receptionist or cashier. In other words, the team had found a lot of room for improvement in this process, as shown in Figure 4-6.

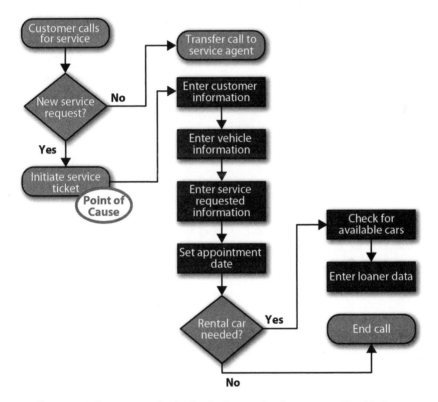

Figure 4-6. *Current state for the Service Request Intake process at New Horizons*

Nancy stood up and moved to the whiteboard. She restated what the team had told her, then said, "So if I'm hearing you correctly, if we were to isolate the point of cause, it would go something like this, right?" as she wrote the following:

> Service request calls are randomly routed by the automated phone system to the first available person in the service department. That person then becomes responsible for entering and completing the service ticket (either within the service request intake system or by generating a handwritten ticket), as well as printing it for review and verification by the customer on the day of service, before any work is performed.

The team agreed that the whole process felt very random; there was no means of guaranteeing that the same agent would service the same customer from one visit to the next, which meant that customers were not getting consistent, personalized service. Considering that the dealership was selling high-end luxury brands, customers expected stellar service, but were receiving far less than they expected from the service department.

Step 3: Set Targets (Plan)

The team was now ready to move on to the next step: setting concrete, measurable, and challenging targets that could be objectively tracked over time. The challenge was to think about what their ideal outcome would be if they were to solve this problem, and then ratchet that up a notch or two. Nancy encouraged them to set aggressive targets because, after all, the team was on a quest for perfection. The question then became what the team could expect to accomplish from the most optimistic perspective possible. Or in simpler terms, what outcome was New Horizons trying to achieve, and by when?

Jim, the owner, had spoken with Nancy about getting to the root of the dealership's problems and addressing them within 90 days. The team decided to push even harder than that and make the target 75 days. Having all agreed to go after this target, Jannie drew a box above the problem statement and wrote out the stated target (Figure 4-7).

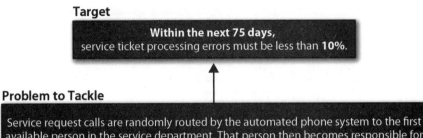

Target

Within the next 75 days,
service ticket processing errors must be less than **10%**.

Problem to Tackle

Service request calls are randomly routed by the automated phone system to the first available person in the service department. That person then becomes responsible for entering and completing the service ticket (either within the service request intake system or by generating a handwritten ticket), as well as printing it for review and verification by the customer on the day of service, before any work is performed.

Figure 4-7. *Step 3: Set targets*

Step 4: Perform Root Cause Analysis (Plan)

The next step was for the team to determine the problem's root cause. This was a crucial step, because if they ended up misidentifying the root cause, the team would risk solving for the wrong problem—or worse yet, solving for a symptom instead of the actual problem.

The team met in the break room again the next morning, and Nancy asked what conclusions they had reached about possible root causes. Rick took the lead and turned around the whiteboard, which revealed the assessments shown in Figure 4-8.

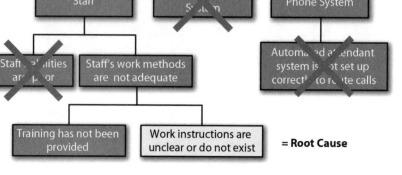

Figure 4-8. *Step 4: Perform root cause analysis (Plan)*

Donna explained how Jannie—who, you'll remember, had worked with Nancy before—had shown the team how to do the 5 Whys technique so that they could develop a deeper understanding of the problem and identify the root cause. They had gone through each of the causes they'd identified and continued to ask *why* until they could precisely state a cause that was strictly supported by facts. The process allowed them to identify the actual cause and effect relationship. The 5 Whys for the root cause of "Work instructions are unclear or do not exist" are illustrated in Figure 4-9.

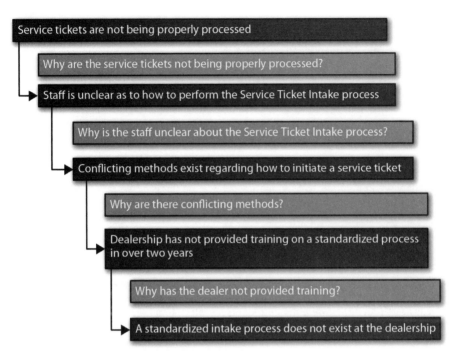

Figure 4-9. *Results of the 5 Whys*

Donna shared that by going to the gemba, they could verify that a direct cause and effect relationship indeed existed, ensuring they had the correct root cause—or at least the one that was highest priority. When they asked the service agents about whether they had been trained on a standardized process, most said that the most recent training had been done awhile back by the previous service manager, who was no longer at the company. However, that manager had not encouraged them to use the service request intake system, so most of them stopped using it either because it was slow and cumbersome or they hadn't received training on it in the first place.

"OK, well then, I guess you all have this under control," Nancy said with a smile as she started to get up from the table. The team looked somewhat startled, but then realized Nancy was kidding when she said, "All joking aside, this is great work!"

OJD and Nancy's Approach

Later that day, Jim mentioned to Nancy that he had seen the team working in the break room earlier. "You all were so deep in conversation that I didn't want to interrupt, so I just now went back in there, and your team has covered the walls with a lot of posters. I took a moment to check them out, and I have to say, I am very impressed." He congratulated Nancy on her great work.

Nancy, however, noted that the work was not hers—it was the team's. It was their idea to post everything so that Jim could visually see their progress, and they wanted everyone in the dealership to understand what they were doing and that they were inviting everyone to look around, ask questions, and even contribute. Visual management is essential when it comes to Lean methods, because TBP is a "we" effort. Nancy reiterated that Jannie, Rick, Randy, and Donna did all that work, and most of it was under Jannie's direction.

Nancy also explained that she was modeling on-the-job development. She said that eventually Jannie would be able to develop others in this manner as well, and she could already see Rick had developed some, and Randy wasn't far behind. She had chosen Jannie, Rick, and Randy for a reason, and the team had been astute enough to pull in Donna, since the loaner car program was a big part of the service department. Nancy said that if they were going to get the dealership off probation and avoid revocation of Jim's dealer's license, then they were going to have to address the issues in those areas as well over the next six months. The Service Request Intake process was just the beginning.

Jim pondered this. "I think there are some words of wisdom in there for me as well," he admitted. "I've been so busy trying to sell and monitor our monthly sales quotas that I forgot the entire dealership needs care and feeding as well." He said he wanted Nancy to walk the entire leadership team through the eight steps at the next staff meeting. "It's time we all start to think about our customers and how to create value for them."

I note this exchange here because Nancy was implementing the OJD approach from the beginning, and she would continue to do so throughout the rest of the process, even though the team might not have been explicitly aware of it at this point.

Step 5: Develop Countermeasures (Plan)

Now that the team had identified a root cause, they had to determine effective countermeasures using fact-based analysis and sound judgment, all while considering their customers, stakeholders, and the possible risks involved. Nancy reminded them that, as in step 1, the team was limited only by its creativity and imagination at this stage, because vetting the countermeasures would happen next, in step 6. Step 5 was only the planning stage.

Nancy called on Donna to lead a brainstorming exercise to come up with countermeasures. After about 15 minutes, the team generated the list depicted in Figure 4-10.

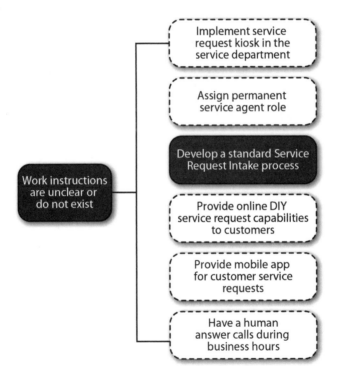

Figure 4-10. *Step 5: Develop countermeasures*

Nancy asked the team which of these countermeasures seemed most feasible. Some looked very doable, but which one would most effectively solve the root cause problem? She had them take a marker and put a star next to the one that each team member thought was most feasible.

The team unanimously chose "Develop a standard Service Request Intake process." Nancy then proceeded to ask why.

Randy explained their reasoning: while some of the other countermeasures were doable and good ideas, they would take a long time—the mobile app and website form options, for example. The team had only 75 days—fewer than that, at this point—to make an impact. Likewise, assigning a permanent service agent and having a person always answer customers' calls were also good ideas, but they were just *symptoms* of the root cause. The countermeasure with the "biggest bang for the buck"—both for the dealership and for its customers—was developing a standardized process.

Since the team was in agreement, the next step was to present this course of action to the stakeholders involved and discuss the risks and benefits before moving forward with the countermeasure. Nancy stressed that the team needed to ensure they built consensus on the plan of action, as the decision would impact everyone. She asked them to identify the stakeholders that would be affected if the countermeasure was implemented.

Jannie said that developing a standardized process would affect the whole service department, so the team needed to meet with the service agent, loaner car, and service technician teams to get their buy-in. Rick also noted that Jim would need to buy in as well.

"Sounds like a plan," Nancy said. "I'll take Jim and you all can meet with everyone else. Let's take tomorrow to get these meetings done, and we'll regroup on Friday morning."

The next day, the team set up meetings with each of the groups and asked them to come to the break room, which by this point the team had dubbed the "war room." They proceeded to walk each team through the five Planning steps of TBP they had performed so far. Everyone was allowed to voice their concerns or hesitations about this course of action. To the team's surprise, there wasn't a single person who raised an objection or concern; they received great comments and feedback they could incorporate back into the plan. They expanded their knowledge of the problem and gained deeper insight into how to solve it.

At the end of the day, Nancy caught up with the team in the war room and asked if they could stay a little while longer to walk Jim through the plan. They were a little surprised because the deal was that she would talk to Jim, but by now, the team knew Nancy well enough to know that there was a deliberate reason that always backed up her words and actions—so there must be a reason for this change in the plan. She walked down to Jim's office and came back with him a few minutes later. They both sat down at the end of the table, and Nancy asked the team to walk him through the work they had performed to date.

Jannie kicked it off by walking Jim through the first graphic on the wall, which showed the eight steps of the Toyota Business Practices. Pointing to step 5, she mentioned that they were about to come out of the Plan phase and move to implementation of the Do phase, which meant building consensus for the plan before they started. "So we've met with each of the teams in the service department and walked them through everything you see on the walls around you. Now I'd like Donna to cover steps 1 and 2, Randy steps 3 and 4, and Rick will close us out with step 5."

One by one they came up and covered the corresponding graphics hanging on the wall for each step. When Rick finished step 5, Jim stood up and started clapping. "Great job, team!" he said. "You have my full support to move forward!"

Step 6: See Countermeasures Through (Do)

Nancy reminded the team that the first five steps of TBP were very important to ensuring they were taking the right action: "Plan your work, then work your plan for success," which applies when using TBP to solve major problems like the one the team was facing. The next step was to test for the most viable countermeasure—also known as a hypothesis—iteratively and incrementally, incorporating the feedback they gathered from each round of experimentation and pulling it back into the process to improve upon it.

The first step was to develop the new standardized process flow, which the team had already discussed the day before. Jannie got up and spent a few minutes walking Nancy through their proposed process, as depicted in Figure 4-11. Nancy instinctively saw a few places where the process would probably need to be tweaked, but TBP is both a learning and development and a problem-solving method. So, she'd have the team implement the process the way it stood now to see what would happen, recognizing that challenges represent growth opportunities.

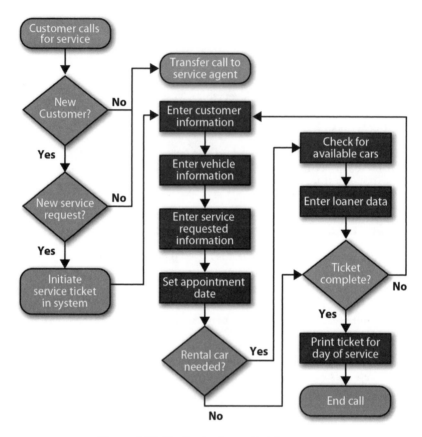

Figure 4-11. *The Service Request Intake process*

Nancy asked which service agents would be the guinea pigs to try out the new process; Jannie replied that Terry and Andrea were game. She and Randy would sit with Terry and Donna, and Rick would take Jan. They then agreed to regroup at 10:30 a.m. and check their progress.

The team headed out to the service agent area and spent about 30 minutes going over the process with Terry and Andrea to help them with the flow, until they got the hang of it. Then off they went to test the process.

Step 7: Monitor Both Results and the Process (Check)

The two teams spent the next couple of hours testing their countermeasure. However, it quickly became obvious that if this process was going to work, the call-routing process needed some changes. Terry and Andrea had been told not to alter their daily routines in any way, which meant they were away from their desks attending to customers or in the garage receiving status updates more than they were at their desks. The first three calls rolled over to the receptionist, because the service agents were either on the phone or away from their desks. When the receptionist answered a service request intake call, that tied her up as well. Frustrated, the team decided to call an emergency meeting to discuss the results they had observed.

Rick pointed out that, to make this countermeasure work, the team would have to make an immediate change in how the phone system worked. Customer calls were bouncing all over the place, and there was no rhyme or reason as to how they got answered. The team had identified this as a countermeasure but had prioritized it lower than the process itself, deeming it something of a "cart before the horse" thing. Rick added, "I think to realize the importance of the call routing issue, we needed to have a process in hand to test. I look at it as part of the feedback and learning cycle you talked to us about, Nancy."

"That is a great attitude to take," Nancy replied, "because if you had looked at it as a failure or missing the mark, you would have also missed the feedback and learning part. So good for you! And yes, I thought that might be the case. But like you said, who really knows until we test it out. So what are you proposing?"

Rick walked over to the process diagram and took out a marker. He inserted several new steps, adjusting the process so that the receptionist now answered all of the incoming calls. With this change, a customer's call would be correctly routed and assigned to the appropriate service agent. The result is shown in Figure 4-12.

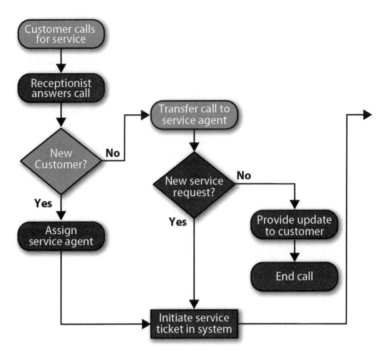

Figure 4-12. *The revised Service Request Intake process*

Rick noted that it would take tech support only about 15 minutes to turn off the auto-response system and that he would discuss the process change with Gail, the dealership's receptionist, as well. He pointed out that they needed to remove her from the queue of folks that do intake, since answering calls and routing them would become a full-time job.

An hour later, Rick had everything switched over, and Gail began to answer all incoming calls in the service department. If it was an existing customer, she began to ask if they knew the name of their service agent. Surprisingly, most did or gave the name of the last service agent they had contact with at the dealership. As the calls began to funnel in, the teams were able to observe the service agents using the new process. Since Gail could enter this information into the service intake system, Nancy would now be able to monitor their workloads, ensuring customers were evenly distributed across the six service agents.

The next major hurdle the team encountered was the service request intake system itself. Since it was now mandatory to enter all service requests into the system and generate a service ticket, it quickly became painfully obvious that the majority of the service agents had no idea how to use the system. Upon observing them struggling with the system, Gail pulled Jannie aside and said,

"I think I'm the one who knows that system the best, since I think I'm the only one using it. I could do a quick tutorial with Terry and Andrea to get them up to speed. If you could answer the phone, that would free me up to work with them. Just hold their calls for now."

Jannie agreed, and Gail spent about 30 minutes walking Terry and Andrea through the system, with the team observing the process as well. "Jannie," she said, "please route the next service call to Terry."

The next call came in, and Jannie routed it to Terry. Gail sat next to him with the customer on the speakerphone, as Terry filled out the electronic form in the system. Terry was a little overwhelmed with the new process and system, but he handled it well and was able to get through the call. The team observed Terry, taking a lot of notes as he worked through the process.

The next call that came in went to Andrea. Having the benefit of both the training and observing Terry, she was able to pick up the pace a little and finished the call a couple of minutes sooner than he did. As she hung up, the team gave each other high fives for successfully getting through their first two calls.

Randy had timed Terry and Andrea on each step so that the team would have a benchmark to track the improvements. The total average time from start to finish was about 20 minutes for Terry and 19 for Andrea, giving an average of 19.5 minutes. The team decided it would be useful to track their times through the process and see what their average was consistently.

The team spent another hour with Terry and Andrea; then it was time to regroup with Nancy in the war room. When they arrived, she was already there with Jim. Sensing the team was a little surprised by his presence, she explained that she had invited Jim to listen to their feedback so that he could help make any decisions they might need as to next steps.

The team spent the next 15 minutes with Nancy and Jim, briefing them on the results from the experiments they performed with the Service Request Intake process. Jannie wrote their conclusions on the board:

1. The call-routing system is impersonal, and the routing algorithm does not fit the business outcome of personalized service from a luxury, high-end auto manufacturer.

2. The service agents lacked the training needed to enter tickets into the service request intake system.

3. The system was slow, and the agents spent a lot of time waiting on the screens to refresh between steps.

4. The average time through the process was 19.5 minutes. Over half that time was spent waiting on the system to refresh the screens.

5. The agents' level of customer service was inconsistent. To ensure a consistent level of service, they might benefit from receiving customer service training.

Jannie reminded Jim and Nancy that the team had already implemented countermeasure #1 and received positive feedback from customers along the lines of "It's nice to call in and talk to a human" and "Thank goodness I don't have to be bounced around because of that awful automated system."

Jim was impressed with the team's progress, so they decided to regroup in the morning and discuss standardizing the process in step 8.

The team filed out of the war room, but Nancy hung back to speak with Jim. She confided that she had not wanted to put him on the spot in front of the team, but to get the results he was looking for, the team needed to tackle countermeasures #2 through #5 before standardizing and implementing this process. The intake system was painfully slow; the average customer was not going to want to spend at least 20 minutes on the phone to schedule a service appointment. She thought it was crucial that they make the necessary changes now: the hardware was old and out of date, and the service agents needed professional customer service training. The cost for the training and the changes would be $50,000, and the software and hardware could both be installed next week. Nancy also recommended a colleague, Lisa, who could conduct the training.

Jim thought that $50,000 sounded like a lot of money, but he also recognized that he really didn't have much of a choice. He agreed it was time to invest in the company's future.

Step 8: Standardize Successful Processes (Act)

The next week saw a lot of activity in the service department. IT worked with the software vendor to update the system, and Nancy worked with Jannie to replace all of the computers throughout the department with faster models that met the software vendor's specifications. Additionally, all of the service agents received customer service training from Nancy's colleague Lisa after work on Wednesday afternoon, and process and system training on late Thursday afternoon, which was traditionally a slow time for them. The final process that was implemented is depicted in Figure 4-13.

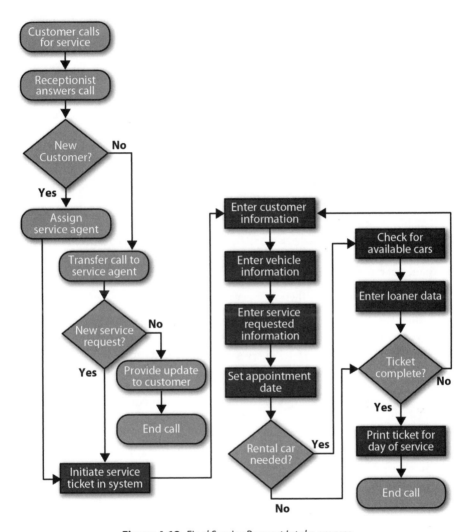

Figure 4-13. *Final Service Request Intake process*

On Friday morning, when the service department opened its doors, the service agents performed like a well-oiled machine. Calls were being routed, tickets were being entered into the system, and customers were leaving with smiles on their faces. That day, Nancy didn't receive a single complaint, and things continued to improve over the next two weeks. The team continued to meet every day as they monitored progress and determined who needed a little extra help with the system or process to ensure things continued to run smoothly.

The next day, Jim got new numbers from the auto manufacturer on customer satisfaction and processing error rates. He was ecstatic: over the last month, New Horizons' net promoter score had increased 25 points, and the error processing rate dropped 40 points. The manufacturer said it was the biggest single monthly drop they'd ever seen for any dealership since they began to keep those stats five years prior. That day, Nancy posted the report in the war room. She called the team together and informed them of the results. There were a lot of woot woots, high fives, and fist bumps among the team members.

"We've made great progress, team. You should all be very proud of what you've accomplished," Nancy said. "So let's get to work to figure out how we can drop the rate by an additional 25 points this month to hit our target of less than 10% within the next 30 days."

At that point, Randy chimed in and said he had some ideas on how to make the handoff between the service agents and service technicians smoother, which might help lower the rate even more. Donna added that they still had issues in the loaner car program as well.

"OK, team," Jannie said, "then let's get to work!"

As well as Nancy's team was performing, not everyone was on board: she had been observing her service agents throughout the eight steps of TBP, and everyone except for Angela had participated and helped to improve the process, as well as trying their best to adjust to the new system. However, Angela was still writing tickets out by hand, showing up late, and leaving early. It was clear to Nancy that Angela was not going to make the cut, so Nancy had to make the tough decision to let her go. Again, it wasn't an easy decision, but it was necessary. A Lean enterprise needs buy-in across the board to work, and as a Lean leader, it is up to you to make these kinds of decisions for the greater good of the organization.

Using OJD to Develop Others

Hopefully, this case study has shown you how the TBP steps can play out when implemented. I also want to point out that since Jannie had been through several TBP initiatives and knew the process well, it might be time for her to assume the role of the OJD student at the end of this first iteration of the eight steps of the TBP process; it's time for her to learn to coach and mentor other developing leaders, like Rick, Randy, and Donna. Nancy would be the most likely candidate to be Jannie's OJD teacher. And hopefully you recognized the opportunities Nancy provided to her to develop her abilities to independently lead the team wherever possible, as the team moved through the eight steps of TBP.

An OJD student is expected to coach and mentor a developing leader who either is leading a TBP team or is an individual contributor. Through this process, the student becomes the master and the master becomes the student, as they are also mentored and coached by their teacher.

In this manner, the developing leader is likened to being an apprentice who learns their craft under the wise guidance and watchful eye of a master craftsperson. Learning is accomplished by doing, not by merely sitting in a classroom and being lectured to. There is a time and place for that, and classroom education is important, but at some point you must learn by actually "doing" —by being mentored and coached by a master teacher through your process of trial and error, allowing you to learn and grow along the way through feedback, which is the most direct way to master your craft.

However, keep in mind that before you can begin OJD, you must first master TBP; it's a prerequisite. By first practicing and honing your TBP skills, you not only learn TBP but also how to lead kaizen or continuous improvement teams, developing both yourself and team members along the way. The final assignment for OJD students is to act as the teacher within their workplace, to mentor and coach a potential leader through leading a TBP improvement effort. Using the four steps of OJD, it's now your turn to act as the sensei, both receiving and giving feedback and coaching from your teacher, as well as giving it to the leader you are developing. Let's take a closer look at the four steps involved in OJD, which again follow the PDCA cycle.

Step 1: Pick a Problem with Your Team (Plan)

Based on the strategic goals of the organization, the TBP team leader and OJD student (or aspiring coach) must pick a problem that ties into the company's overall goals and also challenges and stretches the skills and abilities of both the leader and the coach. Going back to our case study, Randy had mentioned that he had some ideas on how to make the handoff between the service agents and service technicians smoother, which might help lower their processing error rate even more. In this situation, Nancy would act as Jannie's OJD coach and Jannie would be the OJD student, while Randy would be the potential TBP leader in training.

Step 2: Appropriately Divide the Work Among Accountable Team Members, Making the Direction Compelling (Plan)

The TBP team leader (Randy) being coached by the OJD student (Jannie) must understand the crucial tasks and targets required to accomplish the improvement effort. Then, both must convey the purpose of each objective to the team members, allowing them to determine how to perform the work in both a meaningful and achievable way, challenging and stretching their skills and abilities. As the OJD teacher, Nancy observes Jannie and provides feedback on her performance, helping her to grow and challenging her to make sure the team grows and learns as well.

Step 3: Execute within Broad Boundaries, Monitor, and Coach (Do and Check)

This is the phase in which the leader (Randy) and team execute the steps within TBP. The leader must constantly observe how team members carry out the work, understanding what issues they're dealing with and what is and isn't going well from a people and process perspective. Jannie, as the OJD student, coaches Randy in understanding and identifying corrective steps to improve both individual and team performance to ensure a successful outcome. Nancy again, as the OJD teacher, observes Jannie and provides feedback on her performance while interacting with Randy's team.

Step 4: Feedback, Recognition, and Reflection (Act)

If the TBP leader (Randy) or team ventures near or just beyond the established guardrails or boundaries set for the effort, Jannie, the OJD student, has the opportunity to perform a course correction by using a teaching moment to get them back on the right track. This practice allows Jannie to observe how a leader or team experiences failure, digests it, and understands it to move on as quickly as possible to continue the search for what does work. Also, both Randy as the leader and Jannie as the OJD student must ensure they are both providing adequate feedback when evaluating team and individual performance, supplying recognition when the goal is achieved. They both must ensure they are having honest and direct dialogues regarding individual performance.

The final evaluation is a 360-degree one based on both the OJD student's (Jannie's) reflection of their own performance and feedback from the person (Randy) that was coached and mentored and from the teacher (Nancy) or sensei. A simple grade of pass or fail is given. If you're the OJD student, receiving a passing evaluation means you're now able to lead TBP teams and act as an OJD coach. A failing evaluation means you will need to go back and begin again with another potential leader. In either case, the feedback received is fed back into your development plan, as you continue to work with your sensei to further develop and hone your leadership abilities.

Conclusion

Lean enterprises need Lean servant leaders who can help evolve an organization into a consultative, service-oriented place in which everyone participates and contributes to achieving the organization's mission, vision, and value proposition. Lean servant leaders play a linchpin role in the development of individuals and teams by respecting their people and practicing kaizen. They naturally—and continually—play the roles of teachers, mentors, and coaches who create a safe space in which problem solving through listening, observing, experimentation, and learning from mistakes is not only acceptable but encouraged. They think with a kaizen mind and understand it's not a "one-and-done" event because continuous improvement is a way of life. The quest for perfection through the removal of waste is never-ending, and there's always room for further improvement. You can hone your problem-solving abilities by mastering the TBP method and then moving on to OJD to form a two-step Lean servant leadership development system. With OJD, TBP master teachers (or senseis) teach and develop potential leaders in an apprentice-style fashion, learning through hands-on application and by solving real-world problems. Learning happens best at the gemba, or where work is performed. Lasting change happens when it's initiated and instigated by those closest to the work. Through the use of this system, leaders first learn to serve and then can develop others to lead, ensuring a steady stream of leadership talent within the Lean enterprise, well into the foreseeable future.

Now that we've addressed developing yourself as well as others, we can turn our attention to developing a customer-centric approach for the Lean enterprise.

CHAPTER 5

Leading Outside In

Do you consider your company to be customer-centric? Do you think about satisfying your customer regularly? Are you providing high-quality customer service after each purchase to drive repeat business, customer loyalty, and increased profits? These are all questions you should be routinely asking yourself as a Lean leader because Lean is all about being keenly focused on creating loyal and satisfied customers every day.

However, the determination of true value doesn't come from inside your company. Value is determined by your customers. Therefore, taking an outside-in or customer-focused perspective is fundamental to creating an excellent customer experience that results in high customer retention rates.

But what does it mean to be truly customer-centric? It means you care about every interaction you have with your customers, from initial inquiry to a purchasing decision to servicing the product/service afterward. You must always be thinking about how to add value-creating interactions that differentiate you from your competition. Your ultimate goal is to create a customer for life by building intimacy and fostering familiarity. In the end, you achieve long-lasting and valuable relationships on both sides, ensuring your product/service creates high levels of customer satisfaction on a repeated and continuous basis.

This chapter will explore strategies for putting your customers squarely in the center of your business by understanding who they are, what is important to them, and how you can bring their wants, needs, and/or desires to the forefront through the creation of exceptional customer experience every time they interact with you.

Measuring Success in Customer-Centric Companies

At this point, you might be asking yourself, "But how do I go about figuring out and then measuring whether or not my company is truly customer-centric?" There are three important metrics that you must track and monitor to help you find these answers. They are:

- Churn rate
- Customer lifetime value
- Net promoter score (NPS)

Churn Rate

Acquiring new customers is very costly, not to mention time-consuming, and it's becoming more and more difficult as global competition heats up. Many leaders are realizing that it's more cost-effective to focus their attention on maintaining their existing customer base, known as *customer retention*, than it is to constantly go out and find new customers, referred to as *customer acquisition*. According to the *Harvard Business Review*, bringing in new customers can cost 5 to 25 times more than keeping existing ones, and increasing your customer retention rates by just 5% can increase profits anywhere from 25% to 95%.[1] A 2% increase in customer retention has the same effect on profits as cutting costs by 10%, as well as experiencing about a 10% customer churn or turnover rate each year.[2] The end result is that companies with higher retention rates grow faster because they're acutely focused on understanding why people leave, as well as why they stay.

Your churn rate is rather easy to calculate. It's the number of customers who left in the last 12 months divided by the average number of total customers (during the same period). It's an invaluable metric to help you understand when you should be concerned about your customers' behavior, why they're coming or going, and the underlying reasons for both situations. This allows savvy leaders to either make course corrections or continue to do more of what they're doing to lower churn rates, which signals higher levels of customer centricity, because this metric is measuring how well you're managing your customer relationships. Once calculated, ask yourself these questions to effectively analyze the situation:

---

1 Amy Gallo, "The Value of Keeping the Right Customers" (*https://oreil.ly/pMXSz*), *Harvard Business Review*, October 29, 2014.

2 Ibid.

- Do you understand your customer churn rate?
- Is it trending up or down?
- What steps do you need to take to stop a downward trend?
- What things do you need to continue to enhance to keep an upward trend going?

Calculating and then watching this metric frequently tells you whether you're headed in the right direction, as well as whether any course corrections are required.

Customer Lifetime Value

CLV represents the total amount of money a customer is expected to spend on your products/services over their lifetime. It's crucial to know this metric when making decisions about how much money to invest in acquiring new customers and retaining existing ones. It's calculated by taking the average value of a purchase multiplied by the number of times the customer will buy each year multiplied by the average length of the customer relationship (in years).[3] This metric gives you a benchmark as to how much profit is associated with a particular customer relationship or segment. It also aids in understanding how much you should invest to maintain this type of customer relationship.

For example, as a business traveler, I'm a loyal customer of a well-known global hotel chain. If I stay an average of 100 nights a year and the hotel makes $100 profit on each night, then that amounts to a total profit of $10,000 a year. I've been a loyal customer for 10 years now, which means my CLV to date is $100,000. When you look at it in these terms, the hotel chain should be working hard to retain my business in comparison to the leisure traveler that might stay 5 nights a year over 10 years, which is a CLV of $5,000. Again, when you think about it in these terms, it's easy to see which customer the chain should be heavily investing in. So if the chain for some reason loses 100 business travelers with similar CLVs, that means $10 million in lost profit!

Calculating the CLV for different customer types or segments helps you to apply sound business judgment to determine:

- How much you should spend to acquire similar customers and still have a profitable relationship
- What kinds of products/services customers with the highest CLVs want

---

3 Customer Lifetime Value (CLV). www.Shopify.com, accessed May 7, 2019.

- Which products/services have the highest profitability
- Who your most profitable types of customers are

Net Promoter Score

NPS is an index ranging from –100 to 100 that measures the willingness of customers to recommend a company's products/services to others. It's used to understand and gauge a customer's overall satisfaction level and brand loyalty. It's calculated by asking customers one crucial question: "On a scale of 0 to 10, how likely are you to recommend this company's product/service to a friend or colleague?" Based on their answer, customers are classified into one of three categories:

1. *Detractors* score lower or equal to 6. These are people who probably won't purchase your product/service again for whatever reason and could quite possibly damage your company's reputation through negative word of mouth.

2. *Passives* give a response of 7 or 8. They're neither overly negative or positive about your product/service and could easily be lured away by what your competitors have to offer, if given the opportunity. They're less likely than detractors to spread negative thoughts or feelings by word of mouth, but they're not enthusiastic enough to say anything nice either.

3. *Promoters* respond with either a 9 or 10. In short, they love you and your product/service and consistently make repeat purchases, and enthusiastically sing your praises to all those who will take the time to listen to them.

To calculate your NPS, you simply subtract the percentage of customers who are detractors from the percentage who are promoters, which generates a score of between –100 and 100. If all of your customers scored lower than or equal to 6, that leads to an NPS of up to –100. If all your customers answered the question with a 9 or 10, then the total score would be closer to 100.

Recently, NPS has come under heavy criticism because it's such a simplistic measure of customer satisfaction. On its own, it doesn't tell you much, since the true yardstick would be measuring yourself against your competition. It's best used over a period of time to gauge whether you're trending up or down. Also, the old phrase "The squeaky wheel gets the most grease," applies here. That is, customers who are most dissatisfied are more likely to respond to your survey. So keep this in mind as you calculate and apply the NPS to your customer satisfaction levels. Finally, low NPS scores can tell you there's a problem; however, they do little in the way of pinpointing the root causes. It's up to you to dig deeper into the problems and issues, using other means like TBP or customer experience journey mapping (CXJM), which we will discuss later in this chapter.

So, in taking a look at these three metrics, it becomes very easy to judge whether or not your organization is truly achieving customer centricity. The numbers don't lie—you just have to be brave enough to calculate them and then make the appropriate business decisions and actions to reverse adverse effects through countermeasures, or to stay the course in the case of more positive metrics. It's all up to you to lead the charge toward customer centricity!

Zeroing In on Your Target: Customer Experience

Customer experience (CX) is defined as the sum total of *all* interactions across *all* channels your customers have with your organization. It encompasses all end-to-end, front-, middle-, and back-office processes that ultimately influence customer perceptions and beliefs, forming either positive, neutral, or negative thoughts and feelings regarding your product/service.[4] It's critical to have a view of the entire CX, not just individual interaction points, from the initial contact all the way through to troubleshooting and servicing after the purchase. The benefits of understanding your customer and the complete end-to-end experience include increased customer satisfaction and employee satisfaction, reduced churn, and more revenue to your bottom line, which increases your overall competitive advantage through delivering both business and customer value.

But how many companies deliver an excellent CX? Unfortunately, not many. This was the conclusion reached by a study conducted by the Temkin Group. They found that the number of companies that scored either a "Good" or an "Excellent" rating was down from 45% in 2017 to only 38% in 2018.[5] Upon further investigation, this shift occurred because customers have come to expect a great experience from the companies they interact with, not just occasionally but *every* time they interact with them. They're starting to take for granted that their experience with a company should always be excellent, and that trend is expected to continue as the bar continues to rise in the coming years. This means that tying all of these interactions and touchpoints together into a cohesive messaging and branding campaign across your entire customer experience life cycle (CXLC) is more important than ever.

---

4 Jim Tincher and Kate Kompelien. "Designing a World-Class CX Approach: Creating Your Customer Experience Approach for Maximum Impact" (*https://oreil.ly/lW3Wq*), CXPA, accessed May 7, 2019.

5 The Temkin Group, *2018 Temkin Experience Ratings*, March 2018.

Understanding the Eight Stages of CXLC

CXLC includes all the stages a customer goes through in interacting with your product/service. Figure 5-1 illustrates the eight stages of a typical CXLC: Awareness, Research, Evaluate, Purchase, Onboard, Service, Advocate, and Dispose/Repurchase.

Figure 5-1. *The eight stages of the customer experience life cycle*

Awareness

Realizing there's something you want, need, or desire and that it's missing from your life is how the buying process begins. There's a void or gap that needs to be filled, whether you're solving a problem, filling a business or personal need, or looking to make your life easier or more enjoyable. This is the trigger that starts the buying process.

Research

Performing a product/service inquiry to determine what's currently available in the marketplace and which one might satisfy your want, need, and/or desire, often via online searches, in-person vendor/merchant location visits, social media investigations or inquiries, conversations with friends, neighbors, and colleagues, and so on.

Evaluate

Evaluating the options that are out there by asking questions and finding answers to ensure the potential product/service you might choose fills the existing need or gap; your questions might include:

- How do the different products/services compare?
- Is one better than the other in filling the gap?
- What do other people think of each product/service?

You might also reach out to the merchant or use social media and conversations with friends and family to discuss or weigh the pros and cons of purchasing, or you may go to look at or touch a product, or you might speak to a company representative or salesperson in some manner, say, by telephone or in person.

Purchase

Making a buying decision. This is the point of purchase, when you now own the product/service.

Onboard

Putting the product/service into everyday use, by which the customer becomes a consumer and determines whether it does or doesn't generate value.

Service

Getting help when something goes wrong or the product/service malfunctions and requires repair or service to return it to its original working condition.

Advocate

Being a supporter of the product/service to the point that you would recommend it to other people or could possibly make repeat purchases, if you've derived value from it.

Dispose/Repurchase

Disposing of or disconnecting from the product/service or possibly repurchasing the same or different products/services from the company, either at its "end of life," because it has served its purpose, or for some other reason, like being dissatisfied with its quality level or receiving poor service.

Considering the type of experience you want to build and maintain across these eight CXLC stages allows you to get a complete picture of the CX and how you want it to develop and unfold as you interact with current and potential customers, known as your customer experience strategy (CXS). It's also crucial for establishing, maintaining, and retaining customer business and loyalty to your brand, instead of having to go out and continuously acquire new customers. Understanding the experience you create does translate into tangible benefits. Forrester found that leaders who spend the time to understand these experiences enjoy, on average, a growth rate of 17% compared to a growth rate of only 3% for those who don't.[6] That should be enough to get your attention and convince you that your CXS is a crucial element to the overall health of your company and well worth your time and energy.

---

6 Tincher and Kompelien, "Designing."

Identifying Customer Personas

The first step in developing an effective CXS is to humanize your customers by bringing them to life so that you understand how to build that connection from a behavioral and emotional perspective. In his book *The Inmates are Running the Asylum* (Sams), Alan Cooper describes how the creation of what he calls "archetypes," also sometimes referred to as either customer segments or *personas*,[7] are helpful in identifying and describing common characteristics. These characteristics can include behaviors, tasks, goals, and emotions present among all potential customers that are relevant within a given market segment as they make purchasing decisions. In short, they're fictitious representations of real people and their characteristics, behaviors, and emotions. Having a clear mental picture of an actual customer persona, instead of some vague notion of who your customer might be, goes a long way toward helping you make informed business decisions. By personifying your customers, you give them depth and can take into consideration the multiple dimensions of humans so that you can spot relationships and patterns to truly understand what attracts and retains them. This view of your customer then becomes a crucial asset when undertaking efforts to develop and implement:

- Branding and messaging
- Customer market segmentation
- Omnichannel selection strategies
- Marketing and sales efforts
- Omnichannel content development activities

Developing Relevant Customer Personas

Personas are derived through studying and interviewing real people while conducting market research that is captured on a one- or two-page description that can include behavior patterns, goals, skills, attitudes, emotions, and environmental factors, along with a few fictitious personal details to bring the persona to life.[8] Figure 5-2 depicts a persona template that you can use.

---

7 Alan Cooper, *The Inmates Are Running the Asylum: Why High-Tech Products Drive Us Crazy and How to Restore the Sanity*, 2nd Ed. (Indianapolis: Sams Publishing 2004).

8 Kim Goodwin, "Perfecting Your Personas" (*https://oreil.ly/w8CzN*), *Cooper Journal*, May 15, 2008.

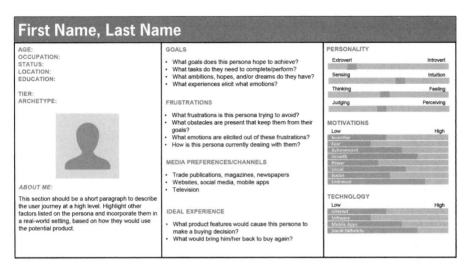

First Name, Last Name

AGE:
OCCUPATION:
STATUS:
LOCATION:
EDUCATION:

TIER:
ARCHETYPE:

ABOUT ME:
This section should be a short paragraph to describe
the user journey at a high level. Highlight other
factors listed on the persona and incorporate them in
a real-world setting, based on how they would use
the potential product.

GOALS

• What goals does this persona hope to achieve?
• What tasks do they need to complete/perform?
• What ambitions, hopes, and/or dreams do they have?
• What experiences elicit what emotions?

FRUSTRATIONS

• What frustrations is this persona trying to avoid?
• What obstacles are present that keep them from their
  goals?
• What emotions are elicited out of these frustrations?
• How is this persona currently dealing with them?

MEDIA PREFERENCES/CHANNELS

• Trade publications, magazines, newspapers
• Websites, social media, mobile apps
• Television

IDEAL EXPERIENCE

• What product features would cause this persona to
  make a buying decision?
• What would bring him/her back to buy again?

PERSONALITY

Extrovert   Introvert
Sensing   Intuition
Thinking   Feeling
Judging   Perceiving

MOTIVATIONS

Low   High
Incentive
Fear
Achievement
Growth
Power
Social
Status
Embrace

TECHNOLOGY

Low   High
Internet
Software
Mobile Apps
Social Networks

Figure 5-2. *Customer persona template (large format version (https://oreil.ly/leadingLean-figs))*

Going back to the New Horizons dealership case study from Chapter 4, after much discussion and after conducting a lot of quantitative and qualitative research on the different types of people that buy this particular make of vehicle, the kaizen team decided to focus on owner types, which seemed to make the most sense. As a result, they identified the following five unique customer personas:

1. Luxury sedan owner
2. Sports coupe owner
3. SUV owner
4. Truck owner
5. Van owner

The team decided to prioritize the list by customer lifetime value (CLV), ensuring that the most value-generating personas get the right level of attention as they move forward. Then they went on to develop all of the detailed customer personas. The sports coupe owner persona is depicted in Figure 5-3.

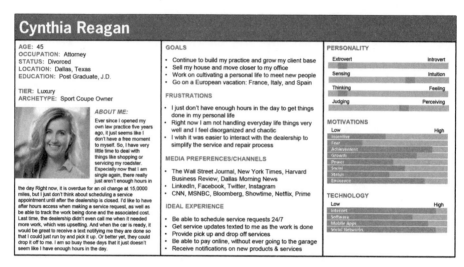

Cynthia Reagan

AGE: 45
OCCUPATION: Attorney
STATUS: Divorced
LOCATION: Dallas, Texas
EDUCATION: Post Graduate, J.D.

TIER: Luxury
ARCHETYPE: Sport Coupe Owner

ABOUT ME:
Ever since I opened my own law practice five years ago, it just seems like I don't have a free moment to myself. So, I have very little time to deal with things like shopping or servicing my roadster. Especially now that I am single again, there really just aren't enough hours in the day Right now, it is overdue for an oil change at 15,0000 miles, but I just don't think about scheduling a service appointment until after the dealership is closed. I'd like to have after hours access when making a service request, as well as be able to track the work being done and the associated cost. Last time, the dealership didn't even call me when it needed more work, which was upsetting. And when the car is ready, it would be great to receive a text notifying me they are done so that I could just run by and pick it up. Or better yet, they could drop it off to me. I am so busy these days that it just doesn't seem like I have enough hours in the day.

GOALS
• Continue to build my practice and grow my client base
• Sell my house and move closer to my office
• Work on cultivating a personal life to meet new people
• Go on a European vacation: France, Italy, and Spain

FRUSTRATIONS
• I just don't have enough hours in the day to get things done in my personal life
• Right now I am not handling everyday life things very well and I feel disorganized and chaotic
• I wish it was easier to interact with the dealership to simplify the service and repair process

MEDIA PREFERENCES/CHANNELS
• The Wall Street Journal, New York Times, Harvard Business Review, Dallas Morning News
• CNN, MSNBC, Bloomberg, Showtime, Netflix, Prime

IDEAL EXPERIENCE
• Be able to schedule service requests 24/7
• Get service updates texted to me as the work is done
• Provide pick up and drop off services
• Be able to pay online, without ever going to the garage
• Receive notifications on new products & services

PERSONALITY
Extrovert — Introvert
Sensing — Intuition
Thinking — Feeling
Judging — Perceiving

MOTIVATIONS
Low — High
Incentive
Fear
Achievement
Growth
Power
Social
Status
Eminence

TECHNOLOGY
Low — High
Internet
Software
Mobile Apps
Social Networks

Figure 5-3. *Sports coupe owner persona (large format version (https://oreil.ly/leadingLean-figs))*

In New Horizons' situation, writing personas as the first step in the CX process makes a lot of sense. The team seeks to understand what vehicle owners want and how they think about and make service requests. In Cynthia's situation, she's a busy professional with very little free time. Being newly divorced, she's in the process of getting her life back in order and has no time to think about things like servicing her car, though she understands that to keep her high-performance sports coupe running well, it needs to be serviced and maintained, which impacts both her motives and her behaviors. However, since the car is still under warranty, she understands she needs to take it back to the dealership where she purchased it for service to maintain the integrity of her service and repair record. But she is frustrated because the dealership just doesn't seem to understand the needs of its clientele, with the service department being open only from 8:30 a.m. to 5 p.m., Monday through Friday. Those are not convenient hours, since leaving work is difficult for her during the day. The event trigger here could be either opening her own practice or becoming divorced. Either way, it means she has less time to get things done outside of normal business hours. The behavior motive is ease of access when taking her car in for service. Life doesn't happen in a vacuum, and discrete, independent behaviors are few and far between. So remember to think about the events, interactions, and dependencies, as well as the behaviors and motives.

Keeping Personas Simple

The opposite of not creating personas at all is creating too many. The general rule of thumb is seven personas, plus or minus two, for any given product/service. If you find yourself creating more than that, try to combine or eliminate a few to reach an easy-to-maintain level. Remember: keep it simple.

Along these lines, I once worked with an organization that told me they had 35 personas—and yes, that was for one product line! The look of horror on my face must have been evident because the product manager I was speaking with then stammered, "Well, we are trying to pare that down some. The UX folks keep the list, and they've been working on it for some time now." However, when I asked the UX director for the list, he had no idea what I was talking about, and unfortunately, this was not an isolated incident. I've had the same conversation over and over again during the last couple of years as I've worked with leaders on their CXS.

So remember that the good old rule of thumb, 7 +/– 2, is there for a reason. That means five to nine archetype personas are all an entire company (or division, depending on its size) should develop. I tend to gravitate toward the lower levels myself because many of the ones you identify can be rolled up into categories, such as "clerk." There are many subtypes or categories within this persona, such as legal clerk, finance clerk, and human resources clerk, but they're all clerks who perform the same general functions, just in different disciplines. Common sense must be applied when developing personas, to guard against going hog wild. And remember that whatever number of personas you develop, they must *all* be maintained, which requires periodically investing time in revalidation and verification to ensure your customer demographic hasn't changed.

Once you've identified your personas, as you develop possible product/service ideas, requirements, or additional customer channels, you'll use them to understand the CX journey they will take as they interact with you across your CXLC.

Designing Customer Journeys That Matter

Customer journeys are individual interactions that a customer has with your organization across a channel, involving the touchpoints or "moments that matter" that result as part of that journey within the CXLC. Well-written customer journeys are a strategic planning and prioritization tool you can use to capture your customers' perceptions, needs, and expectations. They assist you in seeing and assessing the gaps in your customers' experience between touchpoints and within channels so that you gain an awareness of where you need to improve and optimize their experiences. Then you can effectively invest the time, energy, and money where they matter the most and have the greatest impact.

The business benefits of performing CXJM are numerous, as proven by a recent Aberdeen Group study, which found that companies with a formal program realized the following year-over-year growth statistics:

- 18 times faster average sales cycles
- 56% greater cross-sell and up-sell revenue
- 10 times improvement in customer service costs
- 5 times greater revenue from customer referrals
- 54% greater return on marketing investment (ROMI)[9]

Being mindful of the experiences your customers have with you and optimizing them across your CXLC is a must for Lean leaders nowadays. However, the same study found that only 26% of companies have a formal CX program,[10] making instituting one a huge opportunity to create competitive advantage for your organization. A shocking 86% of customers are willing to spend more on products/services that offer a great CX, per another recent study conducted by the Aberdeen Group.[11] So ensuring your customer's experience is a positive one is well worth your time and effort.

Keep in mind, though, that a customer journey is not the same thing as a customer experience. A customer journey is specific to a phase of the CXLC, whereas the customer experience addresses the entire end-to-end experience. For example, going back to New Horizons, the service request intake mobile application that the team is thinking about building addresses the customer journeys within the service phase of the dealership's CXLC, such as:

- Schedule an appointment
- Drop off a car
- Pick up a loaner car

---

9 Omer Minkara, "Customer Journey Mapping: Lead the Way to Advocacy" (*https://oreil.ly/oi1c7*), Aberdeen Group, November 2016, 2.

10 Omer Minkara, "Customer Journey Mapping: Lead the Way to Advocacy," 2.

11 Omer Minkara, "The Customer Experience Value Chain: Paving the Way to Advocacy Report" (*https://oreil.ly/S1YPc*), Aberdeen Group, October 2016, 6.

These are all from the customer's perspective, not that of the dealership. Keep in mind there would also be journeys within each CXLC phase, such as "Purchase a vehicle."[12]

Research

- Compare manufacturer offerings
- Research vehicle reviews
- Decide on a vehicle make
- Decide on a vehicle model

Evaluate

- Schedule a dealership visit
- Conduct a test drive

Purchase

- Negotiate the vehicle loan
- Accept vehicle delivery

And finally, it's important to keep in mind that customer journeys are written from the perspective of the customer. So you need to put yourself in your customers' shoes and understand how they think, feel, act, and behave as they interact with your products/services across the CXLC. Then you can collect and analyze their feedback to improve upon the journey and the overall experience.

The Role of Emotions in the Customer Experience

Before we explore how to build journeys, let's take a few minutes to examine the role of emotions in the customer experience. Understanding how to create emotional connections that elicit customer brand loyalty is very important when identifying the interactions and touchpoints you want to build across your CXLC. Emotions play a big part in the buying experience because they shape the attitudes that drive human decisions. A recent *Harvard Business Review* study[12] found that emotionally engaged customers are:

---

12 Scott Magids, Alan Zorfas, and Daniel Leemon, "The New Science of Customer Emotions" (*https://oreil.ly/UtG7j*), *Harvard Business Review*, November 2015.

- At least three times more likely to recommend your product/service
- Three times more likely to repurchase
- Less likely to shop around (44% said they rarely or never shop around)
- Much less price sensitive (33% said they would need to be given a discount of over 20% before they would consider defecting)

Customer loyalty is a product of emotional attachment because customers remember what emotions are elicited as they use the product or service. Lean leaders who win the minds and hearts of their customers outperform their competition by 85% in sales growth[13] by focusing on creating "moments that matter," or MTMs, that build these emotional connections. MTMs are what turn the average customer into an advocate for your product/service. But how do you figure out which MTMs inspire and elicit strong customer emotions? There are four types you should focus on:

- What do they want to know?
- Where do they want to go?
- What do they want to do?
- What do they want to buy?

You have a wealth of data at your fingertips to help you answer these questions and find these MTMs, and you can uncover a plethora of answers to these questions through analysis of:

Search data
   What are your customers searching for online when it comes to your product/service? What types of questions are they asking? Cost? Features? "How-tos"?

Survey data
   Directly asking your customers to answer questions about what's important to them has always been an invaluable tool.

Interview data
   What would your customers say about your product/service if you asked them directly? Going directly to the customer can be very insightful in helping you understand how to create lasting emotional connections.

---

13 Ibid.

Employee-gathered data

What do your employees say your customers are asking about or indicating is important to them? The people closest to your customers, whether it be in your stores, online, or in customer service, are an invaluable source of information that's readily available to help you identify and create memorable experiences for customers.

Let's now turn our attention to how to design journeys that matter, in order to win both the hearts and minds of your customers, generating their loyalty and creating customers for life.

Conducting Customer Experience Journey Mapping (CXJM)

When thinking about undertaking this type of effort, you must assemble a team that has representation from all major areas of your business, such as CX, UX, customer service, marketing, sales, service, technology, and operations. It's important to form a well-rounded team so that no portion of the journey is inadvertently missed, underrepresented, or misinterpreted. Once your team is formed, you can kick off your CXJM initiative.

Step 1. Define the scope and objectives of the journey mapping exercise

Whether you're mapping your journeys for the first time or optimizing them, you must determine the business drivers and pain points that are motivating you to look at the journey in the first place. Ask yourself:

- What am I trying to get out of this mapping exercise?
- Is it more streamlined interactions?
- Have the trigger events or MTMs changed (expanded or contracted)?
- Do the customer touchpoints feel "rough" or lacking?
- Does analyzing customer feedback or analytics point to problems that must be resolved in the interaction or channel?
- Does your CXS naturally flow from one phase to the next in your CXLC?

An effective CXJM initiative starts with defining the scope and a clear set of goals or business outcomes. Clarify how you want to improve upon both the CX and the overall CXS across your entire CXLC. For example, with New Horizons, the scope of the initiative is contained to the service department, and the business outcome that the team is looking to achieve by building a new service department mobile app is to bring their NPS up by 25 points and their service ticket processing error rate down below 10%, all within 90 days after launch. As you can see, the scope is well defined and the business objectives are quantifiable and measurable within the given timeframe. However, be mindful of guarding against too broad a scope, since context is important and you don't want to water down or accidentally gloss over important details that have more meaning in a tighter frame of reference.

Step 2. Perform research to analyze and evaluate existing customer data

Conducting this type of research helps you to gain an understanding of who your actual and potential customers are as well as providing insights on the current CX. A recent survey conducted by the Customer Experience Professionals Association (CXPA)[14] found the top five sources of customer data when doing CXJM are:

- In-person interviews (53%)
- In-person focus groups (41%)
- Web-based surveys (38%)
- Workshops involving customers (35%)
- Phone-based interviews (26%)

Lesser sources of data can also include:

- Call center logs
- Usability test results
- Contextual inquiry observations and reports
- Customer satisfaction reports
- Customer care reports
- Market value studies

---

14 "Driving Change Through Journey Maps: Discoveries from the Initial Journey Mapping Best Practices Survey" (*https://oreil.ly/iDq7x*), Heart of the Customer, 2016, 5.

Step 3. Identify the personas you'll use to map the journeys

Based on your analysis of the data, your findings should aid you in defining a set of baseline personas that can be for a specific customer type (persona), a potential or target customer, or a segment of customers, depending on the purpose of your CXJM initiative. If you recall, in the New Horizons mapping exercise, the team defined five specific personas:

1. Luxury sedan owner
2. Sports coupe owner
3. SUV owner
4. Truck owner
5. Van owner

Step 4. Conduct a CXJM workshop to create the initial maps

The goal of a CXJM workshop is to create the initial maps that you will continuously refine and eventually optimize as you iterate on each persona across the CXLC, with the sole purpose of building a shared understanding of the customer and how they interact with you during this journey. The end result is the development of a solid CXS for each persona type. Figure 5-4 depicts the end-to-end (E2E) CXJM template that you can use to create your CXJ maps.

Persona: Title

Version: X.x

	Stage 1	Stage 2	Stage 3	Stage 4	Stage N+1
Customer Expectations	• Your Text	• Your Text	• Your Text	• Your Text	• Your Text
CX Journey					
Customer Goals	1. Your Text	1. Your Text	1. Your Text	1. Your Text	1. Your Text
Dept #1					
Dept #2					
Dept #3					
Dept #N+1					
Touchpoints & Emotional Responses	① Your Text ② ③	① Your Text ② ③	① Your Text ② ③	① Your Text ② ③	① Your Text ② ③
Overall Customer Experience	Positive / Neutral / Negative				Positive / Neutral / Negative
Improvement Ideas	1. Your Text	1. Your Text	1. Your Text	1. Your Text	1. Your Text

Figure 5-4. *E2E CX journey map template (large format version (https://oreil.ly/leadingLean-figs))*

The template consists of the following seven sections:

Customer expectations
Defines what the customer expects during each stage of the CXLC for this journey.

CX journey
Denotes the CXLC stages that apply to this journey. You should fill this section out with your core team in advance of your workshop.

Customer goals
States what the customer wants to achieve during each stage. Understanding their goals at each stage allows you to empathize with them to ensure you're addressing their pain points from their perspective.

Business functions
Lists the areas of the business that interact with the customer during this journey. This section is important because it identifies which business areas require process improvement initiatives to address any issues that might be identified.

Touchpoints and emotional responses
Denotes the MTMs and the associated emotions that are elicited from each interaction. This is where you humanize the journey and could quite possibly be the most important section on the whole map. Don't gloss over it. Make sure you truly understand both to ensure you're addressing the right issues.

Overall customer experience
Displays graphically the touchpoints and emotions experienced during each interaction. This is where you'll be able to see the actual journey your customers experience as they move through the different stages, as well as what is and isn't important to them.

Improvement ideas
Captures the possible ways the journey can be improved upon.

For workshops, what I like to do is print the template out on poster-sized dry erase paper and then give one copy to each team so they can work with the boards to construct their maps.

Workshop attendees and materials
Determining who attends the workshop is one of the most important decisions. Depending on how many customers are in attendance, I usually form three to four teams with two to three customers in each, not to exceed five to nine customers in total. Putting more than 25 people in a room is hard to manage. Make sure everyone who is invited participates—

no wallflowers allowed! Onlookers or bystanders have an unnerving effect when people are asked to be honest or emotional about their experience. Do make sure to include all of the relevant areas of your business in each team as well as the business process owners to ensure you are collecting the perspectives of all those involved in this journey. Stock up on pads of sticky notes and markers for the tables as well.

Scheduling the workshop

When scheduling your workshops, arrange them by persona, because each workshop should be focused on one persona at a time. Then begin by reviewing the persona you're focusing on for this workshop. In our New Horizons example, the team picked Cynthia Reagan, sports coupe owner persona (Figure 5-3).

Conducting the workshop

During the workshop, you can follow this simple format for getting the template filled out. Break the day into seven sections of 1 hour each, with a half hour for lunch and two 15-minute breaks. Take the first 10 minutes or so to provide an explanation of the section and discuss the content that's being sought. Then allow the teams to work independently for the next 50 minutes. Have each team member write down their own thoughts on the notes and place them on the board in the appropriate section. Allow 10 to 15 minutes, or until no one is writing anymore. Then have the members of each team discuss the feedback amongst themselves, consolidating the sticky notes and writing their final responses directly on the board for the next 20 minutes. Take the last 20 minutes or whatever time is remaining to have a couple of the teams present their findings and discuss them with the entire group.

The final section, Improvement Ideas, is where the magic happens. This is where you want the teams to let loose and use their imaginations to come up with possible improvements that could be made to enhance the customer experience. Challenge them to come up with ideas that will provide competitive advantage and new and innovative ways to address the issues identified during the workshop. Spend at least 30 minutes on discussing this as a group to see whether any other ideas can be generated collectively.

Following the workshop, assemble your journey mapping core team and create a single, combined CXJ map for the Sports Coupe Owner persona. Figure 5-5 depicts the New Horizons team's end-to-end service vehicle CX journey map.

	Evaluate	Purchase	Service	Advocate	Dispose/Repurchase
Customer Expectations	I want to find a reputable garage or dealership that offers high-quality repairs and professional service.	I don't have a lot of time to take my vehicle in for service, so scheduling an appointment should be simple.	I should be promptly greeted, and the check in process should be simple and accurate, with items correctly done.	I expect great service, high quality, and professionalism to gain my loyalty and repeat business.	Picking up my vehicle should be quick and easy, and I should receive an accurate itemized final bill.
CXJ: Service Vehicle	Evaluate	Purchase	Service	Advocate	Dispose/Repurchase
Customer Goals	1. The service light on my dashboard has lit up, stating my vehicle needs repair and/or service 2. Ask friends, family, coworkers, etc, who provides their service 3. Find a few reputable garages or dealerships where I can get it fixed 4. Research each option and determine a short list of possibilities	1. Evaluate my short list based on reputation, service quality, location, and professionalism 2. Make a decision as to which one I will use in my area 3. Give the garage or dealership a call to schedule an appointment 4. Arrange for a loaner vehicle the day of service	1. I am greeted promptly and they are prepared for my visit 2. The service is performed within the specified timeframe 3. I am informed of and approve/decline additional work 4. Service is done right the first time 5. I receive an itemized bill and am walked through the work performed	1. I will refer this business to my friends, family, coworkers, etc., if: • I am treated fairly and with respect • The staff is professional • My repairs and/or service are completed on time and within the original estimate • Dealership is professionally managed (clean and safe)	1. The deciding factor: I may/may not do business with this dealership again 2. Excellent service will win my business again 3. Poor service means I will go elsewhere next time
Branding					
Sales					
Service					
Financing					
Touchpoints & Emotional Responses	① There is something wrong with my vehicle ② Speak to people for referrals ③ I think I found a reputable dealer to fix it	④ I am going to schedule an appointment at New Horizons ⑤ I just scheduled an appointment for next Monday ⑥ They also hooked me up with a rental...score!	⑦ The service agent was rude ⑧ No rental car...UGH!!! ⑨ Stuff was added to my bill without my approval...very disappointing ⑩ Some repairs were not performed; I will have to take it in again	⑪ I would not refer this dealership if my life depended on it. The way I was treated is inexcusable ⑫ The service manager called and apologized ⑬ She scheduled a 2nd appointment to get the missed items fixed	⑭ I am only lukewarm on using New Horizons again, after everything I went through to get my vehicle properly serviced and repared
Overall Customer Experience	Positive / Neutral / Negative (line graph plotting points 1–14)				
Improvement Ideas	1. Develop a mobile app to make finding information about service and repairs easy to find	1. Make scheduling an appointment and arranging for a rental car available on the app	1. Provide training to the service staff 2. Upgrade the rental car system 3. Send repair progress notifications 4. Provide viewable bill on app	1. Send out feedback survey on app 2. Offer coupons/discounts on next visit 3. Do random follow-up customer calls	1. Provide push notifications when next service is due 2. Call customers who have not been back for over a year

Figure 5-5. *Service vehicle customer experience journey map (large format version (https://oreil.ly/leadingLean-figs))*

Step 5. Validate the CX journey map using your customer research

Now that you have your combined map, you must go back and validate your assumptions with the research you conducted in step 2 above. How do they compare when running a side-by-side comparison? Does the data prove out the map? If not, why? Conducting additional customer interviews or sending out additional customer surveys to get to the bottom of any discrepancies might be helpful.

Also, keep in mind that as you move through this process, the baseline personas should also be continuously updated and modified as you learn more about your actual and potential customers. If a new persona is identified in the process, you must then organize and run another workshop to ensure you have all of them represented.

Step 6. Publish and socialize your CX journey maps

Once you've finished your maps, you should publish them to a corporate site where everyone in the organization can view them. Remember, a Lean culture is based on continuous improvement, so put the maps in the hands of the people that can make the best use of the information contained in them. That could be any number of teams, from sales to operations and on through to technology. Socialize them and incorporate the feedback from these parts of your organization. Be creative! You're only limited by your own ability to harness your imagination and put it to good use.

Step 7. Prioritize and implement your improvement ideas

Finally, make good use of all of those great ideas by forming kaizen teams in the areas where improvements have been identified. Go through and prioritize them first, and then use the Lean TBP process discussed in Chapter 4 to figure out how you can iterate on these ideas and bring them to life. For the New Horizons team, they will be moving their maps to the product development phase, which we'll discuss in Chapter 7.

Building a Mindful Omnichannel Customer Experience Strategy

A great omnichannel customer experience strategy (OCXS) defines the actionable plans you must put in place to deliver a consistently positive and meaningful experience to your customers across every interaction, touchpoint, and channel. Its ultimate goal is to improve both the customer experience and the relationship you have with your customers. However, building an OCXS is a full-contact sport that must include the entire customer-centric Lean enterprise —that is, both the customer- and noncustomer-facing parts of the organization, collaborating together to build a holistic strategy that requires identifying the components and then building the processes, operations, and behaviors that support a customer-first culture.

How Do You Define Omnichannel, Anyway?

A channel is how you bring your product/service to market. Leaders can choose to create and then operate within both traditional and digital channels. Traditional channels include wholesalers, distributors, brick-and-mortar stores, print, telephone, radio, TV, etc. Digital channels consist of websites, blogs, mobile applications, email, search engines, social media (Twitter, Facebook, YouTube), pay-per-click (PPC) advertising , and video. So *omnichannel* refers to using all of these ways of marketing, distributing, and selling your product/service in a connected way that provides an integrated customer experience.

A great example of an OCXS is when customers enter a traditional brick-and-mortar store but then pull out their mobile devices to look for in-store coupons or to conduct online product research, using a search engine to find product information or reviews, checking YouTube for "how-to" videos, or even sending a tweet out to get responses back on product quality and durability. Mind you, all this happens before making a buying decision. An OCXS, when done well, blurs the lines between traditional and digital channels, ensuring a seamless switching back and forth through customer touchpoints.

A multichannel experience is not necessarily an omnichannel one—it comes down to how well all of your channels integrate across your customer experience. That is, you can have a website, a social media presence, and even a brick-and-mortar store, but unless the messaging is consistent across all of these channels, that won't be considered an OCX. And yes, all omnichannel experiences use multiple channels, which means you must focus on perfecting each channel and then diligently working to integrate them all to create a well-thought-out and mindful OCXS. That means that to deliver an integrated experience, you must work to align your product/service goals, objectives, design, and messaging across each channel.

BMW, "The Ultimate Driving Machine"

BMW's brand is built on the slogan "The Ultimate Driving Machine." This is a great example of strong branding right out of the gate. The word "ultimate," per the *Merriam-Webster* dictionary, means the best achievable or imaginable of its kind.[15] When paired with "driving machine," it implies the best achievable machine for driving purposes imaginable. That's a pretty tall claim to

---

15 *Merriam-Webster*, s.v. "ultimate (adj.)" (*https://oreil.ly/_z2c4*), accessed May 7, 2019.

make. However, if you've ever driven one, this car truly lives up to that image. I should know, because I owned a black BMW Z3 Roadster at one time.

For me, the car did live up to its name, and in casual conversation, BMW's branding would always come up when people learned I owned one. Two things would usually follow: the catchphrase of "The Ultimate Driving Machine" would be uttered, or a question would be posed: "Is it really the ultimate driving machine?" To that, I would always answer an emphatic "YES!" It was an amazing car to own and drive. (However, we will not discuss my speeding tickets while I owned this car...uh hum, moving on...)

BMW has created a brand that's very recognizable and consistent within a context they have set and cultivated, across a series of both traditional and digital channels. It's truly a differentiated and interconnected OCXS.

For example, when I recently went to the BMW website (*https://www.bmwusa.com/*), it had a flash banner that immediately began to play at the top of the page, displaying multiple, high-gloss-finish models parked together on a black background. In two- to three-second clips, you see multiple views of the different cars, both inside and out. The rich interiors and stylish fine lines and details of each model appear in short, accentuated glimpses. However, the camera always comes back to one image, which is a quick, partial glance as it pans across cursive lettering on one of the cars that says, "BMW individual manufactured." If that isn't suggestive marketing, I don't know what is, as the subtle hints make you want to find out more about how you too can build your own "individually manufactured" BMW.

BMW's Crystal-Clear Messaging

The focus is on the "BMW Difference." Individuality, performance, style, quality, and innovation are what they're selling. When you own a BMW, the manufacturer's brand pitches a lifestyle that equals success and high standards. You're a discerning and unique individual who seeks luxury, quality, and performance. That's the messaging they're conveying to both their current and potential customers. And yes, you too can join this club if you make a buying decision to purchase one of their fine automobiles. BMW is selling an image as much as a physical product because ultimately you want to be associated with it. I bought my Z3 for the quality and performance. I drove all of the other convertibles on the market at the time, such as Porsche, Mazda, Honda, and Infiniti; and yes, driving a BMW is a true experience. The thing that sealed the deal for me was the interior and the overall handling of the car, which is all part of BMW's image, product quality, and brand reputation.

The BMW OCXS

Now, to prove there is an OCXS at work here, go ahead and open a browser window and search for "BMW." The results that came back for me included YouTube, Twitter, blog posts, US and international websites, etc., as well as your local dealer sites. If I click on the YouTube result, a just over two-minute video of the BMW 7 series driving down the road begins to play. Again, short, two- to three-second clips of the car from every angle inundate me, just like the images that were on the BMW website. You can almost feel the quality and luxury of the car in the images you're viewing. A distinguished older man with a five o'clock shadow stops the car and steps out. He has parked it outside of an airplane hangar, and he is dressed in dark jeans, a black, untucked button-down, and black jacket; he throws his black gym bag into the cockpit, as if he intends on jetting away for a weekend adventure, as he gets into what looks like a small Lear jet. The camera cuts to him preparing the plane for takeoff, as the frame cuts back and forth between the instrumentation panel on the plane and that of the car he had just gotten out of. The implied comparison comes through loud and clear.

Just as he is about to take off, an air traffic controller tells him he is grounded due to the storm front that is passing through the area. Disappointed, he gets back into the car and starts it up. The scene then cuts to him flying down an implied runway as he punches it, as if he were about to take off. As the miles per hour on the speedometer approach 150, a rear shot of the car in the clouds implies it is now flying. There's even an angled shot as the car clears the clouds. It has now stopped raining, and the sun is starting to peek out from between the clouds. The video comes to an end as the music crescendos, and the words "The 7" appear in the upper lefthand corner and "BMW" in the lower right. There is no announcer, no parting words to tell you to go buy the car—just the front lower- to upper-angled shot of it says it all.

The whole clip is geared toward pulling in your passion for driving a high-performance car that's as beautiful inside as it is out. Its craftsmanship and luxury are built for the discerning and unique individual, and it invokes your senses to the point that you can even feel your adrenaline building as you watch the driver race down the runway and the car magically begins to fly!

The brick-and-mortar stores are the same. Lots of high-gloss, gorgeous cars parked at angles on a white high-gloss floor, with the slogans "The Ultimate Driving Machine" and "The BMW Difference" with the BMW emblem posted on the banners overhead and on glossy floor displays. The whole process of buying a BMW took me about two hours, from test drive to signing the loan papers. BMW has streamlined the process because they understand their customers are busy people who don't have the time to spend an entire day in a dealership, buying a car.

Taking a quick look and experiencing these different channels confirms that BMW has an excellent OCXS across both its traditional and digital channels. Digitally, they do an excellent job with a physical product to show you virtually what it is like to own and drive a BMW. They have also seamlessly carried that over to their dealerships with consistent messaging and touchpoints across the different stages of the customer experience. Can you say that about your omnichannel customer experience? Does your messaging and branding carry over between channels? Are you depicting a consistent image of your brand to your potential or current customers, across channels, no matter the platform? Are you building rapport and empathy with them so they can enjoy an experience like that? If the answer to any of these questions is "no," you've got some work to do if you intend on staying relevant with your customers and competitive in your marketplace.

Considerations for Building a Mindful OCXS

Building an effective OCXS is not all about the channels or messages themselves. It's also about the customers and giving them a pleasant experience by understanding who they are, what they are about, and what they are looking for. Building empathy and rapport across the multiple experiences allows customers to make informed decisions that build the relationship with you, your company, and your brand. Let's spend a few minutes discussing some of the considerations you need to keep in mind when building an effective OCXS.

Simplicity and fluidity

First and foremost, a key element in building a successful OCXS is to ensure the experience flows easily and seamlessly across both your traditional and digital channels and from one interaction or touchpoint to another, producing a pleasant and enjoyable customer experience. You must pay attention to customers' channel preferences, usage, and experiences that matter to them, building your branding and messaging from their perspective, not yours. So take the time to determine what you want the customer experience to look, feel, and sound like across all channels, from the first impression to purchase and support, to develop a more fluid and contextual overall experience. Ask yourself the following questions:

- Does your OCXS cover all phases of the CXLC, from initial contact through to service and support?
- Does one channel flow into the next in a consistent and meaningful way?
- How complicated it is to interact with you in a traditional and/or digital manner?

- Is it easy to find something? Make a purchase? Get help? Have questions answered? File a complaint? Return an item under warranty? Get service?
- Are your processes straightforward and consistent across your various channels?

Reachability

Reachability means meeting and engaging with your customers where they are right now. This is extremely important when building empathy and generating a shared context with your customers, so that you are rewarded with their loyalty and an increase in competitive advantage that has the potential to last in the long run. Engaging with them on their terms also makes it feel more natural and less forced or artificial. It's very important to figure out what their engagement preferences are and then provide the right channels to ensure you make it into their field of awareness. When evaluating and determining reachability, ask yourself the following questions:

- What channels do your customers frequent the most?
- Do you have a presence within those channels?
- What channels have the highest rate of success?
- Is it easy to engage with you?
- Are you there when they reach out for help?
- Are you responsive when they do reach out?
- How long does it take you to respond?
- Is the experience generally pleasant?
- Do you sufficiently satisfy each customer?
- Can you effectively engage with them when they show the most interest?
- Is it easy to initiate product inquiries or pose questions?
- Are product/service issues handled on a timely basis?
- Are customers usually satisfied with the end result?
- Are there channel combinations that are more or less effective than others?
- Do you monitor engagement across all channels?
- What communication mechanisms are you currently using? Chatbot? Email? Telephone?
- How effective are they at communicating with your customers?

Personalization

Knowing your customers well is critical to understanding how to differentiate their experiences as they interact with you and your brand. Then turning around and using this knowledge to solve their problems and offer them products/services they might not even realize they want, need, or desire enhances their experience with you by uniquely catering to them. Netflix is a great example of custom personalization because it keeps track of what you've viewed in the past, so that when you log in again to watch a show or movie on its app, the cover page is built based on your previous viewing history. That is, a customized page is generated through the use of an algorithm that harnesses the power of technology—artificial intelligence (AI) and machine learning (ML)—to search for similar shows and movies that you might enjoy watching. This type of personalization is a very powerful tool! So when thinking about personalizing your products/services, ask yourself the following questions:

- Does a differentiated customer experience exist, or is it more a "one size fits all" approach?

- Are you thinking about and addressing the different needs of your customer segments, also known as personas?

- What customer data is easily available that's generated through your interactions and touchpoints?

- Can it be leveraged to create personalization or customization scenarios?

- How can you consistently align those touchpoints with the available data across the entire end-to-end customer experience?

- What technologies are available to assist you in automating data collection and analysis?

Purchase convenience

How easy or difficult is it to buy something from you? After all, that's why you're in business in the first place...right? Take for example my recent experience in a national convenience store (C-store) chain located inside a major international airport. C-stores are supposed to be places where you can pop in, quickly grab something, check out, and be on your way. Unfortunately, there was nothing convenient or quick about this experience! I popped in before my flight to pick up a bottled water, and as I moved toward the coolers, I had to navigate through a line of at least 20 people who were standing in front of the coolers waiting to be checked out. During the busiest time in the morning, the C-store had one register open, and the store filled up with customers. There was so much merchandise scattered around, displayed in very narrow aisles, that there was nowhere for a line to form except in front of the coolers. As it grew, it began to snake around the store until the customers standing in line were now in the way of the shoppers who had yet to make a product selection. I looked around the store and saw another clerk over in the corner stocking shelves. The woman at the register had to stop what she was doing to go get her. By the time she got to her register and opened it up for business, many of those waiting in line had already left, dropping whatever they were holding on the nearest shelf.

When your business model is built on convenience and ease of purchase, especially in an airport where people have flights to catch, the last thing customers want to do is wait in a long queue at the register. The lack of cashier support forced them to choose between buying what they were holding or forgoing their purchase in favor of catching their flight. And because of this experience, I've found myself shying away from reentering one of their stores, because it has left a lasting mark on my subconscious mind. So when thinking about purchasing convenience, ask yourself the following questions:

- Is it easy to check out when a customer is done shopping (either online or in-store)?
- Are product/service facts and specifications easy to find, ensuring that customers understand the purchases they are making?
- Is navigation, either physical or virtual, simple and easy?
- Once a customer selects items for purchase, is there a way to suggest complementary items that the customer might also be interested in?
- Are there enough resources (cashiers, transaction services, customer service agents, etc.) to handle the volume at peak times?
- Are your stores, websites, mobile apps, etc., built with the customer in mind as far as "fit for purpose"?

Service Convenience

In this age of empowered customers who have vast amounts of knowledge at their fingers and many products/services to choose from, it's becoming increasingly important to be able to offer service support in a timely and convenient manner—again, on the customers' terms and at the moment they need it the most. That means you must put as much energy into servicing your products/ services as you do during the purchase process. Great customer service does not happen by chance. Taking a customer's money and disappearing is the fastest way to lose market share, especially in this day and age where it's easy for consumers to rate the service after the sale and give voice to their opinions on social media channels. Keeping poor customer service a secret is no longer possible in our connected world, which means asking yourself these questions:

- Is your service convenience strategy as strong as your purchase convenience strategy?

- Do your customers need 24/7 live chat capabilities to ensure their questions, issues, and concerns are addressed and answered any time of the day or night?

- Do you need to create an online, up-to-date knowledge base on your website to ensure customers have access to self-service capabilities?

- Can your customers research and resolve issues on their own?

- If they can't resolve problems on their own, is it easy to switch to live chat or to give your support center a call?

- How convenient is it to request and get help on your product/service?

- Do you need a 1-800 number for product/service support?

- What types of support systems need to be in place to ensure timely resolution of customer issues?

- Do you have mechanisms in place to track the level of product/service defects encountered after the sale?

- Do you use the data to form insights on how you can improve the quality and service levels of your products/services?

- Does this information make its way back to your product/service management organization?

Building a Comprehensive OCXS in Eight Steps

Now let's turn our attention to how we can put all the things we've discussed in this chapter together to build a comprehensive OCXS.

Step 1. Create a clear OCX mission and vision across the entire CXLC

The first step in developing your OCXS is to have a clear picture of who your customer is and then work to create a focused OCX vision that acts as your guiding principles and that can be communicated to your customers and your entire organization. That means you must identify the customer segments you intend to serve by analyzing the personas you've identified. Then understand, empathize, and connect them to the interactions and touchpoints across the CXLC to ensure you're taking into consideration all the key elements that bring your vision to life, allowing you to accomplish your mission.

Going back to the team at New Horizons, they realized that they needed to focus on becoming a 21st-century company that builds and executes on a vision and mission that is acutely focused on their customers, one that will and must change and evolve. As a result, in addition to the five previously identified customer personas, they added two more (#6 and #7 below), for a total of seven that are important to them:

1. Luxury sedan owner
2. Sports coupe owner
3. SUV owner
4. Truck owner
5. Van owner
6. Employee
7. Community

This plays directly into the company's very simple vision of "Dedicated to customers and driven by excellence." The company's mission statement is just as simple: "To become the world's most renowned center for customer service in the automotive sector." And so are the company's values, which consist of:

- The customer is number one.
- We make things happen.
- Everyone counts.
- We think ahead.
- We do it together.

Step 2. Identify your CXLC

Once you know your personas, you can start to decompose the stages they pass through as they interact with your organization. Think about what's important to them and what the experience you want to build looks and feels like. Using the eight CXLC stages (Figure 5-1), determine which ones apply to your customers' experience. In the case of New Horizons, the team identified the following five stages:

1. Evaluate
2. Purchase
3. Service
4. Advocate
5. Dispose/repurchase

Step 3. Create your CXJMs using your personas

Using the techniques described above, you can then use your customer segments or personas to identify your CX journeys across both your traditional and your digital channels by thoroughly understanding the customer's decision-making process. In the case of New Horizons, the team mapped the service vehicle customer experience journey, as depicted in Figure 5-5.

Step 4. Create your brand that integrates well across all channels

Now that you understand who is important to you, you can go about the task of creating a brand that appeals to them. But what is a brand? The Business Dictionary defines a brand as a "unique design, sign, symbol, words, or a combination of these, employed in creating an image that identifies a product and differentiates it from its competitors. Over time, this image becomes associated with a level of credibility, quality, and satisfaction in the consumer's mind."[16] So the first and most important task that you must undertake is to decide on and create your brand—that is, the image, reputation, characteristics, or unique traits you want your products/services to be associated with.

Being given the choice to consciously mold and shape your brand is a much better idea than allowing it to haphazardly evolve over time. So you must ask yourself, "What type of image and reputation do I want my product/service to have and leave in the minds of my current and potential customers?"

In the BMW example we discussed earlier, the automotive manufacturer made a conscious choice to focus on two themes, "The Ultimate Driving Machine" and "The BMW Difference." Then the company built and employed images of its cars as part of a lifestyle, which elicits strong emotions through visualizing what it is like to be sitting behind the wheel of a BMW. You must think carefully about your branding because it's something that you'll be known for in the long run. This branding message must be consistently applied across all of your channels to ensure you are delivering a seamless, uninterrupted, and predictable experience, no matter the platform.

Step 5. Build out and/or revise your channels

Once you have your journeys mapped, you can identify how these journeys play out across your various channels, both traditional and digital, and then work to either revise or build them out as needed.

---

16 *Business Dictionary*, s.v. "brand" (*https://oreil.ly/fn7NX*), accessed May 5, 2019.

Step 6. Capture customer feedback and gather insights in real time

It's extremely important to understand and gain an insightful view of your customers to form a complete and accurate picture of their likes and dislikes, as well as their buying habits and preferences and how they behave across all channels.

By collecting and analyzing relevant customer data and then feeding it back into the process, you have the opportunity to continuously evolve and enhance their experience. This data will also help you to understand and hone your customer personas, developing a more and more accurate picture of who your customers are within the CXLC and what type of OCXS most appeals to them. Of course, it's crucial to test out the strategies you've created, as well as validating them through the eyes of your customers, ensuring the experience is seamless, simple, and free of obstacles. Some of the different methods to gather feedback include:

- In-store apps that scan an item's barcode, pulling up customer reviews and offering added incentives to purchase, such as discounts or free gifts
- Follow-up email or coupons printed on the back side of a receipt offering a discount on the customer's next visit or purchase
- Online surveys accessed through a code printed on the receipt and offering a discount on the customer's next purchase
- Customer service representative follow-up calls to gain feedback on the product/service experience

Step 7. Personalize the experience across your channels

It's your mission as a Lean leader to figure out what promotions, discounts, and combination of channels are most popular and well-received by each persona type. Determining which personas are more likely to utilize social media channels, share experiences, post "likes" on your Facebook page, and tweet using your hashtag about the great deals they received either online or in your stores is priceless when it comes to furthering your brand. Figuring out creative ways to encourage them to share can be achieved through personalization. Also, creating memorable experiences in your traditional channels, such as in stores, can be accomplished by adding the human touch to the shopping experience. You must recreate the ease of online purchasing in your physical stores, while adding to it as well, to get your customers coming back time and time again. And unfortunately, if you don't accomplish this through personalization, there could very well be no reason to step foot in your stores. There's a vast array of technology out there that can help you effectively tap into and exploit the benefits of personalization.

Knowing how to combine your channels to optimize the CX through personalization is the next great wave of customer centricity. The easiest way to begin personalizing your channels is to start with a single one that focuses in on a single business outcome, such as driving an increase in sales within that channel. The benefits of taking this approach include the ability to track the results of your personalization strategy through the collection of sales data, because there's a direct cause and effect relationship. In this case, by analyzing the sales data before and after the personalization efforts went into effect, you can see whether or not your sales increased as a result of these efforts. A single channel with a single business outcome makes it much easier to derive insights that can be shared across your organization.

With the first channel under your belt, you can then move on to additional channels and outcomes, such as cross-selling, migration, retention, loyalty, etc. As you increase channels and personalization objectives, you increase the number of insights exponentially. Using them to further understand customer behaviors, like abandonment or bounces and why they are occurring, can point you in the right direction regarding fixing these issues. As you become better and better at personalization initiatives, you can then move to optimize customer experiences by using forecasting and simulation software, as your data and insights grow over time.

Step 8. Constantly strategize, monitor, and scale

As your customers become even more empowered in the next several years, having a well-crafted OCX will continue to grow in importance. That means the amount of time you spend on strategizing, monitoring, and scaling will also continue to grow, because a successful OCXS is not a one-and-done exercise. It's an area that constantly needs your attention, care, and nurturing to reap its many positive benefits. Adopting a regular cadence to revisit your OCXS is a must. Assembling your team and conducting weekly, monthly, and quarterly OCXS reviews is not overkill. After all, this is your customer we're talking about, and being a customer-centric Lean enterprise means there's nothing more important to you than your customer.

However, depending on your budget, it may not be feasible for you to build a presence in every channel imaginable. Monitoring the channels you're in for cost versus benefit helps you avoid squandering your resources on less effective, underperforming channels that do little outreach when acquiring and retaining customers. Therefore, deploying and distributing your resources accordingly requires awareness.

Finally, any OCXS that you build must be scalable. If you're a small startup, you may not have the money to invest in costly software in areas like personalization and analytics. However, that shouldn't stop you from building a strategy such that, as your business grows, so too will your OCXS.

Conclusion

From dealing with the customer relationship to understanding the level of loyalty and buying patterns to interacting with your customer, customer centricity is complicated, to say the least. The many moving parts of customer centricity should now be apparent to you. From understanding how to measure it to building customer experiences that matter through persona identification and CXJM and developing an OCXS, your potential and current customers are more than worthy of your time and attention.

To that end, we'll now turn to the next level of Lean leadership: leading enterprise wide.

CHAPTER 6

Leading Enterprise Wide

Leading enterprise wide means fostering and achieving alignment across all levels of the organization through the development of a centralized decision-making framework that clearly states who you are, what you're after, and how you're going to get there as an organization. It acts as your "Enterprise True North" by rallying the entire organization around your common purpose: the pursuit of perfection in all you do in the quest for value creation and delivery.

Have you defined your strategic mission (why your company exists), vision (the future state you're trying to create), and value proposition (proposed value you're after)? Do the people who follow you understand your vision and how you propose to get there through the execution of your mission?

Without a written, well-thought-out plan, it becomes nearly impossible to mobilize others toward your common goals, known as *strategic objectives*.

In this chapter, we'll spend some time discussing how you can build a centralized strategic decision-making framework that ties your mission, vision, and value proposition to your strategic objectives. You can then use the strategic roadmap and release plan to mobilize the Lean enterprise toward the realization of its value proposition. First, though, we'll discuss the need for aligning all areas of your enterprise, and why that's at the heart of this element of Lean leadership.

Recognizing the Importance of Enterprise Alignment

A lack of alignment and collaboration has caused a lot of friction within 21st-century companies, as they struggle to redefine their operating models around digital products/services. Over the last ten years, as executives have worked to grasp the impact of how technology has changed the nature of business, how things get done, and how products/services are delivered to the market, shadow technology organizations that report directly to business leaders have arisen. This practice of circumventing in-house technology organizations has become more and more common, as business leaders feel the pressure of disruption and the need to directly control the product development process as a result. Many technology leaders continue to struggle to change and become more responsive to this new, more collaborative way of working. Gone are the days when the technology organization could independently build and deliver products/services with little to no active input from the business. To some, that might sound like radically odd behavior, but the relationship between the business and technology has never been so strained. When you think about how much is spent on digital transformation (over $1.3 trillion in 2018),[1] the lack of alignment becomes a major problem. In my opinion, this is the main reason why so many digital transformations fail. An astonishing seven out of eight Forbes 2000 companies that have attempted to transform have failed, per a study recently conducted by the PulsePoint Group.[2]

No matter what seat you occupy within the business, technology, or operations, enterprise alignment must be a priority for you as a Lean leader. The rapid change that demands flexibility and responsiveness on your part is here to stay. To ensure enterprise alignment is happening, all parts of the Lean enterprise must be on the same page and under the watchful eye of its Lean leaders, who are capable of working together to foster and deliver value to both its customers and company alike. It all begins with having a frank discussion concerning your innovation strategy. What expectations do leaders have for each other when it comes to innovation?

Understanding the Importance of Alignment and Engagement

Lean leaders on both sides of the table—technology and the business—understand that collaborating to get alignment on expectations and strategic direction is one of the simplest ways to ensure both sides understand how bringing in new technologies and new ways of working to address disruption is going to be handled. One CIO I worked with in the past was faced with a dilemma. He had a $40 million budget to provide technology services and support to a $1 billion business division of a major US-based company that wanted to develop cutting-edge robotic capabilities for its customers. The problem: internally, his

---

1 Michael Shirer, "IDC Forecasts Worldwide Spending on Digital Transformation Technologies to Reach $1.3 Trillion in 2018" (*https://oreil.ly/Pxwud*), ICD, December 15, 2017.

2 Bruce Rogers, "Why 84% of Companies Fail at Digital Transformation" (*https://oreil.ly/jo5d4*), Forbes.com, January 7, 2016.

organization didn't have the technical savvy to handle the development of both the hardware and software that would ultimately result in an end product delivered to its customer base. Like many internal tech shops over the last ten years, his department had fallen victim to the outsourcing trend of the early-to-mid 2000s, and he just didn't have the people or the ability to attract the type of developers that could deliver such a complex solution.

Instead of throwing up his hands and giving in, he decided to work with the SVP of the business line to proactively build a vision and strategy that would manage expectations about the product/service expertise he could offer them, as well as how his department could help the business leaders execute on it. This CIO realized he could use his knowledge of the business to act as an internal technical consultant and ensure that a practical and cost-effective solution could be developed, on time and on budget, that delivered the competitive edge the business was looking for. After all, the business leaders had a business to run, and they weren't technical in nature. By partnering together, these leaders created a win/win situation for both their customers and the company.

He assembled a small team to work with the business leaders to define their high-level product/service requirements. Then he and his staff consulted with and advised the product managers to identify a technical partner that had the expertise to work with them to develop the product. He found a small startup in Silicon Valley and gave them seed money to develop a prototype. Every month, he conducted a site visit to check on the project and the progress the startup was making through its build/measure/learn loop. He also invited the business leaders to accompany him to get a firsthand look at the progress. Together they were slowly building the next generation of this product line for the organization. By engaging the business leaders, the technology leader was able to maintain transparency and visibility as to where the money was going and what progress was being made, which had been a long-standing concern between the two departments, with the business leaders feeling, more times than not, like they were throwing money down a black technology hole.

Moral of the story: smart Lean leaders must insist on enterprise alignment to ensure the survival of their organizations. They must think outside the box as to how to achieve it, as the pace of change continues to intensify, causing global market disruption and fierce competition. The only response is to counter with alignment, agility, creativity, and innovative ways of getting the work done to meet the demands of today's continuously evolving business climate.

But how do you go about creating alignment inside the Lean enterprise? The best way to start achieving this goal is to think about where you ultimately want to end up.

Starting with the Endgame in Mind

Whenever I engage with a new client, the first question I ask the senior leaders of the organization is, "What are the customer outcomes you expect to achieve by undertaking this effort?" This question is of paramount importance and must be answered in a mindful way to ensure my team and I are achieving the right results for our clients. Having a keen understanding of what you're after when it comes to your customer is the fastest way to achieving real and meaningful business results, because it crystallizes what you're after and acts as a guiding theme for you and your organization.

But what are customer outcomes, and how are they developed? A *customer outcome* is an achievable end state that has measurable results that can be observed and verified from the customer's perspective. From the Lean enterprise's perspective, customer outcomes must be described as top-level strategic objectives with actionable initiatives tied to them that can be traced down through the organization and then back up again, as they are achieved through an ongoing measurement process. Only one senior leader is held accountable for creating the desired end state within a given timeframe through the application of a holistic approach that engages the entire organization to achieve the desired outcome.

Take, for example, the New Horizons situation we've been discussing. The persona analysis rendered the customer outcome of:

- High-quality vehicle service and repair work done accurately and on time, in a professional and respectful way

The team's analysis unfortunately showed that this outcome was failing to happen more times than could be tolerated by the dealership's customer base, thus causing customer satisfaction scores to drop through the floor. The problem wasn't the quality of the product itself, since customers weren't bringing these well-known, high-quality luxury vehicles in for out-of-the-ordinary service and repair work. The root cause of the issue was the dealership's way of handling the vehicle servicing, warranty, and repair work. Jim Collins, the owner of the dealership, charged Nancy, the new service manager, with figuring out why both customer satisfaction and retention rates had dropped. He set two outcomes for Nancy, both to be achieved within the next six-month period, based on the persona findings and manufacturer's reporting:

- Decrease the service request error rate by 65%
- Increase the NPS by 25 points

These outcomes are both specific and customer-focused, and Jim can easily measure whether Nancy achieves them or not within the given timeframe. I know this all might sound pretty basic, but you'd be surprised to find how many senior leadership teams I've worked with only vaguely define the outcomes they're trying to achieve, in a manner that is neither specific nor measurable. Common outcomes, such as increasing productivity and/or revenue and cutting costs, are often mentioned without an understanding of exactly how to make those things happen or even why they're important in the first place. I think if you went out and asked many leaders today to define the outcomes they're seeking, you'd probably see those three in their top ten lists, with little or no direct link back to customer and business outcomes and without understanding the full picture as to how to produce the desired results. Throwing vague or unobtainable outcomes around does little to help or mobilize your workforce in the long run. So let me ask you this: as a Lean leader, have you defined a clear set of outcomes you're driving toward to mobilize and lead those that follow you?

Building a Centralized Strategic Decision-Making Framework

Strategy is the process of forming common goals that unite people to ensure everyone within your organization is working together toward achieving both customer and business outcomes. It offers a systematic way to determine how your organization's resources will be used to accomplish these goals, as well as how success will be measured. Without a well-composed strategic framework, there's no way to determine whether you're creating and delivering value. The famous saying by Helmuth von Moltke, a general in the Persian army in the 1800s, later paraphrased by Correlli Barnett in 1963—"No plan survives contact with the enemy"[3]—was about strategy. I've modified it some and have often said to my clients and teams that "No plan survives contact with the customer!" However, that doesn't mean you just throw planning out the window altogether. On the contrary, it means you must be flexible and able to adjust as you interact with your customers within their environment, because you must meet them where they are and on their terms, not yours. Strategic planning is continuous improvement at its best. It's a continuing process of adjustment and waste removal, and it must be constantly performed to ensure your goals adjust and change to accommodate contact with your customers. Strategy is not a static thing; it must change and evolve to propel the Lean enterprise forward.

---

3 Wikipedia, s.v. "Helmuth von Moltke the Elder" (*https://oreil.ly/1kesY*), last modified October 10, 2019, 08:42.

Strategy empowers everyone in the organization and reduces the time it takes to make decisions. It pushes decision-making capabilities to the people performing the work at the gemba (place of work). With a framework in place, there's no more waiting on top executives to make decisions so that work can proceed. On the contrary, informed decisions are made on the ground, in real time, at the point when they're needed. Laying out and maintaining a well-formulated strategy builds a centralized strategic decision-making (CDSM) framework that can be used within the organization to make decisions in line with a company's vision, mission, and value proposition. Take, for example, Amazon's vision and mission statement, which was created over 18 years ago by its founder, Jeff Bezos:

> Our vision is to be Earth's most customer-centric company; to build a place where people can come to find and discover anything they might want to buy online.[4]

Given that Amazon's product and service offerings are so vast, it has a suite of value propositions, based on those product and service offerings:

Kindle
Easy to read on the go

Prime
Anything you want, quickly delivered

Marketplace
Sell better, sell more

Plus many other Amazon product/service value propositions, such as Amazon Music's "Music and More."[5]

Bezos's mission was to build a place where people could find anything they might want to buy online, and his value propositions were convenience, speed, and choice.[6] He has publicly stated he believes the company's success has been greatly influenced by its unwavering commitment to its vision and mission and its relentless pursuit to fulfill its value propositions. He also believes they represent the guiding lights behind his leadership decisions and have greatly contributed to the company's tremendous success, because everyone at

---

4 Barbara Farfan, "Amazon.com's Mission Statement" (*https://oreil.ly/XD2Gp*), The Balance Small Business, March 20, 2017.

5 Guerric de Ternay, "Amazon Value Proposition in a Nutshell" (*https://oreil.ly/rKvZc*), FourWeekMBA.com, accessed June 8, 2019.

6 Patrick Heer, reply to "What is Amazon's unique value proposition?" (*https://oreil.ly/w7qkN*), Quora, June 14, 2017.

Amazon knows why the company exists, what it wants to become, and the value it attempts to create for its customers. There's no guessing or uncertainty because Bezos made it very clear from the start. Everyone works together toward achieving a common set of strategic goals, and any decision at any level is made with those goals in mind.

The success of companies like Amazon is a testament to the effectiveness of a proactive strategic planning process and the development and implementation of a strategic framework in general. Have you taken the time to develop these tools of empowerment and accountability for your workforce? Or are you stuck in 20th-century thinking that says managers much be omniscient, omnipotent, and omnipresent? Let me tell you, those days are gone. So let's roll up our sleeves and get to work on creating your strategic framework.

Understanding the Strategic Planning Process

A CSDM framework gives an organization the ability to define and then socialize all of its important decision-making elements to ensure everyone in the Lean enterprise understands where it's headed, how it's going to get there, and what value it intends to create for both its customer and the company. Its purpose is to empower everyone in the organization to not only do the right things but do them for the right reasons as well.

Building your framework requires all parts of the organization to participate in the strategic planning process. It's not something that's handed down from the executives (the proverbial "mountaintop") and then precisely executed by the masses. It's a plan that must work in the trenches, where it will be adjusted "on the fly" by an empowered workforce that's in direct contact with your customers. These workers must understand the guardrails within which they can operate to satisfy customers and create a differentiated experience. Informed decision making is what your strategic framework and planning process is after, not precise execution. A well-developed framework grows and changes as everyone in the organization gains more and more knowledge about your customers.

This framework must also embrace nimbleness and agility in the sense that it must be adaptive and designed so that you can quickly respond to both internal and external opportunities and threats. It's not a one-and-done activity or something that's written in stone. It's usually constructed to span at least a 12-month period. Going out any farther than that is a waste of your valuable time and energy because things are changing so rapidly. Also, keep in mind that you must revisit it every quarter to ensure its direction and destination remains relevant to the overall goals and objectives of the organization, as well as updating it for the next quarter's work to ensure you have a 12-month rolling plan at all times.

If a change occurs and a course correction becomes necessary, you must have the courage to make the tough decisions to ensure the company is still creating value through the opportunities it chooses to develop. It doesn't do anyone any good to continue down an outdated or obsolete road just because it was once thought to be the right direction. The world is changing so rapidly that building a strategic framework and then periodically examining and adjusting it must become part of a healthy strategic planning process to remain competitive.

To build a viable framework, you must focus on all the layers of the Lean enterprise, as depicted in Figure 6-1.

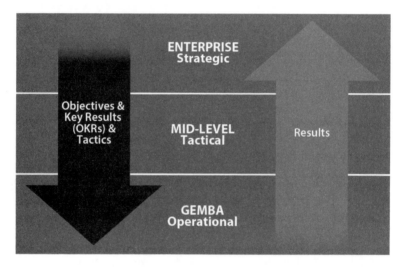

Figure 6-1. *The strategic planning cycle*

Strategic direction must flow from the senior leadership team to tactical middle management and through to the operational level at the gemba. Then, as results are achieved, they must flow back up through the enterprise to report progress against plan and to make sure any course corrections or changes in strategy are also known to senior leaders, to keep them informed as they continue the planning cycle. This cycle repeats itself over and over again, allowing Lean leaders to learn and adjust from the feedback they receive, continuously honing and improving upon the strategic elements throughout the life of the organization. Overall, the CSDM framework consists of the following components:

- Strategic planning canvas
  - — Mission, vision, and value proposition
  - — Strategic objectives
  - — Competitive opportunities
  - — Key results (KRs), tactical plans, and operational tasks
- Investment strategy
- Strategic roadmap
- MVP release plan

Let's look at the practical steps for creating your strategic planning canvas.

Nine Steps to Creating Your Strategic Planning Canvas

The strategic planning canvas is the first of four tools used to create your CSDM framework. Its purpose is to help you clearly define your:

- Vision, mission, and value proposition to ensure you have a clear picture of what you want to become in the future, how you're going to get there, and the value you want to create as a result of this process
- Strategic objectives that are the overarching goals and objectives you want to achieve that fulfill your vision
- Competitive opportunities that give you a leg up on your competition if achieved, and that are tied to your strategic objectives
- Objectives and key results (OKRs) so that you can quantifiably measure progress and make adjustments if necessary
- Tactical plans and operational tasks that must be performed to complete the work on your opportunities

Building your strategic planning canvas is a nine-step process, as depicted in Figure 6-2. It's based on the Lean Plan/Do/Check/Act (PDCA) cycle to ensure it continuously evolves, allowing the Lean enterprise to remain relevant and competitive.

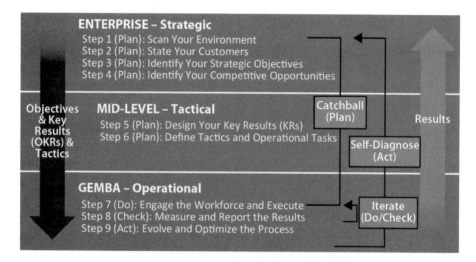

Figure 6-2. *The strategic planning canvas process*

The first four steps are performed by senior leaders at the enterprise level, which encompasses the first part of the Plan phase. Understanding your environment and customers and then identifying your strategic objectives and competitive opportunities both happen at this level. Once complete, this information is passed down to the mid-level tactical managers to complete the Plan phase, by identifying your key results (KRs) and building the tactical plans and operational tasks necessary to achieve them. All of this information is then passed down to the gemba level, where the work is performed for execution, measurement, and reporting. Optimization of the whole process occurs as feedback is pushed back up to the enterprise level, which triggers the whole process to begin again, allowing the organization to constantly evolve in a natural, well-organized way. It's an infinite loop within the Lean enterprise. The strategic planning canvas depicted in Figure 6-3 is the tool used to document this planning process. It acts as a visual aid to assist in documenting your findings as you move through the nine steps.

Lean Enterprise Strategic Planning Canvas

| Step 1: The Environment State our mission, vision, and value proposition 1 | Step 3: Strategic Objectives What are we trying to accomplish? 3 | Step 5: KRs How do we define success? 5 | Step 6: Tactics and Tasks What actions are most effective to accomplish our goals? 6 | Step 8: Measure & Report How do we measure success? 8 | Step 2: Customer /Persona Identification Who are our potential and current customers (personas)? 2 |
| Competitive Landscape? Who do we compete against? What are their/our strengths and weaknesses? Marketplace Challenges and Trends? What gives us a "leg up" in the marketplace? | Step 4: Competitive Opportunities List our identified opportunities to exploit. 4 | | Step 7: Workforce What is the best way to engage our workforce? 7 | Step 9: Evolve & Optimize What ideas will continue to evolve and optimize our plan? 9 | |

Figure 6-3. *Lean enterprise strategic planning canvas*

Step 1 (Plan): Scan your environment

The first and most important step is to thoroughly understand the environment that you exist and operate within. Building the picture of who you are, what you do and provide, who you compete against, and how your environment operates within the context of your mission, vision, and value proposition provides a clear picture of the environmental factors you're facing and must address.

1. Creating/revisiting your mission, vision, and value proposition generates alignment across the entire Lean enterprise, acting as a communication tool to help everyone understand what it's about, where it wants to go, and what value it will deliver to its customers and for the company.

2. Analyzing the competitive landscape by researching and identifying how your competitors are working to satisfy your customers' wants, needs, and/or desires builds an understanding of how you could serve them better through differentiation.

3. Evaluating marketplace challenges and trends helps you to identify distinct advantages your company possesses that give you a competitive "leg up" in your marketplace.

Crafting your vision and mission statements for your organization is not an easy endeavor. What you're after is a one- or two-sentence paragraph that provides a concrete way for stakeholders and employees to easily understand why your company exists and what aspirations and guiding principles you have for your business. For example, New Horizons has a very simple vision of "Dedicated to customers and driven by excellence." Its mission statement is just as simple: "To become the world's most renowned center for customer service in the automotive sector." Simple, directional, aspirational, and inspiring are the qualities you're looking for in well-crafted vision and mission statements.

As for the dealership's value proposition, it's just as simple and consists of "Easy to buy and obtain service." When you look at the value it's trying to create, the issue becomes clear with the problem in the service department. Overall, the dealership's behavior is way off base and inconsistent with all three, which has created a sense of urgency to fix these problems. The dealership is not living up to its vision and mission statements, and it sure isn't creating value for its service department customers.

As far as competition, the dealership doesn't have any, since it's the only one within a 150-mile radius. However, another luxury vehicle brand is building a new dealership in the next town over, but that's at least 25 miles away from New Horizons. Jim and his team don't think this turn of events poses an immediate threat, since there is a significant difference as far as distance goes, not to mention his location is much more convenient, being right in the center of town.

Step 2: State your customers

The strategic planning process is all about satisfying your customers' unmet wants, needs, and/or desires in a better way than your competition to ensure you create and maintain a competitive advantage that keeps you at least one step ahead of them. This is the point at which you bring your customer personas into the process by clearly stating who they are, based on your previous persona identification work. If you haven't identified who your potential and current customers are, now is the time to go back and perform this work. Personas are a crucial element in the process, since everything you do must be grounded in creating and generating value for your customers and stakeholders.

During the CXJM activity performed by the New Horizons TBP team, the following seven personas were identified:

1. Luxury sedan owner
2. Sports coupe owner
3. SUV owner
4. Truck owner
5. Van owner

6. Employee

7. Community

The next step is to apply these personas when developing your strategic objectives.

Step 3: Identify your strategic objectives

Everything that happens in the Lean enterprise should tie back to what you're trying to accomplish—everything else is waste. To build a plan that delivers value, you must start with your ultimate goals in mind. By first identifying the customer, business, and stakeholder outcomes you're trying to achieve, you can work backward to mobilize your organization to produce tangible results for all those involved. Then, by translating those outcomes into strategic objectives that can be broken down into opportunities and executed at both a tactical and operational level, the Lean leader puts a system in place that allows the organization to achieve its goal of creating and delivering value. That's what the Lean enterprise is all about!

But what exactly are strategic objectives? They're the main high-level business objectives that form the basis of the organization's business strategy.[7] When developing objectives, it's important to remember they represent the strategic results an organization is seeking to achieve, based on its value proposition. If a purposed product/service idea doesn't tie back to at least one strategic objective, then inherently it's not a strategic fit and should not be considered for funding. Investing in nonstrategic ideas creates waste, and very little value, if any, drops to the bottom line. The strategic objectives must be deeply rooted in and supported by both the company's vision and and its mission so that everyone understands the journey and can help with charting the course, as well as contributing to their achievement.

Strategic objectives exist at the enterprise level. They represent three to five enterprise-wide "big bets" that a Lean enterprise is trying to accomplish to fulfill its mission and turn its vision into reality. Their purpose is to help organize or group related business initiatives into categories that measure that organizational effectiveness of delivering on your business results. To create them, you must:

1. Evaluate your product/service quality and value creation and delivery, identifying your strengths and areas that need improvement

---

7 Gail S. Perry, "Strategic Themes—How Are They Used and WHY?" (*https://oreil.ly/HxsQk*), Balanced Scorecard Institute, 2011.

2. Conduct brainstorming sessions to identify desired customer and business outcomes from your strengths and development areas

3. Roll the results up into categories to form three to five strategic objectives you will work on over the next year

Remember, your vision, mission, and value proposition frame the discussion around the development of strategic objectives as you determine the top three to five enterprise-wide ones that will be used to make decisions between competing priorities and to determine strategic fit for investment allocation purposes. They act as a yardstick to measure progress toward creating and delivering value. They can also be thought of as guardrails to ensure leaders stay on course and don't veer off into uncharted, non-value-adding side trips.

According to a 2016 Price Waterhouse Cooper CEO innovation survey, innovation leaders that follow an intentional process forecast two to three times higher growth outlooks than those who don't, predicting a growth curve of over 62% (versus the global average of 35%) within the next five years.[8] So unless you put some thought behind what moves the needle, there's no way you'll ever be able to measure whether you're truly succeeding at value creation and delivery.

Returning to New Horizons again, Jim and his leadership team worked to identify the following four strategic objectives for the dealership:

- Increase quarter-over-quarter sales
- Increase our quality of service to our customers
- Increase the use of technology to effectively run our business
- Modernize our facilities

Keep in mind these are overall objectives that apply across the entire dealership and not just the service department, since they are set at the enterprise level.

Step 4 (Plan): Identify competitive opportunities

Competitive opportunities are the things you want to become better at in order to generate increased competitive advantage and accomplish your strategic objectives. A great place to look for these is in the Improvement Ideas section of your customer experience journey (CXJ) maps that you developed, after identifying your personas. Understanding how to appeal to your different segments allows you to differentiate yourself in their eyes, as well as strengthen

---

8 "Whitepaper: Is Keeping Pace the New Standstill?" (*https://oreil.ly/4p6w3*), Pricewaterhou-seCoopers, 2016, 1.

the areas in which the market considers you to be weak. In the case of New Horizons, when the TBP team documented the sports coupe owner persona, they identified the following opportunities (a few of which can be combined to come up with a final list):

1. Develop a service and repair mobile app
   a. Schedule an appointment capability
   b. Provide arranging for a loaner car capability
   c. Send repair progress notifications
   d. Provide viewable bill capability
   e. Push out a feedback survey
   f. Offer coupons/discounts on next visit
2. Provide push notifications when next service is due
3. Provide training to the service staff
4. Upgrade the loaner car program system
5. Do random service customer follow-up calls
6. Perform lapsed service customer follow-up inquiries

After identifying your opportunities, you must tie them back to your strategic objectives to ensure there's a strategic fit and to prioritize them so that you don't waste resources on efforts that don't add customer or company value. For the service journey, the tie back to the dealership's strategic initiatives are prioritized in the following way:

- Increase quarter-over-quarter sales
  — Perform telephone customer inquiries on lapsed service
- Increase the quality of our service to our customers
  — Provide training to the service staff
  — Develop a service and repair mobile app
  — Do random service follow-up customer calls
- Increase the use of technology to run our business
  — Upgrade the rental car system

Now that you've identified your strategic objectives and competitive opportunities, it's time to identify your key results (KRs).

Step 5 (Plan): Design your key results

KRs provide a way of tracking progress made toward accomplishing your objectives and creating additional competitive advantage through completing your opportunities, represented by critical customer, business, and stakeholder outcomes that drive both activities and behavior within the Lean enterprise. Lean leaders use KRs at multiple levels to evaluate their success at reaching their targets. High-level KRs focus on the overall performance of the business through the progress made toward your strategic objectives, while mid- and lower-level KRs focus on progress made on accomplishing your competitive opportunities through acheiving your tactical plans and operational tasks.

KRs also have a considerable ability to drive behavior, so choose them very carefully. It's essential to think through whether the KRs you select and focus on will drive the desired behavior and outcomes that you expect, without any unintended side effects. For example, focusing on productivity to keep the line running but ending up with large stockpiles of inventory is counterproductive. Keep in mind the rule of cause and effect relationship when setting your KRs. You must be vigilant and guard against creating any undesired consequences.

When writing KRs, keep in mind they must be concise, clear, and relevant, as well as measurable, from both a quantifiable and a qualifiable perspective. That is, each KR must meet the SMART criteria:

Specific
   Is it objective?

Measurable
   Are you capable of measuring progress?

Attainable
   Is it realistic?

Relevant
   Is it relevant enough to the organization?

Time-bound
   What is the timeframe for achieving it?

Taking the strategic objectives developed in step 3, Jim and his leadership team developed the following set of KRs, at the tactical level, for the New Horizons service department:

- Increase quarter-over-quarter sales by 5%, for a cumulative total of 20% within the next 12 months

   — Increase service department sales by 2% per quarter by implementing a service follow-up program

- Increase service department sales by 3% per quarter by implementing a lapsed service inquiry program
- Increase the quality of our service to our customers within the next 6 months by:
  - Decreasing the service request error rate by 65%
  - Increasing the net promoter score by 25%
- Increase the use of technology to effectively run the business by:
  - Launching the first release of the service and repair mobile app by the end of Q1 and the second by Q2
  - Performing an upgrade to the loaner car program system by the end of Q4
- Modernize our facilities
  - Upgrading the computer hardware in the service department within the next 90 days

Step 6 (Plan): Define tactics and operational tasks

Tactics are management plans developed to determine how the levels will accomplish the identified opportunities. They can be thought of as tactical plans, such as project plans or to-do lists that identify the discrete steps or operational tasks required to achieve the completion of the opportunity, which is usually time-boxed within a 12-month period. While it's the responsibility of enterprise leaders to lead strategic planning efforts, it's the managers and employees who will ultimately be responsible for executing on it. So involving them in the process is crucial, to ensure they're able to provide input as a means of becoming more invested in achieving the end result. At a departmental level, tactical managers evaluate the opportunities identified by enterprise leaders and then develop tactical plans and operational tasks that will best achieve the desired results.

An important aspect of this process is known as "catchball" (see Figure 6-4), which is an exchange of ideas when developing tactics. The exchange occurs between the organizational levels as they toss ideas back and forth among the leaders within a given level or up and down between levels, returning the "ball" with their input and ideas to the originating level. This process repeats itself as many times as necessary to reach consensus between and within leadership levels. In the Lean enterprise, it's a way of working collaboratively to identify tactical plans or implement/modify operational tasks that achieve the enterprise's strategic objectives through the completion of identified opportunities. It's a participative process that uses iterative planning sessions to field questions, clarify priorities, build consensus, achieve alignment, and ensure that the strategic objectives, competitive opportunities, and KRs are well understood, realistic, and sufficient to achieve the organization's objectives.

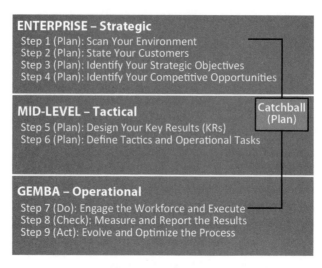

Figure 6-4. *Active levels in catchball*

In a typical catchball series, the identified opportunity is tossed around by enterprise leadership first. Then it's tossed down to the mid-level tactical management layer, where they repeat the process amongst themselves or toss it back up to senior leaders or down to their team leaders and so on, until the tactical plans and operational tasks have been cascaded, vetted, and adjusted (both across and up and down throughout the organization). In the end, everyone has contributed at all levels, and clear tactics and operational tasks have been identified and created with everyone's involvement. This is a much more collaborative and inclusive approach, instead of having enterprise-level leaders throw objectives down from the top layer, expecting the organization to execute things they have little to no input or understanding about.

Finally, keep in mind that tactics and operational tasks are subject to change throughout this process, which means flexibility and adaptability are important characteristics to allow the process to effectively render the desired results. Holding regular progress reviews at least once a month, depending on the volume of changes occurring to the plan, is a helpful activity to manage the change aspects. During each review, results are evaluated, and the tactical plans and operational tasks could need recalibration, followed by another round of catchball.

In Chapter 4, "Leading Others," the kaizen team at New Horizons enabled a rather lengthy game of catchball, as it used the Toyota Business Practices (TBP) method to work through the issues with the Service Request Intake process. TBP is just one of the methods that can be used to put together the tactical plan and operational tasks required to achieve the completion of the opportunity. Others include both traditional and Agile project management methods. The types of plans are identified and listed below for each opportunity.

1. After service customer follow-up call program: traditional (waterfall) project management plan, combined with TBP/process improvement methods

2. Service lapsed customer call program: traditional (waterfall) project management plan, combined with TBP/process improvement methods

3. Service and repair mobile app plan: Agile/Scrum project management plan, combined with TBP/process improvement methods

4. Service staff training plan: traditional (waterfall) project management plan

5. Loaner car program system upgrade: Agile/Scrum project management plan

As you can see, one method will not fit every type of opportunity. At the beginning of step 6, the team should discuss which method is best suited for achieving the desired results. The service department tactical plans developed by New Horizons are depicted in Figure 6-5.

Increase quarter-over-quarter sales (12 months)	Increase the quality of our service to our customers

1. After Service Customer Follow-up Call program
  o Write follow-up call script
  o Pilot follow-up call script
  o Revise script Based on findings
  o Launch follow-up call program
2. Service Lapsed Customer Call program
  o Write follow-up call script
  o Pilot follow-up Call script
  o Revise script based on findings
  o Launch follow-up call program
	(6 months)
	3. Service & Repair Mobile Device Application
	  o Conduct TBP effort on mobile device processes
	  o Build "Customer Register and Log-In" capability
	  o Build "Schedule an Appointment" capability
	  o Build "Arrange for a Loaner Car" capability
	  o Build "Send Repair Progress" notifications
	  o Build "Viewable Bill" capability
	  o Build "Push Feedback Survey" capability

Increase the use of technology to effectively run our business (6 months)
5. Loaner Car Program (LCP) System Upgrade
  o Install new system software
  o Configure new system software
  o Test new system software
  o Perform gap analysis on features & functionality
  o Revise/update LCP processes (if necessary)
  o Conduct LCP processes training (if necessary)
  o Launch new LCP system
	o Build "Offer Coupons/Discounts on Next Visit" capability
	  o Build "Push Notifications for Next Service Due" capability
	  o Pilot/revise Service & Repair mobile device application
	  o Launch Service & Repair mobile device application
	  o Solicit Feedback from customers
	  o Incorporate feedback into the mobile device app
	4. Service Agent Customer Service Training
	  o Determine training vendor
	  o Negotiate and sign contract
	  o Schedule training class
	  o Conduct training class

Figure 6-5. *New Horizons service department tactical plans*

Step 7 (Do): Engage the workforce to execute the strategy

Team leaders and members work out the operational details or tasks needed to implement the tactical plans laid out by the mid-level tactical managers. This is the phase in which objectives and plans are transformed into results. That means tactical managers must stay closely connected to the activity happening at this level. They must regularly practice genchi genbutsu, or "management by walking around," to stay close to the work.

Going back to our New Horizons canvas, the team identified which department will be accountable for the tactical plans and operational tasks for the following opportunities:

#1: Service department and technology

#2: Service department and outside customer service firm

#3: Loaner car program and technology

#4: Service department

#5: Service department

By specifically naming the departments within the organization, the leaders and teams become responsible and accountable for the results they achieve as they work to complete the opportunities that accomplish the strategic objectives determined at the enterprise layer.

Step 8 (Check): Measure and report the results

Measuring results is a must in the Lean enterprise. Establishing measurements and then employing the rigor to measure, analyze, learn, and finally adjust is at the heart of the iterative cycle that exists at the gemba (Figure 6-6). The measurements established and collected at this level feed up to the KRs established in step 5 and which contribute to the success or failure of the strategic objectives.

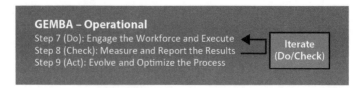

Figure 6-6. *The gemba Do/Check iterative process*

As you analyze the results at the end of each measurement period, course corrections and adjustments are inevitable. The ability to change your mind and alter your course is built into Lean methods through the continuous learning cycle that is inherently present. And remember, you perform strategic planning to empower your workforce so that they can make effective decisions at the gemba without having to go find a mid-level or senior leader to help them solve the problem, because they know where the company is headed and why it picked that direction in the first place. So as you iterate through your tactical plan, expect it to change and grow as more and more data becomes available. Plan your work, and then work your plan!

The measurement and reporting frequency will depend on the KRs being tracked, which can happen on a daily, weekly, monthly, or quarterly basis. These progress checkpoints provide an opportunity for adjustment of your tactics and their associated operational details. KRs aren't static. They always need to evolve and be updated or changed as needed. If you're setting and forgetting your KRs, you risk chasing objectives that are no longer relevant to your business. Make a habit of regularly checking in, not just to see how you're performing against your KRs but to see which KRs need to be changed or scrapped completely.

Going back to New Horizons, the team determined that KR measurements will be compiled by the data analytics group and posted in the TBP team war room on the fifth day of each month, by strategic objective and based on a frequency that adheres to the following schedule:

#1: Sales-quarterly

#2: Biweekly

#3: Monthly

#4: Monthly

Stating how and when results will be measured sets realistic expectations and determines the planning and adjustment cycles necessary to take corrective action, if needed. Posting the results in a public place makes them visible and lends itself to transparency, ensuring everyone understands the progress being made and the adjustments being taken in the pursuit of the Lean enterprise's strategic objectives.

Step 9 (Act): Evolve and optimize the process

You must understand both the progress and the results being made at each level and account for adjustments and changes in direction being made at the lower levels. The Act phase of the PDCA cycle (Figure 6-7) allows the Lean enterprise to become both self-diagnosing and self-correcting, relying on both the downward and upward flow of information to create a closed-loop system that enables the learning, control, and adjustment (or in other words, continuous improvement) of the entire strategic planning process.

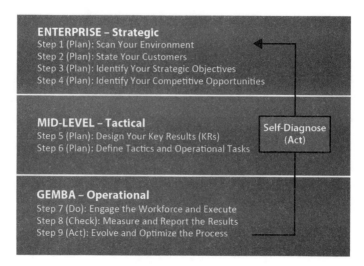

Figure 6-7. *The self-diagnosis loop*

Progress made toward your competitive opportunities and tactical plans, as well as overall direction set by your strategic objectives, must be continuously tracked and formally reviewed on a regular cadence at all levels. Take, for example, the work being done at New Horizons. As the loaner car program team started work on the upgrade of the system, they realized the established processes for the flow of work also needed an overhaul. The new system's features and functionality had changed significantly since the last release, which is now driving the need to update both the processes and the training as well.

This work represents additional effort that must be added to the strategic planning canvas and traced back to the strategic objective that's driving the work being done—that is, opportunity #3, "Upgrade loaner car program system," under the strategic objective of "Increase the use of technology to effectively run our business." Because the hardware is outdated throughout the dealership, not just in the service department, it will need upgrading as well, which ties back to the same objective (#3) and opportunity (#3). Finally, a new tactical plan, #6, "Dealership computer hardware upgrade" (denoted in bold in Figure 6-8), was developed and added to the canvas. As you can see, a change that originates at the team level must be tracked back up through the levels to ensure the strategic fit is maintained.

Increase quarter -over-quarter sales (12 months)	Increase the quality of our service to our customers (6 months)

1. After Service Customer Follow-up Call program
  ○ Write follow-up call script
  ○ Pilot follow-up call script
  ○ Revise script based on findings
  ○ Launch follow-up call program
2. Service Lapsed Customer Call program
  ○ Write follow-up call script
  ○ Pilot follow-up call script
  ○ Revise script based on findings
  ○ Launch follow-up call program
	3. Service & Repair Mobile Device Application
	  ○ Conduct TBP effort on mobile device processes
	  ○ Build Customer Register and Log-In" capability
	  ○ Build "Schedule an Appointment" capability
	  ○ Build "Arrange for a Loaner Car" capability
	  ○ Build "Send Repair Progress" notifications
	  ○ Build "Viewable Bill" capability
	  ○ Build "Push Feedback Survey" capability
	  ○ Build "Offer Coupons/Discounts on Next Visit" capability
	  ○ Build "Push Notifications for Next Service Due" capability
	  ○ Pilot/revise Service & Repair mobile device application
	  ○ Launch Service & Repair mobile device application
	  ○ Solicit feedback from customers
	  ○ Incorporate feedback into the mobile device app

Increase the use of technology to effectively run our business (6 months)
5. Loaner Car Program (LCP) System Upgrade
  ○ Install new system software
  ○ Configure new system software
  ○ Test new system software
  ○ **Perform gap analysis on features & functionality**
  ○ **Revise/update LCP processes (if necessary)**
  ○ **Conduct LCP processes training (if necessary)**
  ○ Launch new LCP system
	4. Service Agent Customer Service Training
	  ○ Determine training vendor
	  ○ Negotiate and sign contract
	  ○ Schedule training class
	  ○ Conduct training class

Modernize our facilities (90 days)
6. Dealership Computer Hardware Upgrade
  ○ **Install new computers**
  ○ **Install new printers**
  ○ **Install new handheld devices**
  ○ **Configure/test hardware & network**	

Figure 6-8. *New Horizons service department tactical plans (revised)*

The New Horizons Strategic Planning Canvas

Figure 6-9 shows the completed New Horizons Service Department strategic planning canvas. Keep in mind that it represents the strategic canvas for a single department within the dealership. Completing it is a major achievement for the organization because it represents "the plan" that is now in place for the next 12 months. Of course, it will need to be periodically refreshed and updated as the tactical plans and operational tasks are executed.

New Horizons Service Department Strategic Planning Canvas

Step 1: The Environment	Step 3: Strategic Objectives	Step 5: KRs	Step 6: Tactics	Step 8: Measure & Report	Step 2: Customer/Persona Identification
Vision: Dedicated to customers and driven by excellence **Mission:** To become the world's most renowned center for customer service in the automotive sector **Value proposition:** Easy to buy and obtain service	• Increase quarter-over-quarter sales • Increase the quality of our service to our customers • Increase the use of Technology to effectively run our business • Modernize our facilities	1. Increase quarter-over-quarter sales by 5 percent, for a cumulative total of 20 percent within the next 12 months • Increase service department sales by 3 percent per quarter by implementing a Service Follow-Up program • Increase service department sales by 3 percent per quarter by implementing a Lapsed Service Inquiry program 2. Increase the quality of our service to our customers within the next 6 months by: • Decreasing the Service Request Error rate by 65 percent • Increasing our Net Promoter Score by 25 percent 3. Increase the use of Technology to effectively run our business by: • Launching the first release of the Service and Repair Mobile App by the end of Q1 2019 and the second by Q2 2019 • Performing an upgrade to the Loaner Car Program system upgrade by the end of Q4 2019 4. Modernize our facilities by upgrading the computer hardware in the service dept. within the next 90 days	Please reference the following tactical plans: 1. After Service customer follow -up call program 2. Service Lapsed customer call program 3. Service & Repair mobile app plan 4. Service staff training plan 5. Loaner Car Program system upgrade plan 6. Dealership computer hardware upgrade	1. KR measurements will be compiled by the Data Analytics group 2. Frequency will be based on the metric collected, based on the following schedule: • #1: Sales-quarterly • #2: Biweekly • #3: Monthly • #4: Monthly 3. Metrics results will be posted in the TBP team war room on the fifth day of each month	1. Luxury sedan owner 2. Sports coupe owner 3. SUV owner 4. Truck owner 5. Van owner
Competitive Landscape? We are the only dealer within a radius of 150 miles in the tristate area that sells and services this make of vehicle **Marketplace Challenges & Trends?** Another luxury vehicle competitor is building a dealership 25 miles from us, in the next town over	**Step 4:Competitive Opportunities** 1. Do random service follow-up customer calls 2. Perform telephone customer inquiries on lapsed service 3. Develop a Service & Repair mobile app 4. Provide training to the service staff 5. Upgrade loaner car program system 6. Upgrade hardware throughout dealership		**Step 7: Workforce** The following staff and teams will be assigned to the following opportunities: 1. Service Dept & Technology 2. Service Dept & Outside Customer Service firm 3. Loaner Car Dept and Technology 4. Service Dept 5. Service Dept 6. Technology	**Step 9: Evolve & Optimize** 1. The Loaner Car program system upgrade will also require all the hardware to be upgraded throughout the dealership 2. The Loaner Car program's processes also need to be revised/modified, as the system undergoes the planned software update 3. Training will need to be developed and conducted to ensure service dept staff is up to date on the new processes	

Figure 6-9. *New Horizons service department strategic planning canvas (large format version (https://oreil.ly/leadingLean-figs))*

Now that the team has completed their canvas, they must turn their attention to developing their investment strategy and building and finalizing the dealership's service department strategic roadmap and release plan.

Creating Your Investment Strategy

Lean leaders must prudently decide, on an ongoing basis, just how much money they need to run, grow, and innovate on their business strategy and then set investment targets based on their strategic objectives and competitive opportunities, developed during the strategic planning process. These targets then drive the investment in intentional (core and enhancements to products/services) and emergent (new or transformational) innovation, based on their strategic objectives, which measures the effectiveness of an organization's investment strategy. Overall, the purpose of developing your investment strategy is to define how you will allocate your scarce resources (time, money, and people) toward developing new product/service ideas, as well as maintaining and enhancing existing ones. It's tied to the Lean enterprise's business strategy and heavily focused on its value proposition through the identification of unmet customer wants, needs, and/or desires, as well as how well the organization delivers customer, company, and stakeholder value.

A well-developed investment strategy is used to:

- Determine how much of an organization's resources are spent on identifying and researching unmet customer wants, needs, desires, target markets, and new product/service ideas

- Make investment and trade-off decisions between core, enhancements, and new product/service priorities at the enterprise level

- Drive the amount of development effort dedicated to bringing new and enhanced products/services to market at the mid and gemba levels

- Determine the size and number of teams and what they work on at the gemba level

However, building the capacity to innovate is not easy, and it's no longer a choice—it's a necessity. Maintaining competitive advantage, once an innovative product/service is released, must also be considered. Success breeds imitation, and lots of it.

Developing a Successful Investment Strategy: Apple Disrupts Sony

The Sony Walkman, released in 1979, was a portable cassette player that ushered in the age of mobility and created the mobile personal devices market. An example of disruption at its best, it allowed people on the go the option to listen either to their favorite radio station or to music recorded on cassette tape while running, walking, commuting, etc. The only option up until that point had been the portable transistor radio, which received only AM/FM radio station signals. As the mobile personal devices market grew, more competitors entered the space. Sony continued to maintain its market leader position by evolving its product line, as the types of storage media changed from cassette tape to compact disc (CD) in the late 1990s, by introducing a CD version with anti-skip technology that allowed the company to maintain its competitive edge.

However, the drawbacks to the device, such as short battery life, heaviness, and size, all contributed to its downfall when Apple introduced the iPod in 2001.[9] The iPod was lightweight, had a rechargeable built-in battery, and was connected to the Macintosh iTunes platform, where users could download music directly into the device's memory in the new MP3 format. Sony, once a disruptor, had become disrupted in a market it had created. Apple had listened to the unmet wants, needs, and/or desires of customers and created something that represented even more value that they were willing to pay for. Sony did release its version of a portable MP3 player to compete with Apple; however, Sony never attained the level of success with this product that it did with the Walkman back in the 1980s.

Apple closely tied its strategic framework to its investment strategy. Even back in 2001, Apple understood the power of connecting its products and services together to create and maintain competitive advantage. The iPod leveraged iTunes, an online music-downloading platform, initially accessible only through a Macintosh computer. By doing so, Apple also disrupted the music industry (which Sony also had a stake in due to its 1987 acquisition of Columbia Broadcasting System [CBS] Records, later renamed Sony Music[10]), killing the vinyl record business in the process. If you aren't innovating, you can bet someone else is and will eventually come along and disrupt you.

---

9 Wikipedia, s.v. "iPod" (*https://oreil.ly/2LL9Q*), last modified October 18, 2019, 21:07.

10 Wikipedia, s.v. "Sony Music" (*https://oreil.ly/qHMeV*), last modified November 11, 2019, 09:20.

A well-thought-out investment strategy helps companies determine how much they want to spend upfront on their current product/service lines, as well as what they're willing to spend on innovating new ones. For example, at Google, 70% of investment funding is allocated to core products/services, 20% to enhancements, and 10% to emerging or new product/service innovation.[11] By clearly stating the target allocations for each category, Google effectively allocates its scarce resources and eliminates competing priorities by setting targets for both intentional (core and enhancements) and emergent (new) innovation. When an organization goes about setting allocation targets, the goal is to minimize risk while achieving the highest possible return on investment (ROI).

Factors to Consider When Setting Your Targets

Three factors exist when setting your targets:

1. Industry
2. Competitive advantage
3. Maturity level

Depending on the industry, investment strategies will vary. Take, for example, the airline industry. Its allocation targets represent a 60/30/10 split,[12] while technology companies represent a 45/40/15 split, and consumer packaged goods represent a 80/18/2 ratio.[13] Each industry is unique due to the nature of its business and operating model. It might cost a little less to develop software compared to the cost of developing airline products/services. Technology companies that are labor versus product (airplanes) intensive must set their investment targets accordingly, because it costs about the same to maintain their core products/services as it does to enhance them.

Competitive advantage is the second factor. Whether a company is considered a leader or a lagger affects its investment strategy. Companies that have allowed their competitive advantage to erode find themselves at a disadvantage and often need to play catch-up to market leaders. For example, to increase its competitive advantage and gain a greater share of its market, a consumer packaged goods company temporarily adjusted its investment strategy from a 75/20/5 target allocation to a 50/25/25 split to develop a new product line that

---

11 John Battelle, "The 70 Percent Solution: Google CEO Eric Schmidt gives us his golden rules for managing innovation" (*https://oreil.ly/1zlvj*), CNN Money, November 28, 2005.

12 Nawal K. Taneja, *Airline Industry: Poised for Disruptive Innovation?* (New York, NY: Routledge, 2017), 7.

13 Bansi Nagji and Geoff Tuff, "Managing Your Innovation Portfolio" (*https://oreil.ly/abvNT*), *Harvard Business Review*, May 2012.

increased its market share and gained back its competitive advantage. The trick here is not to sacrifice one for the other in the long run. Changing your strategy must be grounded in facts and not be done merely for the sake of accommodating someone's pet project. Vetting a new product/service idea takes place at the enterprise level, with senior leaders making the crucial investment allocation decisions.

Maturity, the last factor, is important from the perspective that older, more established organizations have core and adjacent products/services that they must maintain and expand to stay in business. Making big bets on breakout or disruptive new product/service ideas directly competes with maintaining older, more established ones that pay the bills and keep the lights on. However, in contrast, Lean Startup organizations usually invert this model, with 10% going to core, 20% to maintaining, and 70% to new product/service ideas,[14] since there's nothing to maintain and much more to grow when you're first starting out. As organizations mature, the scales tip toward supporting and maintaining core product/service lines, as well as enhancing them, which causes the allocations to shift and be more heavily weighted to the left.

Developing Your Investment Allocation Targets

Setting investment allocation targets correctly may take several budgeting cycles to accomplish. A team comprised of senior and mid-level leaders must work together to establish and then periodically review the organization's targets. The gauge for success is reflected in an organization's price to earnings (P/E) ratio.[15] Comparing industry P/E benchmarks, NPSs, or consumer analytics may help to determine whether the targets need to be adjusted up or down. For example, a drop in NPS may signal too much time and effort being spent on innovation, at the expense of enhancing your core product/service lines.

Also, any changes in the factors mentioned above may be cause for adjusting the allocations as well. A company whose business model was in the Lean Startup phase may move toward becoming more mainstream, resulting in adjustments to the allocations to maintain its market share. Or inversely, an established company that continually loses ground year over year due to market disruption by a competitor may need to adjust its allocations and spend more on new product/service idea generation and development than it has in the past to regain its market share and stay competitive. Therefore, how much is enough in each category fluctuates and will be based on your company's

---

14 Ibid.
15 Ibid.

overall business strategy, competitive position in your industry, and maturity level.

Setting investment targets for New Horizons

Returning to New Horizons, once the objectives were identified, the leadership team revisited their investment strategy to determine what percentage of the available investment capital could be spent on core, enhancements, and new product/service ideas over the next year. Under the dealership's current strategy, its allocation targets had been set at a 70/20/10 split for the last several years. Given the organization's current challenges, Jim and his leadership team believe the targets require adjustment to 65/25/10 to address the pressing issues facing the organization. As you can see in Figure 6-10, the objectives act as levers that can be manipulated by adjusting the spending amounts either up or down, depending on the decisions made during the strategic planning process.

Strategic Objective	Budget		Investment Strategy		
	Percent	Total $$	Core	Enhance-ments	New
			65%	25%	10%
Increase quarter-over-quarter sales	45%	$157.5M	$102.4M	$39.38M	$15.7M
Increase the quality of our service to our customers	15%	$52.5M	$34.0M	$13.12M	$5.3M
Increase the use of technology to effectively run our business	25%	$87.5M	$56.9M	$21.88M	$8.7M
Modernize our facilities	15%	$52.5M	$34.15M	$13.12M	$5.3M
Total	**100%**	**$350M**	**$227.5M**	**$87.5M**	**$35.0M**

Figure 6-10. *New Horizons yearly investment strategy by theme*

Overall, because the dealership sells a physical product that must be bought and enhanced with additional parts at the dealership, it can't bring down the core and enhancement costs much on objective #1 of increasing sales quarter over quarter. The 5% shift from core to enhancements, while holding new spending steady, should be enough to accomplish the upgrades to the dealership's systems and facility. By proactively setting the direction of its innovation and investment spending, Jim and his leaders are intentionally becoming masters of their destiny: defining their mission and vision, setting their strategic direction, and then putting the capital behind these activities to drive value creation and delivery for their customers, stakeholders, and the dealership. Lean leaders must develop the rigor and discipline to proactively plan where their company's money is going to be spent, because innovation, and the value creation that comes from it, doesn't happen by chance. It must be intentional, deliberate, and consistent activity that happens quarter over quarter, year after year.

Developing Your Strategic Roadmap

I once worked with a customer who told me he had just sat through a two-hour meeting in which the leaders of the company hotly debated the spending of another $2 million to finish a project that was a year overdue and $3 million over budget. By the time it was complete at the end of the current year, the opportunity they had been working on had passed them by, and the product that was going to be rolled out at the end of all of this effort was obsolete. However, many of the leaders felt they were obligated to complete it out of a sense of loyalty to the CEO, since it was his pet project. Unfortunately, there are countless initiatives in corporate America that should have been killed, stopped, or cut, but no one had the courage or recognized the need to do so when the strategic direction of the organization changed, or the competitive advantage they were trying to capture ceased to exist. Because of this lack of corporate courage or good stewardship, billions of dollars are wasted every year on initiatives that add very little or nothing to the bottom line. In the situation I just described, the company's leaders will have spent $10 million on something that now creates very little value for the company and its customers. So, to turn the corner and become a value-generating organization, the ability to respond to change must become a part of your corporate DNA.

When developing your strategic roadmap, two constraints must be taken into consideration: your investment strategy and the amount of investment funding available per budget period. Both constraints limit the type and amount of work that can be accomplished in any given budget period. Therefore, an organization's limited investment funding must be appropriately allocated, based on the company's investment strategy and sense of urgency that exists from changing market conditions. The following four key ingredients are necessary to build an initial first-year, rolling wave strategic roadmap:

- Strategic objectives and competitive opportunities
- Tactical plans with delivery timeframes and cost estimates
- Investment strategy and funding allocations

Let's look at how these ingredients come together to assist New Horizons in their efforts to develop their roadmap.

Building the New Horizons Strategic Roadmap

Overall, the strategic direction for the New Horizons service department in the next 12 months focuses on the objectives listed in Figure 6-11, which represents the anticipated investment spending this year across the four strategic objectives and three investment strategy categories. The anticipated spend within the service department is $17.5 million, which, based on total budget estimates (Figure 6-10), makes up about 20% of its anticipated investment spending this year across the three investment strategy categories.

Matching the investment strategy to the yearly strategic objectives, investment allocations, and tactical plans gives New Horizons' Lean leaders a concrete picture of how they will create service department value over the next 12 months. New Horizons' mid-level tactical managers used the cost estimates obtained from the tactical plans to work together to balance these factors and assign funding to the plans, based on the investment allocations and budget targets, to ensure the dealership's investment spending matches its investment strategy. They achieved a balanced budget by remaining within the total yearly budget targets and will be able to add all of the work described in their canvas to their strategic roadmap.

Strategic Objective	Opportunity	Tactical Plan	Timeframe	Cost Estimate & Investment Strategy		
				Cost Estimate	Total	Investment Type
Increase quarter-over-quarter sales	1. Do random service follow-up customer calls	1. After Service customer follow-up call program	Next 12 months	$1.25M	$2.25M	New
	2. Perform telephone customer inquiries on lapsed service	2. Service Lapsed customer call program	Next 12 months	$1.00M		Core
Increase the quality of our service to our customers	3. Develop a Service & Repair mobile app	3. Service & Repair mobile device application	Next 6 months	$6.00M	$7.50M	New
	4. Provide training to the Service staff	4. Service Agent customer service training	Next 6 months	$1.50M		Enhancement
Increase the use of technology to effectively run our business	5. Upgrade loaner car program system	5. Loaner Car Program (LCP) system upgrade	Next 12 months	$5.00M	$5.00M	Enhancement
Modernize our facilities	6. Upgrade hardware throughout dealership	6. Dealership computer hardware upgrade	Next 90 days	$2.50M	$2.50M	Enhancement
		Total Service Department Investment Allocation		**$17.25M**	**$17.25M**	

Figure 6-11. *New Horizons service department investment allocations by theme*

This type of clarity is achieved only through strategic planning at the strategic (enterprise) and tactical (mid-level) levels, allowing New Horizons to lay out a roadmap based on facts and logic instead of hunch and intuition. It's an integral part of ensuring that strategic objectives are well-planned and that they intentionally guide how value is created and delivered. Now the managers are ready to construct the first part of the roadmap, by placing the tactical plans on it, based on their end delivery timeframes. Table 6-1 depicts the New Horizons Service Department Strategic Roadmap at the tactical plan level.

For example, the technology team has three major efforts underway this year: the dealership computer hardware upgrade, the service and repair mobile device app, and the loaner car program system upgrade. Because the first one is due in the next 90 days, it's scheduled to be completed by the end of Q1. The second one is due to be completed within the next 6 months, so this work is placed on the roadmap to be completed by the end of Q2. The last one is set to be delivered in Q4, since its target date was set to be within the next 12 months. Remember, the tactical plans are placed on the roadmap based on their completion date, not their start date. Going forward, the roadmap will be used to communicate out to stakeholders the progress against both the plan and KRs, as well as being used in prioritization efforts to ensure the teams don't get overloaded and require additional assistance (such as contract help) to complete the work.

Table 6-1. New Horizons service department 12-month strategic roadmap

Year 1: Q1	Year 1: Q2
• **Increase quarter-over-quarter sales (12 months)** **$1.25m** 1. After Service customer follow-up call program **$1.00m** 2. Service Lapsed customer call program • Modernize our facilities (90 days) **$2.5m** 6. Dealership computer hardware upgrade	• **Increase the quality of our service to our customers (6 months)** **$6.00m** 3. Service & Repair mobile device application **$1.50m** 4. Service agent customer service training
Year 1: Q3	**Year 1: Q4**
	• **Increase the use of technology to effectively run our business (12 months)** **$5.00m** 5. Loaner Car Program (LCP) System Upgrade
$4.375m/quarter Run Rate **TOTAL: $17.5m**	

The last step in constructing the roadmap is to place the operational tasks on it, to determine the *minimum viable product* (MVP) release plan.

Releasing Value in Increments: MVP Release Planning

All the preceding activities were performed to be able to identify how to chunk the work and release it in stages to create incremental value through the creation of an actionable plan, known as the minimum viable product (MVP) release plan. It's the responsibility of the mid-level tactical managers who work with the teams to clarify the MVP operational tasksets that deliver value within each release. Each task is assigned a priority based on business and customer value and then laid out on a timeline or release plan for execution and delivery. Each time segment in the plan represents a release of bundled tasks, or in other words, the MVP feature set developed to deliver incremental value. The capacity of the teams and the length of the execution window determine how much can be included in each release.

The MVP release plan is prepared by the tactical managers and gemba teams so that it's clear when work needs to occur for each task. It also aids in communicating with other parts of the organization, such as the marketing and operations teams, as to when tasks will be ready to release out to the market. Using this process, a product/service is delivered incrementally, instead of all at once, based on what makes sense to the market and what customers find valuable. Releasing it in chunks also allows the organization to learn about what is valued in the marketplace through customer feedback, along with being able to start to recoup its investment by generating a revenue stream and payback period, sooner rather than later.

Completing the MVP Release Plan

To complete the release plan, the tactical managers work with the gemba teams to determine which operational tasks, located underneath each tactical plan, add the most value. The knowledge gained during the previous phases forms the basis of prioritization in terms of high, medium, and low value compared to each other. The priority of a task also determines the execution windows in terms of near-, medium-, and long-term timeframes. The highest priority, near-term tasks are grouped together at the top of the list, then the medium ones, and finally the lower priority, longer-term ones. In this manner, a prioritized list based on strategic fit, business value, and delivery date is created.

Keep in mind that both the roadmap and the release plan represent a rough estimate of the anticipated work for the next 12 months. As the tactical managers continue to learn more about what's required to deliver each tactical plan through the decomposition and continuous refinement of the tasks underneath, some movement and adjustments may occur. Also, the organization's priorities might shift, or a hot new product/service idea may create a new plan that requires immediate development to seize market opportunity. So changes to both the roadmap and the release plan are inevitable. Remember, nothing is written in stone; responding to change and having the flexibility to quickly shift priorities are why all this planning happens in the first place.

However, the current period investment and budget targets must be maintained. As a Lean leader, you will always be constrained by your investment funding targets because you can't spend what you don't have. If more funding is necessary to seize a market opportunity, then these targets will need to be revisited or some scheduled work from one of the current tactical plans will have to be deprioritized and pushed out. But the timing and feasibility of making a change must be considered. Changing things up in the middle of a release window is not a good idea. If adjustments are necessary, they usually occur at the beginning of a new release cycle. This gives the organization time to complete the scheduled work in progress (WIP) for the current release and then shift its focus and funding before work begins on the next one.

Building the New Horizons Service Department MVP Release Plan

Having developed their strategic objectives, competitive opportunities, and tactical plans, as well as determining their investment strategy, the New Horizons service department budget sits at approximately $17.5 million. With the New Horizons Service Department Strategic Roadmap in hand, the tactical managers meet with their teams to construct their current year, quarterly MVP release plan. Working off the 12-month strategic roadmap, the tactical managers first prioritize the tasks based on business and customer value and then assign a priority based on when they require development effort. They work through all of the tasks on their list in this manner until the top-priority items in the current (Q1 in Table 6-2), near-term (Q2 in Table 6-2), medium-term (Q3 in Table 6-2), and long-term (Q4 in Table 6-2) timeframes are assigned to a release.

Once complete, the gemba teams can begin work on planning the next release, knowing they are working on things that will definitely create and deliver value for New Horizons' customers, stakeholders, and company, which in the end creates the win/win situation that Jim and his team wanted to achieve.

Table 6-2. New Horizons service department 12-Month MVP release plan

Year 1: Q1 MVP Release #1	Year 1: Q2 MVP Release #2
1. After Service Customer Follow-up Call program • Write follow-up call script • Pilot follow-up call script • Revise script based on findings • Launch follow-up call program **2. Service Lapsed Customer Call program** • Write follow-up call script • Pilot follow-up call script • Revise script based on findings • Launch follow-up call program **6. Dealership Computer Hardware Upgrade** • Install new computers • Install new printers • Install new handheld devices • Configure/test hardware & network **3. Service & Repair Mobile Device Application** • Conduct TBP effort on mobile device processes • Build customer register and log-in capability • Build "Schedule an Appointment" capability • Build "Arrange for a Loaner Car" capability • Pilot/revise Service & Repair mobile device application • Launch Service & Repair mobile device application	**3. Service & Repair Mobile Device Application— (Cont'd)** • Build "Send Repair Progress" notifications • Build "Viewable Bill" capability • Build "Push Feedback Survey" capability • Build "Offer Coupons/Discounts on Next Visit" capability • Build "Push Notifications for Next Service Due" capability • Pilot/Revise Service & Repair mobile device application • Launch Service & Repair mobile device application • Solicit feedback from customers • Incorporate feedback into the mobile device app **4. Service Agent Customer Service Training** • Determine training vendor • Negotiate and sign contract • Schedule training class • Conduct training class
Year 1: Q3 MVP Release #3	**Year 1: Q4 MVP Release #4**
5. Loaner Car Program (LCP) System Upgrade • Install new system software • Configure new system software • Test new system software	**5. Loaner Car Program (LCP) System Upgrade— (Cont'd)** • Perform gap analysis on features & functionality • Revise/update LCP processes (if necessary) • Conduct LCP processes training (if necessary) • Launch new LCP system

Conclusion

Leading enterprise wide means spending time to develop your CSDM framework so that you can empower everyone within your Lean enterprise to work toward achieving its strategic objectives. By systematically identifying your competitive opportunities that are completed through the development of tactical plans and operational tasks, you build an organization that allows everyone to participate in the process of setting the course and then fulfilling its vision. All of the activities that a Lean enterprise undertakes must be tied back to its strategic objectives; otherwise, there's no reason to undertake them. In this way, waste is removed, and only value-adding activities are undertaken to fulfill its mission and bring its vision into reality.

When companies don't spend the time to develop their frameworks, it causes organizational drift: the organization drifts aimlessly without direction, hoping the activities it undertakes somehow result in value delivery. Product/service releases become a haphazard cluster of unrelated activities that may or may not deliver value. Hope is not a strategy, and when leaders at all levels within the Lean enterprise forgo making the tough decisions that are necessary to develop a concerted plan, they are not doing themselves or their staff any favors. More often than not, their inability to make the tough calls doesn't mean those decisions aren't made. In this situation, the responsibility falls to tactical managers, operational team leaders, or even the gemba teams themselves to make these decisions and the company continues to exist. If what an organization truly seeks is to create and deliver value, then leadership at all levels must be held accountable. After all, you would never board a ship or get on a plane if you knew that the captain at the helm or the pilots in the cockpit had no intention of doing their job that day—or worse yet, that they weren't fully committed to having a safe and success cruise or flight...right? Those that follow leaders count on them to lead. Period!

So if you think about it, when a company's leadership doesn't develop its "Enterprise True North" and chart its course beforehand, they are in a sense saying, "Sorry crew...you're going to have to figure this one out on your own. We're sitting it out. Best of luck!" It sounds laughable, but when you're out in the middle of the ocean or 35,000 feet in the air, it's cause for panic. As a Lean leader, you must hold yourself and other leaders accountable to give the crew a plan to operate inside of and be able to make sound tactical and operational decisions. That way, if we come upon a storm or hit some rough turbulence requiring the crew to slightly alter course or turn on the seat belt sign, the decisions they make in these situations will be grounded in fact and are well-informed ones.

Don't underestimate the power of developing your CSDM framework because, in the end, it also feeds decentralized decision making through empowerment and transparency, leading to the ultimate goal of creating and delivering both customer and company value.

One of the best ways to create this kind of value is to innovate, which is the focus of the next chapter: leading innovation.

CHAPTER 7

Leading Innovation

Innovating is the heartbeat of the Lean enterprise. And it must beat with vitality and zeal to ensure that disrupting your competition and marketplace is in the forefront of everyone's mind within your organization. That means developing and executing on a strong innovation program to understand how to look for and anticipate change, then embrace and learn to exploit the inevitable opportunities that it brings to you and to the Lean enterprise.

This chapter discusses what innovation and being truly disruptive means to you as a Lean leader. We will cover the qualities of innovation, common sources of disruption, and ways you can harness these things to your strategic advantage through the use of design thinking, voice-of-customer programs, and the Lean product canvas.

Fighting Off Extinction Through Innovation

Innovation is an elusive thing. A recent study by Altimeter (a prominent research organization) found that low digital literacy is restraining the scope and extent of innovation,[1] even though customers have embraced the internet for more than 20 years now. This survey showed that only 40% of companies operated with an executive-mandated steering committee[2] responsible for introducing innovation and accomplishing organizational transformation, even though the Internet of Things (IoT) is beginning to permeate every corner of

---

1 Brian Solis and Aubrey Littleton, Aubery. "The 2017 State of Digital Transformation" (*https://oreil.ly/tG_02*), The Altimeter Group, October 2017, 4.

2 Ibid., 5.

our world. Customers more and more demand the rapid development and release of new products/services that satisfy their constant cravings for innovative new features and functionality, in a way we've never seen before. That's a sad commentary on the state of industry today, and developing the ability of the Lean enterprise to evolve with the times is your responsibility as a Lean leader.

Many companies are still too intensely focused on cutting costs as a means to survive instead of identifying their product's or service's vision and value proposition and then developing a concrete mission to realize that vision and create customer, stakeholder, and company value. Despite the success of companies like Facebook and Amazon, which lost millions of dollars in their early years, first and foremost Mark Zuckerberg and Jeff Bezos focused on filling the unmet wants, needs, and/or desires of this new customer base. "Build products and services that customers find useful and valuable, and the profits will follow" is the mantra of this new generation of leaders. Focusing on value delivery and redirecting a company's workforce to deliver that value in innovative new ways represent the emergence of a new approach to doing business, where innovation and speed to market is the name of the game, with disruption being the sought-after end result.

Innovation Isn't New!

All this talk about innovation might seem like a recent conversation, but it's far from that. The importance of innovation was codified in 1985 by Peter F. Drucker in his seminal book *Innovation and Entrepreneurship*, in which he wrote:

> Innovation is the specific tool of entrepreneurship, the means by which they exploit change as an opportunity for a different business or a different service. It is capable of being presented as a discipline, capable of being learned, capable of being practiced. Entrepreneurs need to search purposefully for the sources of innovation, the changes and their symptoms that indicate opportunities for successful innovation. And they need to know and to apply the principles of successful innovation.[3]

Almost four decades ago, Drucker identified the heart of innovation: exploiting change and viewing it as opportunity rather than as our greatest nemesis. Today, being digitally literate is often seen as a linchpin of innovation, but it's only one piece of the puzzle. Competing in today's marketplace means having a well-rounded strategy that supports your competitive position.

---

3 Peter F. Drucker, *Innovation and Entrepreneurship: Practices and Principles* (New York: Harper and Row, 1985), 19.

It's not just about being a business-to-business (B2B) or business-to-customer (B2C) company; it's about being omnichannel and approaching your business from a strategic, tactical, and operational perspective. The problem is that we've bought into the hype around "digital literacy." Some leaders have latched onto that term like it's some sort of magic bullet or life preserver. You can almost hear them: "If we could only master *digital literacy*, everything would be so wonderful in our organization and our troubles would be over!"

To compete on a global scale, Lean leaders must be bold and innovative, exploiting and expanding into multiple sales, distribution, and customer experience channels. They can do that only by recognizing how to leverage and combine traditional and digital ways of marketing, selling, supporting, and operating a 21st-century company.

Defining the Qualities of Innovation

What does innovation really look like, and what qualities does it possess? That's a tough question. With the subject getting so much attention over the last several years, you'd think it would be easier to answer. When experts define innovation, they usually discuss the qualities or characteristics of those who seek to innovate, or they suggest methods to use when innovating. However, those types of discussions don't really get at the heart of what it takes to succeed in the innovation game. I believe succeeding at the innovation game involves seven things.

Human thinking

Innovation must leverage human thinking; it must put the customer at the center of all your efforts by making them the focus of why you want to innovate in the first place. You must build a picture of your ideal customer so that you can really design and develop products/services that appeal to them. You must not think of them as the human embodiment of dollar signs—your customers will see right through any attempt to merely push a half-baked product/service onto them.

That is no easy task, though, because people are unique creatures. However, they do share collective traits that can be identified and leveraged, by customer type and within a specific context, when designing and developing products/services. You can employ participatory design techniques to bring the human aspect into the design process.

But let's not confuse human-centered design with *design thinking* (discussed later in this chapter). Human-centered design is a philosophy that puts people at the center of the design process. Design thinking is a method of accomplishing this task. In the end, it's all about identifying the behaviors, motivations, and needs that drive people to make "pull-based" buying decisions, from a human perspective.

Context

Solving the right problem in the right context is crucial to being a successful innovator. You must pay attention to the context or framing of the problem in the customer's environment in order to hit the mark with an innovative new product/service. To accurately identify context, you must solve for the root problem, not for its symptoms. Remember, there are many ways to solve a problem, so let your creativity and imagination run wild. Work on your hypotheses to discover the best solution.

By expending the energy to truly understand the real problem in the first place, you give yourself a much better chance of succeeding in designing and building the right product/service in order to solve the right problem within the right context.

Collaboration

The Lean enterprise's innovative spirit thrives when people work together in a collaborative way. Making your team holistic by including representation from every department—including those that will design, develop, market, sell, service, and support the product/service once it is released to the market—produces a team with lots of different perspectives.

Diversity breeds creativity. Getting a bunch of people with different views or perspectives in a room to solve a problem harnesses the power of the collective consciousness. All the beliefs, experiences, behaviors, thoughts, and motivations of your potential customer are represented right there in the room with you, through the diversity inherent within your team.

Iterative and incremental processes

Innovation by its very nature embraces experimentation. Until you actually develop something, such as a working prototype that you can put into the hands of your customers, realizing what does or doesn't work is impossible. This is really the only way to figure out whether you hit the mark or need to go back to the drawing board and try again.

Giving innovators free rein to innovate through experimentation is the greatest gift you can give them. So if you have these folks in your organization, give them the time and space to iteratively and incrementally innovate. Or if you're one of them yourself, figure out who will support you in your quest to "build a better mousetrap." Then partner with them to start building it! That's how innovation happens.

Failure tolerance

Failure is an inherent part of the learning process and should be viewed as finding out one more way that something won't work as you continue to experiment with finding the real solution. Failure is a chance to learn and grow and come up with other, more viable ways to solve the problem. Armed with the new knowledge you've just obtained, you can then try again and again, if need be. Innovation is an iterative, closed-loop process that offers incremental learning as you go. Take advantage of it and cherish the learnings that come from it.

Moxie

Many years ago, my mother introduced the term "moxie" to me. She would use it to describe people whom she admired for their grit, tenacity, determination, spunk, and unwavering conviction to succeed at whatever they set their sights on. If you don't possess moxie, you're probably best staying on the sidelines and not jumping into the innovation game. Innovating comes with a series of ups and downs that will test your patience, resolve, willpower, perseverance, and convictions.

On the other hand, if you light up at the thought of a good challenge and your mind is keenly focused on long-term success, then by all means suit up, my friend, and put yourself in the game. Just remember that innovating must be a part of your DNA.

Disruption

Innovation by its very nature is disruptive. It challenges the status quo by not accepting the notion that this is just the way things are and there is no changing it. Being disruptive involves a constant learning cycle that springs forth from our nature as curious beings who observe, think, reason, and learn by questioning things—and then figure out how to make them better. A disruptive mind is a powerful thing to leverage and cultivate. Innovation is the process of discovering new ways of doing things and making things better than before. But it all begins with one disruptive mind that spends many mental cycles thinking about how to make things better for us all.

Thinking with a Disruptive Mind

Lean leaders lead change. If you've gotten in the habit of looking for opportunities to be disruptive, you're always preparing both yourself and the Lean enterprise to seize and exploit them. You're constantly scanning the horizon for the next great disruptive opportunity. Watching trends in your industry and environment, talking with your peers to get their perspectives, keeping an eye on the global economy and where it's headed—these are all ways to keep your finger on the pulse of potential sources of disruption. Being disruptive is a proactive stance when it comes to anticipating change because change is what's at the core of disruption. As a Lean leader you must learn to spot trends and react to them before they get forced on you and your organization.

There's no way to slow down or stop change. The best strategy is to stay out in front of it because then you'll be ahead of your competitors, negative trends, downturns, and environmental conditions. Thinking with a disruptive mind is an art that you must hone as a Lean leader to stay relevant in your market and ahead of your competition. The sooner you realize this fact, the sooner you'll see that change is a good thing.

Examining the Sources of Disruption

This section explores six areas where you can look to disrupt or, on the flip side, be disrupted yourself. Focusing on these areas and asking yourself lots of questions are important first steps to properly anticipating and preparing for change.

Markets/industry

Your field of play is the first place in which disruption can happen. Understanding what's happening in your own backyard is paramount to staying ahead of the disruption curve, not just on a local level but all the way up to the world stage. Rising and falling trends and patterns impact how you operate in the near to distant future. Understanding that both your markets and your industry possess these multidimensional aspects allows you to clearly see and define proactive measures to remain competitive and lead within your industry.

- What is happening in your market? Regionally? Globally?
- What is your competition up to in your market/industry?
  — Have they introduced a new product/service?
  — What impact is it having on your market share?
  — What are you going to do about it?
- Is there a trend or pattern developing on the horizon?
  — Has it developed to the point that it is now impacting your market?
  — How are you going to respond to it?
- What state is your market in?
  — Is it emerging? Accelerating? Peaking? Declining?
  — What things must you start/stop/maintain in order to address the changes?

- Are you viewed as a leader or a lagger?
  - Do you set trends or follow them?
  - If you're lagging, what are your plans to catch up?
  - If you're a leader, how do you intend to stay ahead of your competition?

Technology

Every company is a technology company nowadays. Understanding and exploiting emerging technologies is a necessity that's here to stay. So staying ahead of the technology and seizing the opportunities it brings in order to disrupt both the way you do business and your competition is a no-brainer at this point.

- What is happening in your industry regarding technology?
  - New innovations?
  - Things on the horizon?
- Who is embracing these new trends?
  - How will you compete against them?
- How do you plan on exploiting technology to gain competitive advantage?
  - Is there a technology that has the potential to completely disrupt your market? Your product/service lines?
  - Are there countermeasures you can put in place to offset this impact?
- Is the next new, hot "IT" thing a fad, or will it have some staying power?
  - Will your competitors seek to exploit or avoid it?
  - Is there a window of technology opportunity open to you that may close soon?
  - What is the likelihood of your competition exploiting it to gain market share?

Economy

Technology has caused the world to shrink, and what happens in one part of the world, from an economic perspective, might well affect other economies halfway around the globe. There's a domino effect in play here, and you can no longer ignore far-off events. By paying attention to the economy at all levels, you'll be better able to cope with the disruptions caused by local and global economic shifts.

- In what direction is the economy headed? Boom, bust, or status quo?
  - How should you prepare for an eventual downturn/upturn?
- What are the stock markets doing in the US? In Europe? In Asia? Around the world?
  - Bullish? Bearish?
  - How will this affect your customers and their ability to purchase your products/services?
- Has there been a natural disaster that will affect the supply of a precious commodity or product ingredient?
  - How will it affect your supply chain? Are there other options available to you?

Political climate

Understanding what's going on from a political standpoint expands your disruptive field of vision into areas that can sometimes remain hidden and in the shadows, only to create situations that pop up at the last minute, when you least expect them and when it is too late for you to react.

- What is happening in politics at the local, regional, state, and federal levels?
- Are there new laws and/or regulations that you'll have to comply with?
  - Are there ways to exploit them to your benefit?
  - What type of effort/cost will you need to expend to be/remain compliant?
- What is happening on the world stage?
  - Is there political unrest? New parties or leaders coming into power in far-off places that may affect you?
  - Are there new world views taking shape?

Workforce

You have to take your workforce into consideration to ensure your continued survival. Properly skilled and trained employees coupled with solid talent acquisition and performance management strategies are necessary to accomplishing your vision, mission, and value proposition.

- What do the members of your current workforce value?
  - Are they intrinsically or extrinsically motivated?

- Is that trend going to continue? Is there change on the horizon?
- What about the generational aspects of your workforce?
  - Is the composition of your workforce changing due to attrition? Retirement?
  - Are you thinking about succession planning?
  - Are you prepared to train the next generation of leaders? Or employees?
- How do they want to be led?
  - Command and control? Autonomously? Somewhere in between?
  - How are you going to train your current leaders to adjust to any trends or changes on the horizon?
- Is diversity supported and encouraged?
  - Does your workforce reflect both your current and potential customer composition?
  - Is there gender parity, and is equal pay for equal work happening?
- Do your talent acquisition and performance management strategies encourage people to stay or leave?
  - What is your retention rate? Attrition rate?
- What is the word on the street about you as an employer?
  - Good? Bad? Indifferent?
  - Do you have a plan to fix any perception problems, real or perceived?

Lean enterprise

Finally, you must examine and evaluate what's going on inside your organization. You need to position your company for continued success and be proactive about adjusting course in the foreseeable future to maintain your competitive advantage.

- Are there budding innovators right under your nose?
  - What are their thoughts on your future and the overall outlook of the company?
  - Do they possess disruptive ideas that you can support?
  - If you funded their ideas, what would be the cost and outcomes?
  - Would it result in a new product/service that could be brought to market?
  - Would it expand your market presence or open up new ones?

- Is your operating or organizational model stale? Are they ripe for transformation to keep up with the times?
  - Do they slow down your ability to quickly make decisions in response to change?
  - Are you stuck in dead-end silos that do not foster collaboration and innovation?
  - Are there fiefdoms or counterproductive behaviors that need to be broken?
  - Do the different departments support or hinder each other's progress?
    - What about the progress of the company as a whole? Is it being impacted by these behaviors?

These questions are intended to get you thinking about all the ways change can affect you, but they are by no means an exhaustive list. By now I hope you realize that you must acknowledge and proactively manage change. Any of the factors just covered could be the source of the next major wave of disruption in your market, industry, economy, environment, or the world. Are you going to exploit it or cringe and wither in defeat? The choice is totally up to you. And remember, choosing not to act is also a choice. Will your competition make that same choice?

Moreover, do you still think you can control the effects of change? Because trying to control these effects is an illusion. Thinking you can control them will end up pushing you toward corporate extinction. Make the choice now to proactively respond to the changes these factors may bring and see them for what they are: opportunities on the horizon!

Finding Disruption in the Voice of Your Customer

To design innovative products/services that are disruptive in nature, you must understand who you're designing them for, why customers would buy them in the first place, and how they will be used. Consider the following questions:

- When was the last time you had a conversation with someone who actually bought your product/service?
- Do you truly understand why that person made a purchasing decision?
- Are your customers being treated like real human beings or just numbers on a page?
- What is it like trying to find something on any of your channels?
- How easy do you make it to actually buy something from you? Return it? Get it serviced in a timely and professional manner?

- Do you think your efforts to date have yielded a connection with your customers? Would they agree with you?

Attracting, acquiring, and retaining your customers is about connection. People buy goods and services from people and companies who create and elicit feelings of positive connection. Our globally connected world has led to the rise of the empowered customer. Today, choices abound for the savvy shopper. Determining what is and isn't important to customers can make or break your product/service right from the start. What better way to form a connection than reaching out and asking them? According to research conducted by the Aberdeen Group (an international customer experience research firm),[4] leaders who have an engaged customer experience and a best-in-class Voice of the Customer (VoC) program register almost 10 times greater year-over-year increases in annual company revenue compared to all others. They also:

- Enjoy 55% greater customer retention rates

- Have an average 23% decrease in year-over-year customer service costs

- Post 292% greater employee engagement rates

A VoC program is about describing the needs of your customers, from their perspective, by capturing what they're saying about your business, product, or service. It's about taking the time to listen to your past, present, and future customers so that you can connect and engage with them across all of the touchpoints that make up your customer experience (CX). That's how you figure out which types of products/services they want to buy and consume from you. Confirming your customers' wants, needs, desires, perceptions, preferences, and expectations is key to developing a holistic customer-centric strategy so that you're sure you're developing the right products/services, at the right time, to fill the right need. A *need* is nothing more than a description, in the customer's own words, of the benefit to be fulfilled by your potential product/service.[5]

But a need is not a solution, because customers usually describe needs in the form of characteristics, preferences, or expectations of a potential product/service. So in the early stages of your VoC, it's best not to focus on solutioning the needs they express. Doing so may cause you to miss disruptive ideas or creative ways to actually solve their problems.

---

4 Omer Minkara, "The Business Value of Building a Best-in-Class VOC Program," The Aberdeen Group, April 2015.

5 Abbie Griffin and John Hauser, "The Voice of the Customer," *Marketing Science* 12, no. 1 (Winter 1993): 4.

The idea is to improve on your products/services, as well as all stages of the customer experience. Overall, a VoC program helps you to:

- Evaluate new concepts, innovative ideas, and disruptive, market-leading solutions
- Customize your products/services, add-ons, and features to meet the needs and wants of your current and potential customers
- Increase customer retention and acquisition rates
- Serve your customers with products/services they actually want, need, and desire to purchase and consume
- Identify potential brand crises through early warning signs, based on market movements or shifts in competitor strategies

Implementing an ongoing VoC program requires continuous effort. It's deeply rooted in Lean continuous improvement principles. If you aspire to be a customer-centric organization, one that brings disruptive products/services to market, this feedback loop must become an invaluable part of the innovation process, along with building and increasing customer loyalty. It also acts to keep churn rates down and net promoter scores up.

Collecting and analyzing information and feedback from many different sources, such as marketing, operations, customer analytics, and competitor research, can be quite a daunting task, especially if this is the first time you've done a VoC analysis. But when you're done, it provides a wealth of data and information, including the following:

- Who your customers are
- What wants, needs, and/or desires they are most interested in having met
- What various journeys, touchpoints, and connections exist within the customer experience
- How to prioritize where your efforts will have the most impact

Seven Steps to Conducting a VoC Analysis

This section goes over seven distinct steps you can use to accomplish this task.

Step 1. Conduct VoC interviews

The first and possibly most important step is conducting the VoC interviews. For the sake of maintaining focus, you must develop a standard questionnaire so that there's consistency across the interview findings. It's best to limit yourself to 10–15 open-ended questions that spur conversation during a one-hour session. The questions should be considered a starting point, but many times during interviews the answers you receive may take you off in a completely different direction, which is okay, since there are no right or wrong answers. Remember, you're there to gather information, not conduct an inquisition. I like to make sure I get through all the questions so that I can do an apples-to-apples comparison when analyzing the data. I usually end up with no more than 12 questions.

As for the questions themselves, open-ended questions are preferred. For example, ask interviewees to picture themselves using your product/service or channel, shopping in your store, or using your website or a mobile device to shop online. As they respond, ask probing questions that drill down on their needs to obtain more detailed descriptions. That's where their needs will become the most specific. Just asking them what they want won't render the results you're looking for, because most people don't know how to answer that question. Building real and hypothetical experiences they can relate to during the conversation will help you gather the relevant data.

Next, you must identify who you're going to interview. Research suggests that a sample size of approximately 10 to 30 customers (current and potential) tends to be the most beneficial, with the sweet spot being 20 to identify over 90% of the needs.[6] Going above 30 doesn't render additional benefits during this phase of needs collection, so don't waste your time and don't fall into analysis paralysis. Collecting 90% is good enough. Remember, there's a cost associated with this work; it's not free—consider whether or not spending more to get closer to 100% is worth it. Only you will be able to know when you've done enough interviews to render good results, because this process is quite qualitative. These are only guideposts for you to follow.

The interview should be performed by teams of at least two people—one to ask questions and one to observe and take notes. Recording the interviews can also be helpful. Having them transcribed allows you to conduct further analysis afterward. Transcribing also means you can go back and check whether your notes accurately reflect what was said during the interview. Always make sure the interviewees are aware of the fact they are being recorded; it's a good practice to let them know about recording during the selection process, to give them an early chance to opt out.

You can also conduct focus group and mini-group (two to three customers) interviews. Interviewing larger groups of customers will often render even more results as you take advantage of the synergies between the participants,

---

6 Ibid., 9.

resulting in the collection of even more creative ideas. The duration of each interview should be two hours, again with two people leading the interview.

Step 2. Analyze the customer interview transcripts to develop a detailed list of customer needs

Research has shown that if you conduct between 10 to 30 interviews, you'll need a team of approximately four or five analysts to identify 90% of the needs and disruptive ideas expressed by the customers.[7] Keep in mind that the team composition should be varied as well, pulling from the different groups that will use the data, such as customer experience (CX), user experience (UX), product/service development, marketing, sales, service, and others, which will give you a richer variety of perspectives and greater understanding of a larger set of customer needs. Each analyst should go through every transcript and identify the ideas they hear to obtain the detailed list.

Step 3. Sort the list by customer type or segment and importance

Once you have your detailed list, sort it by customer segment, rendering a complete "voice" for each segment. Then go through each segment and rank the importance of the needs for each customer type, keeping in mind that importance is denoted by the desirability of fulfilling that need for that segment.

Step 4. Prioritize and categorize each need

First, sort the expressed needs into the following three customer needs categories:

Basic needs
What the customer assumes the solution will do

Articulated needs
What a customer tells you they want the solution to do

Exciting needs
Needs that, when fulfilled, represent true innovation, both surprising and delighting your customers,[8] as well as disrupting your market and competition

Then prioritize the needs based on what the customer said about each. This can be tricky, but don't worry. The next step is to validate your prioritized list of needs with your interviewees before you move forward with taking action.

---

7 Ibid., 12.

8 Ibid., 4.

Step 5. Validate your findings

Before you go any further, go back to the interviewees and ask them to comment on your prioritized list. Set up a follow-up interview in the same manner as before, but now the focus will be on discussing and validating your list. Show the list to each interviewee and have them review your prioritization efforts, paying close attention to where and why differences might arise. Ask open-ended questions to understand the thoughts, feelings, emotions, beliefs, and perceptions behind each. After this second round of interviews is complete, reconcile your findings to derive the final prioritized list of customer needs and disruptive ideas.

Step 6. Organize the needs into a hierarchy

Structure the needs into a hierarchy, consisting of the following three types:

Primary needs
> These are strategic in nature, the top 5 to 10 used to set the strategic direction of the product/service.

Secondary needs
> Each primary need is then decomposed into 3 to 10 tactical needs, defining what you must do to satisfy the primary need or strategic direction.

Tertiary needs
> These needs are operational in nature and provide the detail you'll need to develop solutions that satisfy the secondary needs.

After completing this step, you will have your marching orders and can move on to determining how to go about fulfilling each of them.

Step 7. Determine how you're going to fulfill each need

The VoC data can be used in many ways to fill customer needs. You can define a new channel to broaden and enhance your customer experience or develop a new marketing campaign to let your customers know that you offer a solution. You can use your data as input to develop design attributes for a disruptive new product/service. To answer an unmet need and bring an innovative new idea into the marketplace, it's up to you to determine how best to use the data you've obtained.

There are numerous other ways of collecting customer feedback besides committing to the time and expense of performing a VoC analysis. Here are several:

Online/offline customer surveys and reviews
> Putting together surveys and collecting data either online or offline is much easier than expending all the time, effort, and expense of live interviews

(the costliest VoC method). But remember that surveys are often only filled out by disgruntled customers who have not had a good experience, so there's a good chance that the results will be slanted or biased toward the lower end.

Live chat

Speaking to customers while they view your website can be a very effective way of collecting customer data. According to a study done by Forrester,[9] 44% of shoppers stated they think the best feature of an ecommerce website is the ability to chat with someone to get help or have their questions answered right there on the spot. By analyzing the chat sessions, you can figure out what questions they're asking, what products they ask about most, and whether they're looking for something you don't offer, as a way of determining additional unmet customer needs during a visit to your site. You could also follow up with an email survey to ask them more specific questions and get additional, more targeted feedback for further analysis.

Social media

Platforms like Twitter, Facebook, and LinkedIn are great sources for direct customer feedback. You can choose to quickly listen in the background or actively participate in the conversation. It's up to you to determine how best to leverage these media to collect additional customer needs and product/service feedback.

Websites

What do your customers do when they visit your website? By analyzing their behavior, you can harvest a wealth of information about their likes and dislikes. You can check out how they came to your site, how long they stayed, what they lingered on, whether they bought anything, and when they left. You can easily leverage tools like Google Analytics to collect and analyze this data.

Online customer reviews

These types of reviews can be a source of unbiased and unsolicited customer feedback. Sites like Angie's List, Yelp, TrustRadius, ConsumerReports.com, and the Better Business Bureau can all give you this type of information. Just be prepared for both positive and negative comments that may or may not be justified. If a pattern develops and the same issues, problems, and concerns keep coming up, then you have some work to do on either your product/service quality. But again, human nature comes into

---

9 Diane Clarkson, with Carrie Johnson, Elizabeth Stark, and Brendan McGowan, "Making Proactive Chat Work: Maximizing Sales and Service Requires Ongoing Refinement" (*https://oreil.ly/eLoHb*), Forrester, June 4, 2010.

play with sites like Angie's List and Yelp, where a poor review may have sprung from the customer having a bad day or could even have been planted by your competition. Sites like Amazon and Yelp are trying to crack down on fake reviews by verifying a purchase through the use of artificial intelligence algorithms, which is a good approach and something you might want to look into as you move forward.

Recorded call data
Your call center represents a treasure trove of customer information and feedback. By analyzing what customers call about, how they speak about your product/service, and what sort of objections or concerns they raise, you get to the bottom of brand and product/service quality perceptions.

Emails
Sending out either customized or templated emails is an easy way of getting feedback from your customers. Just be prepared for a relatively low response rate, similar to that of sending out surveys, since it's easy for current and potential customers to ignore these types of inquiries.

Collecting this information is just the first step. You must then take action to improve your products, services, and customer experiences. Feed the data back into your customer experience strategy, ideation funnel, and product development practices to ensure you're proactively responding to your current and potential customers. Your overall goal in expending all this effort is twofold. First, you want to improve customer acquisition, retention, and satisfaction rates, and build stronger, more lasting relationships with your current customers while attracting new ones. Second, you want to identify innovative new products/services you can design and develop to disrupt both your market and your competition to grow and maintain/retain your competitive advantage.

The next section examines how to leverage this data to improve on customer satisfaction and how to go about building innovative new products/services that will accomplish these goals.

Achieving Success Through Innovation

New product/service innovation is a product of modern culture. There's a great thirst for one new and innovative product/service after another as technology continues to evolve at an astonishing rate. Innovation has become the norm and is now a customer expectation for companies competing in our global economy. However, a study conducted by the Product Development and Management Association (PDMA) found that failure rates varied among industries, ranging from 35% for healthcare to 49% for consumer goods,[10] although some sources quote a much higher rate—up to 95%.[11] Castellion and Markham's study is considered to be the most reliable to date, while many other, more recent studies are not supported by empirical evidence. Overall, let's say half of all products/services fail after they're brought to market. That means you have a 50/50 chance at success, which makes it appear as if success is merely a flip of the coin.

Failures are a fact of life for companies large and small, and savvy Lean leaders understand that failure is a cost of doing business. Failures are a sign of a company's continuous evolutionary journey, and over time they fade into history and are forgotten. But there's a cost associated with failed products/services, estimated to be over $37.5 billion a year.[12] Some failures are more epic than others, ending with the onset of corporate extinction, either very quickly or very slowly and painfully over time. One long-forgotten failure, to the tune of almost $50 million, was Apple's first personal computer, called the LISA.[13]

Unearthing Apple's Epic Failure

The LISA PC was the brainchild of Steve Jobs, the late cofounder and former CEO of Apple, and was named after his daughter, Lisa. (Jobs insisted at the time that LISA stood for "Local Integrated Software Architecture."[14]) LISA was the first PC to boast a graphical user interface (GUI), giving users the ability to point and click on icons using something called a "mouse," which was attached to the back of the machine, rather than typing in text commands on a command line using a keyboard. It also came equipped with an external storage device that users could save files to, known as a floppy disk drive. (All of this was revolutionary at the time—we're talking circa 1983[15]—but is taken for granted by most computer users today.)

So if it was so revolutionary, why did LISA fail? Design, reliability, cost, and target market demographics all played a major part in its demise. Its clunky design and a screen that was too small to make it practical for everyday

---

10 George Castellion and Stephen K. Markham, "Myths About New Product Failure Rates" (https://oreil.ly/Kc_lV), *Journal of Product Innovation & Management* 30 (October 25, 2012).

11 Marc Emmer, "95 Percent of New Products Fail" (https://oreil.ly/xPfk_), *Inc.*, July 6, 2018.

12 David Keith Daniels, "Failed Product Launches Are a $37.5 Billion Problem" (https://oreil.ly/PU7w-), BrainKraft, February 22, 2018.

13 Martin Stezano, "They Can't All Be iPhones: The Story of Apple's Forgotten Flop" (https://oreil.ly/9tRfZ), HISTORY, June 29, 2017.

14 Charles McCollum, "Logan Has Interesting Link to Apple Computer History" (https://oreil.ly/nFXDi), *Herald Journal* (Logan, UT), October 16, 2011.

15 Stezano, "They Can't All Be iPhones."

business use were major drawbacks when compared to the IBM 80 series towers it was competing against. IBM's design entailed a computer box, or tower, that could either be laid down or be stood upright on a desk or floor, with a 12-inch monochrome monitor that was separate from the computer itself. LISA's hardware was also underpowered, unreliable, and prone to overheating. Moreover, the nearly $10,000 price tag was too expensive for the business market the computer was targeted at. For that price, there just weren't enough benefits or value created compared to cost. In the end, Apple dumped and quietly buried almost 3,000 LISAs in a Utah landfill in 1989, as a tax write-off of unsold inventory[16]—literally a "buried" secret that Apple carries with it today. So you see, even those we consider giants of innovation experience failure, sometimes on an epic scale.

The silver lining to this story was that when Jobs moved off of the LISA project and onto the Macintosh PC project, he brought all of those innovations with him, which contributed to the epic success of this machine when it was released to the market in 1984[17] as the "first" GUI computer. The Macintosh was a game changer for Apple, raising its stature in the PC market and enabling it to compete head-to-head with the IBM machines of the time.

Learning from LISA

Innovation must be driven by understanding the real problem to be solved. The practicality of the LISA PC just wasn't there for the market it was designed for. Knowing what we now know of Jobs's early innovations, we could speculate that the customer wasn't thought of at all in the four years it took to design, build, and release LISA to the market.

This example highlights the fact that you must understand how your customers will use your product/service, as well as the inherent value that must be obvious to them, which is the driving factor for making a buying decision. It also means you must apply some rigor in asking yourself a series of tough questions, centered around the why, who, what, where, when, and how of product/service ideation. Without taking the time to identify these key variables, your chances of product/service success are decreased.

Having to deal with these unknown or unidentified things *after* product/service launch is not in your best interest. If your product/service is not selling, it's your responsibility to figure out why and make the tough decision to continue moving forward, making the needed changes, making it more attractive—or to kill it all together. Maybe the marketing campaign was poor, and your

---

16 McCollum, "Logan Has Interesting Link."
17 Stezano, "They Can't All Be iPhones."

customers weren't able to find your product/service. Maybe the design was flawed, and your customers didn't reap the benefits as expected. Maybe the pricing was well beyond your target demographic's budget. You must set your product/service analytics upfront during the Design phase, then collect and measure them after the product/service is released out to the market to determine:

- What results where you expecting?
- How close did the product/service come to your expectations?
- What actual value did your customers experience by both buying and using it?
- What adjustments need to be made to make it more attractive to your customer base?

After doing your homework, you'll be ready to focus on redesigning and building products/services that create value and ultimately lead to success. Let's spend a few minutes defining what that "homework" looks like in the form of the Lean product canvas.

Designing and Building Innovative and Disruptive Products and Services

The designing and building of innovative new products/services that achieve market disruption requires combining two major Lean techniques that foster and encourage the iterative and incremental design, develop, and release process. These techniques are design thinking and Lean Startup.

Defining the Design Thinking + Lean Startup Cycle

Design thinking is a bottom-up, customer-centric problem-solving approach that uses human-centered design techniques to identify and design possible solutions that ultimately result in products/services that meet or exceed customer expectations. It's not about technical feasibility—on the contrary, it's acutely focused on customer usability, desirability, and putting people first (Figure 7-1).

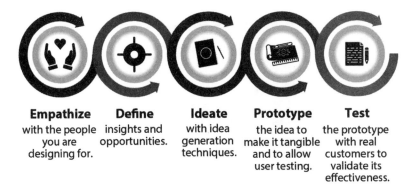

Empathize
with the people you are designing for.

Define
insights and opportunities.

Ideate
with idea generation techniques.

Prototype
the idea to make it tangible and to allow user testing.

Test
the prototype with real customers to validate its effectiveness.

Figure 7-1. The design thinking process

Design thinking starts with putting yourself in your customers' shoes by empathizing with them. From their perspective, you design a set of pressing issues and opportunities and then generate a set of relevant solutions. Only then are you ready to build a working prototype that can be validated for effectiveness by testing it out on your early adopter customers.

On the other hand, Lean Startup, illustrated in Figure 7-2, focuses on building and testing the solution in increments, using an iterative Build/Measure/Learn loop to first build a working prototype and then release it out to a small group of customers (*early adopters*) who measure its effectiveness in solving the problem when it's used by actual people. Finally, the results are analyzed to learn what did and didn't work through the feedback provided, incorporating that data back into the process to make the product/service even more attractive or higher in quality, or to achieve greater customer satisfaction the next time around. The two methods are complementary and can be used together to design, build, and release disruptive and innovative new products/services in an iterative and incremental way.

Figure 7-2. *Build/Measure/Learn loop*

Designing and developing in this manner reduces risk. By releasing small pieces of a product/service, known as *minimum viable product* (MVP) feature sets, to early adopters, you can test your assumptions to figure out what is and isn't appealing to your customer base, without spending a lot of time, money, and effort on things they may not be interested in. The data collected through this type of experimentation is then analyzed and fed back into the process during the next iteration, to move the product/service in the right direction. In employing this method, you make evidence-based decisions by analyzing real customer feedback rather than using subjective guessing or waiting too long to test demand or feasibility in the marketplace. It also starts the payback period (the time it takes you to break even on your investment) much earlier, decreasing the cost of delay and increasing your revenue stream by cutting down on the time to market.

The intersection of the two Lean techniques is shown in Figure 7-3, which depicts the first three phases of design thinking (Empathize, Define, and Ideate) and illustrates how the two methods intersect during the Prototype/Build phases. Keep in mind that moving from design thinking to Lean Startup is a sort of go/no go decision. Both the problem and the solution are validated from a strategic perspective by ensuring the idea matches a strategic objective and represents a valid competitive opportunity. By spending the time to thoroughly vet the idea, you ascertain the feasibility of moving to the next step: devising your tactical plans and defining operational tasks required to build your first MVP.

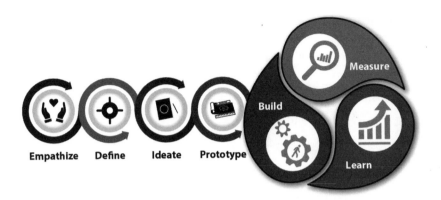

Figure 7-3. *Design thinking + Lean Startup cycle*

Leveraging the Lean Product Canvas

I've found a great tool that really helps to organize my thoughts when design-ing and developing new products/services using the design thinking + Lean Startup cycle. I call it the *Lean product canvas* (LPC). It's built on Alexander Osterwalder's Ph.D. dissertation at the University De Lausanne,[18] which was fully fleshed out in Osterwalder's 2010 book *Business Model Generation*.[19] According to Osterwalder, "A business model describes the rationale of how an organization creates, delivers, and captures value."[20] Ash Maurya later adopted the idea and applied it to Lean product development in his book *Run-ning Lean* (O'Reilly).[21] I've made further modifications to it. Figure 7-4 out-lines my conception of the LPC.

---

18 Alexander Osterwalder, "The Business Model Ontology: A Proposition in a Design Science Approach" (PhD diss., University de Lausanne, 2004).

19 Alexander Osterwalder and Yves Pigneur, *Business Model Generation* (Hoboken: John Wiley and Sons, 2010).

20 Osterwalder, "Business Model Ontology," 14.

21 Ash Maurya, *Running Lean: Iterate from Plan A to a Plan That Works* (Sebastopol, CA: O'Reilly, 2012), loc. 697, Kindle.

Lean Product Canvas

WHY: The Problem Statement Describe the problem to be solved.	WHAT: Value Identification Identify the value for each persona	WHERE: Target Markets & Channels Marketing & Sales strategy for each channel	WHEN: Product Roadmap Product timing, compliance, security, etc.	WHO: Customer/ Consumer (Persona) Identification Target customers and consumers
1	**3**		**5**	**2**
Current Competition? Who has a similar product?	Pricing Identify the potential pricing structure			Targeted Research Methods? VoC? Focus Groups? Observation, etc?
	Revenue Identify potential revenue stream	**4**	HOW: Product Development Solution architecture & production methods	
Existing Solutions? Strengths and weaknesses of each	Cost Structure Fixed and/or variable costs	Key Metrics How do I measure success?	**6**	Early Adopters List the characteristics of your ideal customers

Figure 7-4. *The Lean product canvas*

LPC consists of six parts that address the why, who, what, where, when, and how aspects of product/service design through a series of questions that you answer as you fill out the canvas.

#1. Why: The problem statement

The "Why" part of the canvas addresses the following questions:

- What problem am I trying to solve?
  - — Is there a need for it to be solved?
  - — Am I being realistic about the need to solve it? Is it really necessary?
- What competition exists in this market?
  - — Who has similar products/services?
- What are the strengths and weaknesses of the products/services already in this market?
  - — Why are they doing well?
  - — What are they not doing that could warrant another offering?
  - — What can I learn from what's already being done?

#2. Who: Customer/consumer (persona) identification

The "Who" part of the canvas addresses the following questions:

- Who is interested in the solution? Who is my customer?
  - What customer personas or segments are most likely to buy, and why?
  - What is the process I should use to ensure I've identified the correct personas?
  - Do I understand the customer experiences (CXs) as they interact with the product/service?
- What type of research do I need to conduct?
  - Voice of the Customer (VoC)? Focus groups? Observation?
  - Have I formed a user group, advisory board, or other method of gathering real-time feedback?
- Is there an early adopter market?
  - How will I gather and analyze customer feedback?
  - What is the process to synthesize it back into the development process?
- Is there a difference in who would *buy* (customer) versus *consume* (consumer) it?
  - Does this distinction warrant differentiation when designing, developing, and releasing it?
  - Where do they share commonalities that I can leverage across the two?

#3. What: Value identification

The "What" part of the canvas addresses the following questions:

- What is the value proposition for each persona or segment?
  - What motivators exist to drive them to purchase this product/service?
  - How can I differentiate my product/service in their eyes?
- What price point would be attractive versus the perceived value?
  - Versus the competition?
  - What entrance price point for the product/service makes sense?
  - What is my long-term pricing strategy?
- What value (company revenue) goals am I looking to achieve over the first six months, year, and two to three years?
  - What value expectations and forecasts make sense and are realistic?

— How many units will I need to sell to achieve my value targets?

— How many sales calls will it take to close business to achieve these targets?

- What are the costs associated with bringing this product/service to market?

  — What are the indirect and direct costs? Labor? Materials? Legal implications? Trademarks? Security? Compliance?

#4. Where: Target markets and channels

The "Where" part of the canvas addresses the following questions:

- What is my marketing and sales strategy for each segment?

  — Will I market to existing customers? New customers?

  — What retention rate am I seeking to achieve during the first six months, year, and two to three years?

  — Will customers make multiple purchases?

  — Will this new product/service be attractive to my existing customer base?

- What type of marketing and sales campaigns are needed for each persona?

  — Are they the same, or is some differentiation required?

  — How can I most effectively reach my target market? Inbound versus outbound marketing? Direct? Referral? Organic? Social? Email?

  — What distribution channels exist? B2B, B2C, or other? Digital? Brick and mortar?

  — Can I integrate my marketing and sales campaigns? Point of purchase displays? Online click-throughs?

  — What type of messaging appeals to each persona or segment?

  — How will I communicate to them? What is the frequency?

  — Will I need a sales force to sell the product/service? What skills and expertise will they need?

  — Can my existing sales force sell it? What type of training will they need?

  — Is partnering with a distributor a feasible option? If so, how will I identify the right distributor?

- What metrics and/or analytics can I use to gauge success or failure?

  — What key performance indicators (KPIs) and metrics are valid?

  — Potential to actual customer sales (lead) conversions?

— Click-through rate (CTR)?

— Page views versus bounce rates? Versus sales?

— Search engine referrals?

— Direct customer feedback? (What a novel idea!)

— Email sent versus opened?

#5. When: Product/service roadmap

The "When" part of the canvas addresses the following questions:

- What crucial features would differentiate my product/service from its competition?
  - What is my MVP?
  - What amount of functionality can be released out to the market to gather feedback and begin to generate value?
- Does the product/service have a shelf life?
  - Is there a sense of urgency to bring this to market? When does the first MVP release need to launch?
  - How late can we enter the market and still experience a successful product/service launch?
- Are there any local, state, or federal compliance issues?
  - What is the lead time to get my product/service approved?
  - Will it require legal review?
- Are there any data security requirements?
  - Does the product/service deal with confidential customer data?
  - How can we best go about protecting customers from data breaches?
- What type of release cadence do I need to set?
  - What is the feasible life of the product/service? One year? Two or three years?
  - When does the product/service need to be released to seize market share?

#6. How: Product/service development

The "How" part of the canvas addresses the following questions:

- What key assumptions am I making that must be validated?
  - Are they realistic? What is the process that will be used to evaluate and challenge them?
- What will it realistically take to bring this product/service to market?
  - Who else needs to be involved?
  - Do we have the right skill sets?
- Is the architecture feasible given the current state of technology?
  - What is the best development method?
    - Do I need to partner with a manufacturer? If so, how do I identify potential manufacturers?
  - What type of supply chain function do I need to build?
  - Am I going to need third-party vendors to supply parts? Or will I build them myself?
  - What quality standards do I need to achieve to attract my target demographic?

As you work through your LPC, keep in mind this exercise is geared toward getting you started in thinking through all the details necessary to thoroughly understand whether or not you actually have a feasible product/service. Think of it as being your initial business case as to why you personally would want to throw all of your time and energy for the next umpteen years behind designing, developing, releasing, and maintaining this product/service. Also, if you're going to seek funding, either as an entrepreneur or an intrapreneur, whoever you ask is going to want answers to these questions. "Trust me, it will make money" isn't going to cut it. I've been there and done that! Not being prepared and not having done your homework aren't going to get you the results you're looking for. When you're asking someone to commit to a six-figure number or more, you can bet they will expect you to know these answers. Spending time up front to answer these questions will build a strong case for why someone should put their faith in you and fund your idea.

Speaking from personal experience—having sat in front of bankers and venture capitalists myself and having been turned down multiple times when I made the funding ask—the more solid your new product/service idea is, the more likely your request will be granted. And believe me, getting turned down is the most humbling experience you could ever imagine. I cannot stress to you enough that building your canvas is one of the most important steps in the product/service development process.

The New Horizons Service and Repair Mobile Device App Canvas

In Chapter 4, "Leading Others," the New Horizons kaizen team identified a set of countermeasures (shown in Figure 7-5) that could be implemented to solve the issues they were experiencing in the service department.

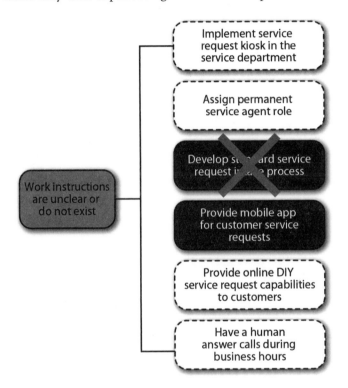

Figure 7-5. *Step 5: Develop countermeasures*

One countermeasure that was suggested during step 5 was to provide a mobile application for customer service request capabilities to customers so they can use their mobile devices to initiate a service request without having to make a call into the dealership. The team is now ready to move ahead on this countermeasure as the next step in their continuous improvement journey. They've gone ahead and developed an initial canvas for this potential service in the form of a mobile device application. Figure 7-6 is the end result of the team's work.

This is the first of several iterations you'll make on your LPC. It is a living and evolving document, not a one-and-done exercise. The LPC evolves and changes as you work through:

- Persevering and bringing the product/service to market
- Pivoting and altering the original concept to suit the market need
- Parachuting or dumping it all together

Service & Repair Mobile Device App Canvas

Date: 6/10/2019

Iteration #1

WHY: The Problem Statement	WHAT: Value Identification	WHERE: Target Markets & Channels	WHEN: Product Roadmap	WHO: Customer / Consumer (Persona) Identification
1. Current scheduling processes are inconsistent 2. Redundancy exists when customers have to repeat themselves if the request is not properly opened & entered into the system 3. Service agents are not following up with customers on status and cost 4. Additional service items are not being approved by customers 5. Write-offs are growing due to lack of obtaining approval **Current Competition?** None **Existing Solutions?** N/A	1. Time saver 2. Greater degree of accuracy 3. Convenience 4. Cost saver **Pricing** There is no cost to the user, so pricing does not apply. **Revenue Stream** Average estimated service request ticket = $500 **Cost Structure** 1. Software development costs 2. Platform costs (Hosting, servers, etc.) 3. Data security/privacy 4. Marketing and PR 5. Legal	1. Auto manufacturer's website 2. Dealership website 3. Point-of-service brochure/flyer 4. Word of mouth 5. Referrals 6. Social media 7. Billboards **Key Metrics** 1. Service requests created/updated per day 2. Total weekly/monthly online service revenue 3. # of new accounts created 4. # of existing users reusing per month 5. # of 4+ star ratings 6. Conversion and retention rates	1. First Minimum Viable Product (MVP) release within 3 months 2. Second MVP in 6 months=take credit cards 3. Third MVP in 9 months=status updates, inquiries, and billing disputes online **HOW: Product Development** 1. Software development company 2. Interfaces with existing systems (service request system, service records, credit card processing, inventory system) 3. Hosting service 4. Marketing & PR firm to develop campaign	1. Luxury sedan owner 2. Sport coupe owner 3. SUV owner 4. Truck owner 5. Van owner 6. Employee 7. Community **Targeted Research Methods?** 1. Focus groups to test out product feasibility 2. Conduct VoC with cross-section of personas **Early Adopters** 1. Interested in saving time 2. Being able to schedule a request at any time, 24/7 3. Concerned about getting the best value or lowest cost

Figure 7-6. *The New Horizons service & repair mobile device app canvas*

If the iteration process proves the product/service idea is viable, once you've developed the first iteration of your canvas, you're ready to validate the information you entered, using a set of Lean techniques that allow you to hone your ideas as you work through the product/service development process.

Developing Iteratively and Incrementally

Developing iteratively and incrementally means you build a little, test a little, measure, and repeat as necessary. This method is keenly focused on taking as few steps as possible to design, build, and release customer-centric and value-creating products/services out to the market. Removing waste (muda) from the process and ensuring the continuous flow of work through managing work in process (WIP) are both key objectives. To employ this process, you must have a relatively good understanding of what you're going to build first, second, third, and so on, by defining your MVPs. Because the team is building a product (the mobile app itself) and providing services through it, they must ensure that they address both as they move forward. This is a very important distinction because the mobile device is a channel to deliver a set of services to schedule and track service appointments and the work performed as a result. It's not just about designing and developing a digital application for the sake of completing and releasing it; the backend processes within the dealership must also be designed and developed to make the app function properly.

This may sound like common sense, but you would be amazed at how many times my developers have programmed a piece of functionality with very little thought given to ensuring that the service processes behind it actually worked. At one point in my career, I almost lost a major account because one of my developers went around the planning process and arbitrarily decided to code something into the program that was requested through his personal relationship with the product owner. When we went to demo it for the client, the backend service processes had not been thought out and developed, which caused the entire program to crash, leaving me with a very irate customer. Ouch!

Returning to New Horizons, we left the team at the point where they had created the first version of their service and repair mobile device app MVP release plan (Figure 7-7). This is no more than the tactical plan to develop out the opportunity identified during CXJM and further detailed during the strategic planning process. Upon further refinement of the plan by the operational team leaders and gemba teams, they decided to break up the MVP releases into four discrete Plan/Do/Check/Act (PDCA) cycles over two quarters to ensure the collection, analysis, and incorporation of early adopter (EA) customer feedback to learn and adjust as they move through the product/service development process.

As you can see, each quarterly release window now has two MVPs associated with it. The first three MVPs will be launched to a dark site and will be available only to EA customers, whereas the last one will be released to both the EAs and the dealership's current customer base.

Year 1: Q1 MVP Release #1	Year 1: Q2 MVP Release #2
MVP #1 • Conduct TBP effort on mobile device processes • Build customer register and log-in capability • Build Schedule an Appointment capability • Launch MVP #1 to dark site • Solicit feedback from Early Adopter (EA) customers • Analyze results from MVP #1 **MVP #2** • Incorporate learnings from MVP #1 • Build Arrange for a Loaner Car capability • Pilot/revise Service & Repair mobile device application • Launch MVP #2 to dark site • Solicit feedback from EA customers • Analyze results from MVP #2	**MVP #3** • Incorporate learnings from MVP #2 • Build Send Repair Progress notifications • Build Viewable Bill capability • Build Push Feedback Survey capability • Build Offer Coupons/Discounts on Next Visit capability • Launch MVP #3 to dark site • Solicit feedback from EA customers • Analyze results from MVP #3 **MVP #4** • Incorporate learnings from MVP #3 • Build Push Notifications for Next Service Due capability • Launch MVP #4 to production • Solicit feedback from EA customers • Analyze results from MVP #4 • Incorporate learnings from MVP #4 • Release and move into production

Figure 7-7. *New Horizons service & repair mobile device app MVP release plan*

Overall, developing products/services in an iterative and incremental fashion allows you to build a little, test a little, learn a little, refine, and release as many times as it takes to arrive at a fully functioning product/service. The alternative would be to wait six months before releasing anything—which may well backfire on you when you figure out there's no market for what you've just built and all that time, effort, and money was wasted. As you can see, MVP #1 is very basic. It lets the team see whether or not their customers would even want to use a mobile device app to schedule appointments, requiring a minimal amount of effort to test out the product/service idea.

In this manner, a go/no go-pivot decision is made at the end of each release after the results are analyzed. At any point, anyone involved in the process can suggest any one of those three alternatives. There's a built-in kill switch within the process that doesn't exist within more traditional methods of product/service development. It can stop leaders from throwing valuable enterprise resources down a black hole that has the potential of not producing the desired or expected results for the Lean enterprise.

Fostering Innovation Through Continuous Learning

Learning and innovation go hand in hand. You identify a problem or challenge, conduct trial and error experiments, measure results, analyze the feedback, experience learning, and then rinse and repeat to incorporate what you have learned back into the process so you can experiment yet again until the best possible solution is found. That's what Lean methods like Toyota Business Practices (TBP), design thinking, and Lean Startup are all about. They're based on the scientific method of the Plan/Do/Check/Act cycle that starts with questioning a problem, issue, or situation and then moving into identifying possible solutions and experimenting with them to figure out what is viable through measurement and reflection. If you cannot validate that it yields results, the whole process starts over again until a viable solution is found. There's nothing mysterious about how you innovate—it's a process that can be learned and taught to others. That's what Toyota's on-the-job development (OJD) is all about. All you need is a curious and disruptive mind to get the ball rolling. So make continuous learning part of your work by integrating it into what you do on a daily basis because that's the key to becoming truly innovative. Without learning, innovation cannot take place.

Lean leaders understand that learning comes first. It's embedded in their everyday lives, and opportunities to learn abound all around us. For the Lean leader, it's a way of life to look at everything with a curious mind and seek opportunities to improve on what's currently being done. To figure out better and less wasteful ways to design, create, and deliver truly innovative new products/services that result in both customer and company value.

Conclusion

Leading innovation inside the Lean enterprise is a complex endeavor. It takes mobilizing the entire organization and getting everyone moving in the same direction to comprehend and define the correct set of customer wants, needs, and/or desires, in order to go after the right things that create and deliver value. Squandering your valuable, scarce enterprise resources on non-value-adding products/services is the fastest way to corporate extinction. You must start the innovation process with a clear understanding of where you're headed. Then diligently build the plan to get there in an iterative and incremental fashion, using the Lean product canvas and design thinking + Lean Startup cycle to release MVPs out to the market that test the delivery of value. This chapter has demystified innovation by building an understanding of the Lean methods and tools that are available to you.

Building disruptive products/services requires building a culture keenly focused on disruptive innovation through continuous learning and adjustment. We will turn our attention to that topic in the next chapter.

CHAPTER 8

Leading Culture

This chapter is all about defining and building a culture that grows and evolves over time. You know you have achieved a state of continuous evolution when your culture takes on a life of its own and is supported and nurtured throughout the Lean enterprise by those inside of it. As a Lean leader assuming the role of change agent, you are signing up to proactively guide the development of your Lean culture—something you must believe is possible from the onset. And whether you realize it or not, you are already equipped with many of the tools you will need to create and evolve your culture that have been discussed throughout this book. This chapter will help you make a conscious connection between Leading Lean and the all-important element of culture, which is so crucial to the Lean enterprise. Let's get started on developing, sustaining, and growing your Lean culture as a Lean leader.

Defining "Culture"

Culture. What a nebulous word. It represents the intangible thing that defines any enterprise, Lean or not. You can see culture when you look at an organization's leaders, by observing what they value, the way they behave, what they say, and how they act. Culture funnels down from the top and spreads out to affect every aspect of the company, positive and negative. It really isn't nebulous after all if you know what you are looking for and spend the time to analyze the four foundational aspects of culture: an organization's beliefs, values, behaviors, and actions. It takes the people inside a Lean enterprise to bring it to life and to care for it, feed it, and protect it as it grows and evolves over time.

Today many management consultants and transformational change agents blame a company's culture for its ills and then go on to state that changing the culture is almost impossible. To me, that attitude is rather defeatist. I believe human beings, given the right motivation, have the innate ability to change whatever they set their minds to. What causes cultural change to fail is the variable of resistance to change. The make-or-break component, the tipping point between success and failure, is whether your workforce embraces the required changes.

Motivation: The Essential Ingredient

Motivation must be present to make cultural change happen. People need to be motivated to change. Motivating people requires determining what motivates them and then incorporating these factors into your cultural change efforts. To clarify something right now, that does not mean getting out a big stick. People cannot be coerced into changing. They must participate in the change, because change done *to* them won't stick, whereas change done *with* them, where they actively participate, will be supported and sustained over time. That kind of change will grow and take on a life of its own. The people inside a Lean enterprise must "own" their culture and actively participate in evolving it at the strategic, tactical, and operational levels. Building culture is not just the responsibility of senior leaders. They do play a major part in defining and developing its strategic direction, but accomplishing real and lasting change requires everyone in the entire organization.

Why is building and sustaining a healthy culture so important? Culture provides a mechanism for survival that defines the norms for socially and professionally acceptable behavior. It sets standards of behavior that are predictable and consistent for everyone who lives and works within it. Without culture, an organization would become a free-for-all, like the Wild West. Without good foundations rooted in your system of beliefs, values, behaviors, and actions, there is no sense of order, and chaos abounds.

Becoming a Lean enterprise is about achieving a state of continuous evolution, brought about by a commitment to continuous improvement (CI) efforts that are geared at accomplishing customer, stakeholder, and business outcomes. Merely going through the motions of implementing some CI projects and expecting to achieve lasting and sustainable results through disparate, disconnected projects does little to move the needle toward this goal. Fully embracing Lean throughout the enterprise takes a concerted, disciplined approach that includes mindful cultural change.

Defining Culture in the Context of the Lean Enterprise

Corporate culture refers to the beliefs, values, and behaviors that determine how a company's leaders and employees interact to accomplish the Lean enterprise's objectives. Many times, culture is implied, not expressly defined, and develops organically from the cumulative traits of the people who are hired by the company over time. However, as it develops, culture reaches to the core of a company's ideology and practice and affects every aspect of its business.[1] Ah, there it is! Yes, people can change the entire culture of a company, because it is PEOPLE that define the culture through their beliefs, values, behaviors, and ultimately their actions. Even one person can have a major impact on the culture of an organization. In the case of the Lean enterprise, that person must be YOU!

Leaders are often more focused on things like improving performance, increasing productivity and profitability, and cutting costs than on changing culture. Yet people drive culture and thus impact overall results. Undervaluing how people feel about their work is a Lean antipattern, because how people feel is a big motivator: thoughts, feelings, and emotions matter. People—both customers and employees—are valued and respected in a Lean culture. This drives productivity, profitability, and sustained growth through innovation. As with your customers, an emotional connection fosters engagement for employees too. Sakichi Toyoda, the founder of Toyota Motor Corporation, understood this principle well. It was the fourth of five main principles he laid out when he started the company: "Always strive to build a homelike atmosphere at work that is warm and friendly."[2]

As a Lean leader, you must build a culture that promotes personal accountability, autonomy, purpose, mastery, and continuous improvement if you intend to build an enterprise that embraces Lean. Define what you want your culture to become—then be guided by your beliefs, model your values, demonstrate the supporting behaviors, and take the actions to make the change happen and become a role model for your workforce.

---

1 Investopedia, s.v. "Corporate Culture" (*https://oreil.ly/Czzb0*), by Sandra Lim, last modified May 7, 2019.

2 "About Toyota" (*https://oreil.ly/6wjnn*), Toyota Aruba (website), accessed June 15, 2019.

Defining the Leading Culture Dimension

Culture is complex and hard to change, with many moving parts and intertwined pieces. To get a sense of what "good" looks like, consider the Leading Culture dimension of the Modern Lean Framework™ (detailed in Figure 8-1). It depicts the beliefs, values, behaviors, and actions that represent the cultural elements of a Lean enterprise. This part of the framework should look familiar: the preceding chapters have systematically discussed three of its four quadrants. The stage has already been set to discuss how to go about developing a Lean culture.

It is called a framework because you will take what applies to you, your followers, and your organization and leave the rest behind. Through this framework, you will create an essential "support structure" for your Lean culture. In Quadrant I are the beliefs that guide us. They create the foundation of a code of conduct when leading self (Chapter 3) and others (Chapter 4) to a Lean mindset while leveraging Lean thinking (both discussed in Chapter 2). Quadrant II contains the values that grow from your belief system. These are supported by the motivating behaviors in Quadrant III. Quadrant IV details all the supporting actions you need to create these behaviors. All of this is rooted in the Plan/Do/Check/Act (PDCA) cycle that is fundamental to Lean.

Quadrant I: Beliefs

Leading Self
- Believe & trust in yourself
- Develop & maintain a healthy mind & body
- Possess a bias toward action
- Face challenges head-on
- Leverage common sense for problem solving & decision making
- Practice Emotional Intelligence (EQ)
- Display persistence & tenacity
- Be a student

Leading Others
- Be a servant leader & teacher
- Respect others
- Think w/a kaizen mind
- Develop others
- Lean Mindset & Thinking
- Embrace innovation/disruption
- Foster experimentation
- Focus on quality, value & flow
- Gather feedback
- Always be improving (People, process, & technology) and learning

Quadrant II: Values

Core Values
- Customer Centricity
- Quality & Innovation
- Respect, Honesty, & Integrity
- Trust & Loyalty
- Accountability & Mastery
- Continuous Learning & Improvement
- Teamwork & Collaboration
- Imagination & Experimentation
- Humility & Graciousness
- Visibility & Transparency
- Observation & Reflection
- Economic & Social Responsibility

Extended Values
- Agility
- Purposefulness
- Adaptability
- Responsiveness
- Inclusion
- Diversity
- Empowerment
- Autonomy & Purpose
- Environmental Awareness
- Practicality & Genuineness

Quadrant IV: Actions

Processes
- Eight Steps to a Lean Culture
- Lean Enterprise Strategic Planning Process
- Objectives & Key Results (OKRs)
- Conversations, Feedback, and Recognition (CFRs)
- Toyota Production System (TPS)
- Toyota Business Practices (TBP)
- On-the-Job Development (OJD)
- Scientific Method – PDCA Cycle

Methods
- Genchi Genbutsu
- Value Stream Mapping
- Voice of the Customer (VoC)
- Customer Persona Analysis
- Customer Experience Journey Mapping (CXJM)
- Omnichannel Customer Experience Strategy (OCXS)
- Design Thinking
- Lean Startup
- Lean Six Sigma
- Agile Methods

Quadrant III: Behaviors

- **Enterprise Alignment**
- **Customer-Driven Outcomes**
- **Business-Driven Outcomes**
- **Centralized Strategic Decision Making (CSDM) Framework**
  - Strategic Planning Canvas
    - Vision, Mission, & Value Proposition
    - Strategic Themes
    - Competitive opportunities
    - Tactical plans and operational tasks
  - Investment Strategy
  - Strategic Roadmap
  - Minimum Viable Product (MVP) release Plan

Plan · Do · Check · Act

Figure 8-1. *The Leading Culture dimension (large format version (https://oreil.ly/leadingLean-figs))*

Establishing and growing a Lean culture requires you to systematically build out and maintain all four quadrants over time. You may be thinking, "Okay, got it! Let's jump into QIV and implement some of the processes and methods. Let's get some immediate and measurable results." Doing that might get you something, but probably not the overall results you were trying to achieve. There is a reason why Quadrant IV is fourth, not first. You cannot force a culture through actions. It needs to spring forth from the collective beliefs and values of the individuals in the organization. Actions will play a big part in growing and maintaining your culture, but you need to be a little more deliberate than that.

Process should never be your starting point, because processes treat the symptoms, not the root cause. You need to first define what you believe to be true (QI: Beliefs), then define what is important to you (QII: Values), build the behaviors that will give you direction and guidance along the way (QIII: Behaviors), and *then* figure out which actions (QIV) will help you accomplish what you're after. If you skip the first three quadrants, you will have no idea which processes and methods (actions) you need. If you rush through the framework, you'll end up a poser, merely "Doing Lean" instead of actually "Leading Lean." This is a fatal error I see repeated over and over again. The place to start is at the beginning, by determining your belief system. Everything springs forth from that, whether you realize it or not.

Quadrant I: Identifying Your Beliefs

Beliefs (Figure 8-2) are assumptions concerning what you ascertain or believe to be true. These form the basis of your Lean belief system.

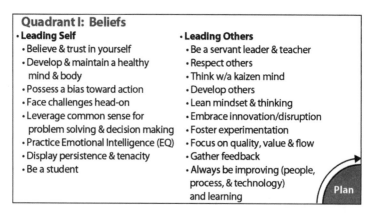

Figure 8-2. *QI: Beliefs*

Beliefs are the things that we, as Lean leaders, hold as self-evident truths. They are ingrained in our values and reinforced through how we behave. To become a Lean leader, you must truly embrace these beliefs. Bring them into your life and own them. Imprint them in the way you think, feel, and behave through repetition. That is how you make them your own. Then they will become habitual behaviors over time.

Quadrant II: The Role of Values in Defining Culture

Values are standards that become generally accepted over time and guide our behavior. Many of the values expressed in QII are present in QI as well. That's because the underlying belief system of the Lean enterprise is formed on what the Lean leaders hold to be their truths. These are solidified into values through behavior in QII (Figure 8-3).

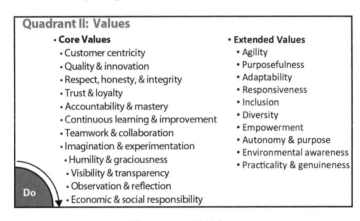

Figure 8-3. *QII: Values*

To understand what you want to become, you need to define what is important to you by determining the values that foster and support the appropriate behaviors and actions that bring about a Lean culture. Values guide and motivate you. When personal and corporate values align, we find truly dedicated employees. If you want to attract people who will live and support your corporate culture, you need to understand and consciously promote them. Recruit people who display and live these values.

Have you ever worked for a company whose values didn't align with your own? I have. The experience was a nightmare. My personal values were in constant conflict with the ones being displayed by the company's senior leaders. Can you recall a time when this happened to you? What was the result? Did you leave in search of a better match? Was it a conscious or unconscious choice? Maybe you felt that something just wasn't right, but you couldn't put your finger on the underlying cause—you just knew it was time to make a change. That is the cognitive dissonance that happens when a values mismatch occurs. People make choices with their feet. If you have a revolving front door and your talent attrition rates are high, it might be time to look at the values that have become synonymous with your organization.

Values have a major influence on a person's behaviors and actions. They serve as broad guidelines for an acceptable code of conduct inside the organization. To develop a culture of continuous improvement, align your beliefs and values with the behaviors that accomplish your corporate vision, mission, and value proposition.

Values also play a crucial role in your organization's decision-making processes, because accountability is pushed down to the gemba, where the work is performed in a Lean enterprise. Because values drive what your people do without clear instruction, it's crucial to identify and promote your values to guide ethical behavior. Making what you value perfectly clear takes the guesswork out of deciding between ethical and unethical behavior. You also may well keep the company out of hot water, or out of the public eye when it comes to being socially responsible and accountable. A negative comment is just 280 characters away on Twitter.

In analyzing Toyota's guiding principles, you can distill what the company's leaders value most; they have explicitly stated it. Extended principles flow out of leading yourself and others and are representative of the Lean mindset and its methods.[3] Introducing Lean into your organization must begin by developing a firm understanding of these values and then identifying which ones to focus on. Remember: beliefs drive values, values impact behaviors, and behaviors promote action.

Quadrant III: Using Strategy to Solidify Your Behaviors

Behaviors drive strategic, tactical, and operational actions. In the context of the Lean enterprise, they create the yardstick by which progress is measured. If your goal is to develop an organization keenly focused on what it values, your values must also be reflected in your behaviors. The expected behaviors must be explicitly stated in your centralized strategic-decision-making (CDSM) framework and supported by developing your mission, vision, and value proposition. Define your strategic objectives, competitive opportunities, and key results (KRs) to give the Lean enterprise purpose and an outcome-oriented culture. Your followers in a Lean enterprise crave purpose and direction. As a Lean leader, your job is to create purpose and direction to drive the behaviors you seek (Figure 8-4).

---

3 Please see the work of Lean thought leaders such as Jeffrey Liker, James Womack, and Daniel Jones.

People often think of Lean (as in Lean Six Sigma) as a set of tools to reduce costs. But once you start thinking culturally, you realize that it is the underlying values, supported by beliefs and translated into behaviors that can be measured, that drive the Lean enterprise forward.

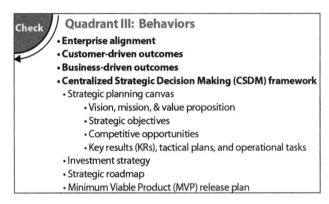

Figure 8-4. *QIII: Behaviors*

Chapter 5 talked about identifying the outcomes you seek to accomplish from both a customer and a company perspective. Chapter 6 discussed achieving enterprise alignment by connecting strategy to execution, building strategic objectives, tactical plans, and operational tasks. We will revisit these tools later on in this chapter to drive home the connection between behaviors and creating and evolving Lean culture.

Quadrant IV: Bringing a Culture to Life Through Your Actions

The way to accomplish anything is by taking action, rooted in the desired behaviors the organization seeks to achieve and based on its beliefs and values. Actions are how you mobilize the Lean enterprise to continuously evolve and improve over time. Figure 8-5 lists the Lean processes and methods for building and sustaining a Lean culture.

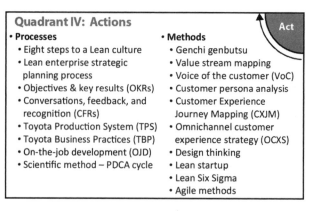

Figure 8-5. *QIV: Actions*

Executing on the Eight Steps to a Lean Culture: New Horizons

Building a Lean culture requires mindful effort. You patiently build it over time. Figure 8-6 outlines the eight steps required to build or change your corporate culture to embrace Lean. As you can see, step 1 starts with understanding your foundation by assessing your current culture. You'll use that later to identify cultural gaps you will need to address. Then, in steps 2 through 4, you work through the quadrants in the Leading Culture dimension of the Modern Lean Framework™. You determine what actions are required to bring your culture to life by formalizing them in step 5. To accomplish your mission and achieve your vision, in steps 6 through 8 you establish accountability by establishing OKRs, conducting CFR check-ins, and measuring and evolving as you go.

Figure 8-6. *Eight steps to a Lean culture*

By repeating this process on a periodic basis, you proactively lead the establishment of a culture that supports the evolution of Lean, in an iterative and incremental way. Ideally, you should move through this eight-step process and all four quadrants of the culture framework at least once a year, to ensure you maintain alignment with your CSDM framework and the behaviors that drive actions. As a Lean leader, it is your responsibility to ensure the continuous evolution and survival of this process.

Jim Collins, the owner of New Horizons, realized that many of the issues in the dealership had sprung from the culture that had taken root before Nancy came in and injected some new life into the service department. He wanted to propagate the Lean aspects that Nancy's kaizen team had been exhibiting throughout the other parts of dealership in order to grow and sustain his business well into the future. That meant taking a proactive stance and resolving to take action. He asked Nancy for help. She recommended Lisa—her colleague who had conducted the sales training the previous month—to help with the culture assessment and overhaul.

Step 1: Assess Your Current Culture

To change, update, or enhance your culture, you must first benchmark your current cultural strengths and weaknesses. Assessing your own culture requires objectivity. You need to remove yourself from it and become an impartial observer as much as you can. In Chapter 4, when Nancy first walked into the New Horizons service department, she witnessed the dealership's culture in action, including the lack of engagement, customer service, and sense of urgency. As an impartial observer, she found it pretty easy to tell that the dealership had an unhealthy culture.

A handy tool for assessing culture is to conduct a Lean enterprise *culture walk*, using the Lean Enterprise Culture Walk Four Blocker template shown in Table 8-1.

Table 8-1. Lean Enterprise Culture Walk Four Blocker

Interactions Observations
Observe how your employees interact with each other, as well as with your customers. Ask yourself:
• How do people inside of the organization interact with each other?
• How do leaders interact with each other? Their employees? Their customers?
• How do employees interact with each other? Their leaders? The company's customers?
• How are meetings conducted? Do they start on time? Are they well organized and purposeful?
• How are conflicts resolved?
• What is the noise level? Do people verbally interact with each other? Is email favored over personal interaction?
• What is the tone of interactions? Formal/informal? Pleasant/hostile?
Work Environment Observations
Walk around and take a look at your physical space. Ask yourself:
• What objects are sitting on desks? Hanging on the walls?
• Does anything seem to be missing? Does anything seem odd or out of place?
• Is it set up for human interaction? Is it sterile and uninviting?
• How is the space allocated? What is the mix between offices and cubicles? Where are the offices located?
• Is the common area inviting? Do people congregate around the coffee machine? Is there a bulletin board? If so, what is posted on it?
• Are there spaces designated for collaboration? Do they have whiteboards?

Emotions Observations

Whether you realize it or not, emotions play an important part when it comes to your values. People do not elicit emotions about things they do not care about. They can be an indication of your current values at work. Ask yourself:

- How do people speak to each other? To customers? Vendors?
- Do they make eye contact as you walk by? Look up from their desks or from what they are doing?
- What are people getting upset about? What caused the conflict?
- Do people seem engaged/disengaged? Happy/sad? Friendly/withdrawn? Excited/bored?
- What is the emotional tone of interactions? Happy/sad? Friendly/withdrawn? Excited/bored?

Organizational Aspects Observations

These questions have to do with the company itself, and you'll need to ask them of both yourself as well as your colleagues:

- Is the organization's mission and vision clear and connected to our daily activities?
- What do you think are the company's values? Do they resonate with you? If not, why?
- Do company leaders live and display our values? If not, why?
- What is the predominant formal management style present in our leaders?
- What informal leadership practices exist that leaders rely on to get things done?
- How are success and failure addressed?
- Are rewards and recognition tied to performance?

The purpose of the culture walk is to give you suggestions about where to look when analyzing the elements of your current culture. It provides areas of focused observation and questions to prompt you, while walking through the organization. Yes, we are applying the Lean method of genchi genbutsu, or *going and seeing for yourself.* What a novel idea, that firsthand observation would be a very powerful Lean tool! The template should include space to record your observations in the following four critical areas:

Interactions
> Observe how employees interact with each other and their customers. Interactions can tell you a lot about your organization's belief system and how it plays into the values being exhibited.

Emotions
> Observing people as they display their emotions (or lack thereof) tells you a lot about how your current values work for or against the culture that has been established to date.

Organizational Aspects

These are things directly associated with the company, such as its vision, mission, value proposition, leadership style, organizational structure, rewards and recognition system, and so forth.

Work Environment

An organization's physical environment can be very telling. Is it warm and inviting? Do people look like they enjoy working at your company—or like they can't wait until five o'clock rolls around and they can jet out of there? Are there common areas to collaborate and take a break during the day? Walk around and look at your physical space from an outsider's perspective. Would you want to work here as a potential job applicant? Would it give you a reason to get up in the morning and come into work?

Analyzing the New Horizons service department's culture

The first step that Lisa suggested for assessing New Horizon's culture was for her and Nancy to perform a culture walk to observe the four elements at play in the dealership: the types of interactions that take place, what emotions are being expressed during those interactions, what's going on in the workplace, and the organizational aspects of the dealership itself. Lisa presented Nancy with the Four Blocker template. Nancy's completed template is shown in Table 8-2.

Table 8-2. New Horizons service department Culture Walk Four Blocker

Interactions Observations
• Leaders spend a lot of time in their offices, which are tucked away down a corridor that is separate from the rest of the service department
• Formal conversations appear to be the norm. For the most part, they are brief and to the point, with little casual conversation being made
• The kaizen team that meets in the war room is well organized and focused. They understood the objective of the meeting, there was an agenda, and notes were being taken
• The service agent and customer waiting areas were very quiet. The personnel in the Parts area had a radio on playing country music over the top of the piped-in music
• Interactions with customers are professional, friendly, and polite
• A conflict with a customer was handled in a professional and thoughtful manner

Work Environment Observations

- Service department war room is covered with work being performed by a Lean Continuous Improvement team, displaying the values of customer centricity, quality, visibility, transparency, and collaboration/teamwork
- The computer equipment in the service department actually looks out of place. Its high tech appearance doesn't match the tired and out-of-date early 80s décor
- The service agents are all clustered together and huddled around small desks that are mostly taken up by the keyboard, mouse, and monitor that sit on each of them. There is little work space and no place to put anything, including personal items
- The service bays are cluttered and disorganized, with parts stacked up against the wall
- The certifications hanging on the wall are old and out of date

Emotions Observations

- Overall, the staff seems to be courteous and polite to the customers. However, there isn't any sense of urgency to greet customers or go the extra mile on the customer service side. They appear to be somewhat withdrawn overall
- A customer became somewhat irritated over a billing inaccuracy and incomplete work. The service agent quickly defused the situation and was able to calm the customer down by offering a 10% discount on the work performed and promised to get the rest of the work done within the next hour, as the customer waited on-site
- The tone across the department appears to be somewhat subdued. Employees are friendly, but they do not seem excited or engaged in or about their work

Organizational Aspects Observations

- When asked to state the dealership's vision, mission, and values, 9 out of 10 employees could not state them, and the one that did was only half right. One employee also responded that she was not aware that the dealership actually had those things in place
- The predominant leadership style appears to be command and control, with very little room for employee input or feedback
- Compensation and rewards are based on longevity at the dealership, not performance
- Discounts that are offered as a way to compensate for poor workmanship and unhappy customers are deducted from employees' pay as a way to encourage better performance
- Learning and development must be done on an employee's day off. Many of the service technicians are not up to date on their certifications or the new tech in the vehicles as a result

Nancy found the experience enlightening. The walk showed her that the department had made some improvements already, but she also saw areas that needed more focused attention, as well as a few places where the new initiatives in the service department might have unintentionally created some undesirable behaviors.

The customer service training showed up in the Interactions and Emotions Observations sections, revealed by how the service agents now handle customer conflicts. Nancy suspected that the new system had taken some of the "fun" out of working at the dealership. Everyone was serious and to the point in their interactions with each other and with customers. Often, in your haste to fix things, you may produce unintended results, thanks to the relationship between cause and effect. That is why it is important to follow all of the eight steps to building a Lean culture.

The Culture Walk Four Blocker findings are a great way to look for symptoms and build your culture. Lisa decided to spend time combining her findings with Nancy's to get a complete picture of what was happening, so that they could collaborate with Jim on building the dealership's cultural future. They then moved on to step 2 and worked on defining their Lean belief system.

Step 2: Establish Your Lean Belief System

If you are not getting the results you are expecting, it's probably because your belief system is not aligned with your values and behaviors and not reinforced by your actions. At the core of a Lean leader is a strongly held belief system that forms through understanding how to lead yourself first and then others. Over time you develop and embrace a Lean mindset through Lean thinking. Therefore, an organization that seeks to develop a Lean culture must actively participate in the development of its people by fostering the conditions that are right to bring about a healthy Lean belief system.

Choosing your weapons wisely

Two processes that can go a long way toward instilling this belief system are Toyota Business Practices (TBP) and on-the-job development (OJD), both of which are based on the PDCA cycle. These processes work at all levels (Enterprise, Tactical, and gemba) within the organization. Using these iterative and incremental actions embraces and supports a Lean mindset and Lean thinking: leaders first learn to lead themselves in a team setting. Then, when ready, they move on to leading others, which develops a kaizen (continuous improvement) mind that fosters Lean thinking. Learning, growing, and improving become second nature, leading to innovation and ultimately to becoming a disruptor in your marketplace.

Kaizen is a way of life. It is not something that is done once or twice a year in an organization. The Western notion of a "kaizen event," where a team comes together to solve a particular problem, is fine and may render results. But those results need to be maintained through continuous improvement efforts. Otherwise, waste will creep in, and those gains will dissolve and possibly even disappear over time.

I've seen a lot of corporate kaizen programs fail because the organization hires an outside training firm to come in and train up a bunch of Lean Six Sigma yellow or green belts, only to release them into the workplace without any supervision or coaching. When the whole effort yields few or no lasting results, senior executives end up saying, "We tried that 'Lean thing' here and it doesn't work." The teams are then disbanded, and it's back to business as usual. Of course that's not going to work. Lean is a mindset, a way of life, not something that can be "trained" into or forced on people. It must be practiced, to hone your skills and become well versed. That is the only way Lean will be embraced and ingrained into an organization's belief system and subsequently its culture.

Developing a *kaizen mind* means honing your ability to see the waste in everything and striving to remove it, one nasty piece at a time. That means respecting people and working as a team to improve the flow of work, eliminate waste, increase product/service quality, and ultimately create greater value for both the customer and the company. That is the essence of The Toyota Way. There is nothing secretive or mystical about it. It is an exciting process that takes patience, perseverance, and persistence (all qualities of a Lean leader). The more success a kaizen team experiences, the more they want to tackle more challenging and complicated problems. As the team continuously improves the organization, so too do its members improve themselves.

Turning beliefs into values through repetition

As we've seen with New Horizons, spinning up kaizen teams is not hard. However, if you are just starting out on your Lean journey, you most likely will not have the expertise inside your organization to support these efforts. Jim was smart enough to realize he needed outside help, so he hired Nancy, who had previous experience. She acted as their first sensei, and she was honing Jannie's ability to lead throughout the TBP process; whether Jannie realized it or not, Nancy was practicing OJD. Jannie was Nancy's apprentice, and both were working to build Lean skills and abilities in themselves, as well as the organization.

Building a Lean belief system that turns into a standard way of conducting yourself, guided by your values, requires repetition. That is how beliefs turn into values. You must give your people the tools to make this happen and then stand back and have the patience to allow it to evolve. When beginning work with a new organization, I like to start by running a TBP initiative as a pilot or proof of concept (PoC) to convince senior leaders that Lean really does work within their company. This approach brings Lean out of the hypothetical shadows and into the light of day through practical application with visibility and transparency. Implementing it where they can actually see firsthand results removes the objection of "not invented here, therefore we are not interested"

—or worse, "Lean is that Japanese thing, and we just don't work that way around here." Toyota is a global company. What its senseis have realized is that Lean must become a part of the culture for it to take hold. It must be adaptive and allow the kaizen teams to embrace it in their own way. It cannot be prescriptive and must flow out of both the organization's and its home country's cultural traits.

Once you start this process, it will take time for Lean to grab hold and spread. Take it one team at a time, and make sure their goals and successes are transparent and well publicized. Keep their work visible by posting it the way the New Horizons team did in their break room, ensuring that everyone in the organization understands its impact.

Preparing for the inevitable culture clash

Old habits die hard, so be prepared to face opposition, even if you undeniably produce results. Some people will emphatically deny that Lean is taking hold and rendering results in your organization. You may just have to live with these naysayers for a while, until you pick up enough momentum that their voices are either converted, drowned out, or possibly even removed by your supporters. Whether you are an external consultant or an internal transformational change agent, you'll need strong convictions and a thick skin to overcome this type of opposition.

Just remember: you are in it for the long haul, so don't compromise on what you know will work. Don't change the process because of pressure or criticism. Adapt to your organization by meeting it where it is and then slowly working to change it. Remain steady in your convictions that Lean does work if it is given the proper time, energy, and support.

Building New Horizons' belief system

Nancy and Lisa took their insights to Jim. Nancy pointed out a marked difference between the employees who had been part of the kaizen team and the rest of the service department: old and new beliefs, values, behaviors, and actions were clashing between that team and the rest of the department. Jim admitted he had observed the same; the kaizen team members had more "pep in their step" and were still maintaining their whiteboards and reporting their progress and improvements. Jim had noticed other employees stopping by the war room to check out the team's materials, too.

Nancy said that was exactly why they wanted to slowly transition the other parts of the service department into kaizen teams that practice TBP and OJD— to build upon the belief system that was beginning to form at the dealership. She said they would identify a leader in each area, form a team, and then provide TBP training at each step, coaching and mentoring them as they moved forward. The goal would be to develop the leader into a sensei who could then take over another team, and so on, until they had moved through the whole dealership.

However, Nancy also stressed the need to set realistic expectations. This process would take some time, and the ultimate goal would be twofold: improving on the Lean ways of working at the dealership, and creating Lean leaders through TBP and OJD who could help to evolve the dealership's belief system.

Lisa noted that, due to their previous work, the dealership had three senseis: her, Nancy, and Jannie. They could spin up three more teams, which would be more than enough to cover the service department and also possibly one more area within the dealership. They asked Jim if he had a preference for where these teams should be formed; he said he wanted to see how his salespeople responded to these methods and training. He asked Lisa how they would know what issues they should work on. She assured him that when they conducted their gap analysis in step 4 and defined their future state, they would identify the things that needed to be worked on next.

Step 3: Identify the Values That Define Your Culture

Values form from your system of beliefs, which means the two are interconnected. So when identifying the values that are important and must be modeled within your Lean culture, the best place to look is your current beliefs. Determine the three to seven beliefs that matter the most to your Lean enterprise. This doesn't have to be a complicated process. You can start by brainstorming a list of values that resonate with you, using the list in Figure 8-1 as a starting point. Vet them with your employees and customers to verify that they resonate with both groups. Once done, post them in a common area for both groups to see, so that you begin to live them through behaviors and actions, making them meaningful and relevant.

Bringing New Horizons' Lean culture to life

Lisa asked to meet with Jim and Nancy in Jim's office the next day. They both looked a little nervous about why she had asked to meet them there instead of the war room. It was because she wanted to discuss the findings of the culture walk in private first, to get their reactions and thoughts. She presented a packet containing both Nancy's and Lisa's Four Blockers, plus a third template that combined both, shown in Table 8-3.

Table 8-3. New Horizons Service Department Culture Walk Four Blocker, combined findings

Interactions Observations
• Isolated and inaccessible leadership • Formal conversational style; casual interaction is minimal • Problem solving differed to supervisor; lack of empowerment • Work is focused on the individual performer; the kaizen team is an island • Respect is given based on formal power and position service department noise level is low; parts area is playing country music • Customer interactions are professional, friendly, and polite • Customer conflict resolution is professional and thoughtful
Work Environment Observations
• Service department war room is Lean Central; pillar of teamwork in action • Posters denote kaizen progress, supporting visibility and transparency • Inconsistent appearance of the dealership overall; outdated décor/high tech equipment looks out of place • Dealership doesn't convey vibrancy; bathrooms are in a state of disarray • Cramped working conditions in the service agents' area; no personal items anywhere! • Cluttered and disorganized service bays; no central storage for parts • Continuous learning not supported; certifications on the wall are old and out of date • Doors are full of fingerprints; paint is rubbing off door handles • Intake area full of stains on floors and walls
Emotions Observations
• Staff generally courteous and polite to the customers • Staff lacks a sense of urgency and ownerships • No motivation to greet customers or go the "extra mile" on the customer service side • Low job satisfaction; employees lack joy and fun in their work • Billing inaccuracies and incomplete work result in irate customers • Discounts given to defuse irritated customers • Irate customers venting to each other in the waiting room • Dealership's tone is solemn and subdued; friendly but disengaged staff

As you can see, Lisa's assessment rendered a lot of information. She had taken the liberty of combining and rephrasing some things on the Four Blocker, as well as adding her own observations to Nancy's, to generate a snapshot of the dealership's current culture. It was not an exhaustive list, but it captured how the staff was interacting with each other, and its customers and vendors; what emotions were elicited as a result of those interactions; how the organizational aspects impacted them; and what role the work environment played in the dynamics of the dealership.

Lisa noticed that Jim was quiet and a bit flushed. She could tell this wasn't exactly what he was expecting, and Nancy's face wasn't far behind. They were receptive to Lisa's feedback, even though it highlighted that they had a lot of work ahead of them.

Sometimes an outside observer can pick up on things that those inside the organization would not even notice. Because Lisa was thinking about the New Horizons brand from both an employee and a customer perspective, she wasn't narrowly focused on one or the other.

Jim admitted that it was hard to digest these truths—that New Horizons was still a ways off from being a Lean enterprise, and that the kaizen team was removed not just from the rest of the service department but from the rest of the dealership.

Lisa agreed and proposed the next step: assembling a cross-functional team to define the values that would support and reinforce the company's belief system as it developed and launched additional kaizen teams. It was very important that employees knew and understood what values the dealership held so they could enact them through behaviors and actions. Lisa suggested they invite Jim's leadership team and Nancy's kaizen team to a session geared toward identifying New Horizons' values. During the meeting, they would:

- Review the company's vision, mission, and value proposition to understand where they wanted to go, how they would get there, and what value they were going to create for their customers and for the dealership
- Explain the Leading Culture dimension of the Modern Lean Framework™ (Figure 8-1) and the predominant Lean beliefs in QI, then brainstorm and categorize the values they identified to come up with a first draft
- Analyze the combined Culture Walk Four Blocker worksheet to identify gaps and determine if there was anything they'd want to add, replace, or delete to define the future state
- Verify that these goals resonated with employees and customers, making any necessary changes

Once this was done, and before training the staff and posting the results in the customer waiting room, they would also perform one last sanity check. During the next step, which is to develop their CSDM framework, they would ensure that they support, and do not conflict with, the behaviors they were trying to elicit and reinforce throughout the department. Making these values visible influences behavior: when customers understand your values and observe counterproductive employee behavior or actions, they can call them out. You'll see this in your customer satisfaction surveys and follow-up service calls. Visibility and transparency are powerful tools in fostering a Lean culture.

That week, the team worked to define and develop the dealership's first draft of its values. Lisa wanted to make sure they kept the dealership's vision, mission, and value proposition in the forefront of everyone's minds as they worked. She had the poster shown in Figure 8-7 made up and hung it in the war room.

New Horizons
Commitment to Excellence

VISION
Dedicated to customers and driven by excellence

MISSION
To become the world's most renowned center
for customer service in the automotive sector

VALUE PROPOSITION
Easy to buy and obtain service

Figure 8-7. *New Horizons Vision, Mission, and Value Proposition poster*

After discussion and brainstorming, the team developed the initial set of values depicted in Figure 8-8. The first two come directly from The Toyota Way, the next three come from the list of core values in Figure 8-3, and the last one is a variation on continuous improvement.

**New Horizons
Commitment to Excellence**

OUR VALUES
Respect for People
Teamwork
Quality
Accountability
Visibility & Transparency
Continuous Evolution

Figure 8-8. *New Horizons values, initial draft*

Step 4: Define Your Motivating Behaviors by Creating Your Strategic Framework

The next step is to build your CSDM framework that clearly spells out where you want to go (mission), what you want to achieve (vision), and the value you want to create and deliver (value proposition) in the next year. Going any further out than that is a waste of time, due to the rate of change in the world today. Chapter 6 describes this framework as consisting of the following components:

- Strategic planning canvas
  - Mission, vision, and value proposition
  - Strategic objectives
  - Competitive opportunities, tactical plans, and operational tasks
- Investment strategy
- Strategic roadmap
- MVP release plan

Strategy and culture are intertwined. Foregoing the creation of your framework does not stop the evolution of your culture. My father once told me, "Jeannie, not making a choice is choosing, and if you don't do it, someone else is going to make it for you." Don't put your destiny in someone else's hands.

If you choose to forego creating your CSDM framework, some sort of culture will still evolve out of that decision. To regain control of your destiny and steer it in the right direction, you must purposefully create your strategy and treat it as your Enterprise True North. Without culture, your framework is just words on a page.

Also, innovation must be supported and aligned to both your culture and your strategy. A 2018 survey found that 71% of companies that understand this alignment experience much faster enterprise growth rates than their competition.[4] On the flip side, 36% of the leaders surveyed stated their innovation strategy didn't align with their culture, and 47% said their existing culture had failed to support their innovation strategy. Those are truly shocking statistics. Innovation has been a hot topic for quite some time now and is a crucial element of corporate survival. Innovation excellence must also be aligned with many of the things we've discussed throughout this book: not just strategy and culture, but also leadership alignment, customer experience, and employee engagement, in particular.

Recapping New Horizons' strategic framework

Jim and Nancy presented New Horizons' strategic framework to Lisa the next day. His team had built the service department's framework using the Lean enterprise strategic planning process that Nancy had taught them to create their strategic planning canvas (Figure 8-9).

As you can see, it clearly states the service department's vision, mission, and value proposition in step 1; the strategic objectives are detailed in step 3; the competitive opportunities they identified are in step 4; the key results are listed in step 5; and the tactical plans are identified in step 6. By developing their canvas, the team established the foundation of their strategic framework, which they all thought was a major accomplishment. They had never done anything like this before, and they felt it was a great first effort toward aligning their strategy to execution, as well as value creation and delivery.

Lisa agreed. The team had also worked on their investment strategy (detailed in Figure 8-10) that allocated how they would spend the funding on the initiatives that had been identified and how they tie this to the strategic objectives on their canvas.

---

4 Barry Jaruzelski, Robert Chwalik, and Brad Goehle, "What the Top Innovators Get Right" (*https://oreil.ly/s8tt9*), *strategy+business*, October 30, 2018.

New Horizons Service Department Strategic Planning

Step 1: The Environment

Vision: Dedicated to customers and driven by excellence

Mission: To become the world's most renowned center for customer service in the automotive sector

Value proposition: Easy to buy and obtain service

Competitive Landscape? We are the only dealer within a radius of 150 miles in the tristate area that sells and services this make of vehicle

Marketplace Challenges & Trends? Another luxury vehicle competitor is building a dealership 25 miles from us, in the next town over

Step 2: Customer/Persona Identification
1. Luxury sedan owner
2. Sports coupe owner
3. SUV owner
4. Truck owner
5. Van owner

Step 3: Strategic Objectives
1. Increase quarter-over-quarter sales
2. Increase the quality of our service to our customers
3. Increase the use of technology to effectively run our business
4. Modernize our facilities

Step 4: Competitive Opportunities
1. Perform random service follow-up customer calls
2. Perform telephone customer inquiries on lapsed service
3. Develop a service & repair mobile app
4. Provide training to the service staff
5. Upgrade loaner car program system
6. Upgrade hardware throughout dealership

Step 5: KRs
1. Increase quarter-over-quarter sales by 5%, for a cumulative total of 20% within the next 12 months
   - Increase service department sales by 2%/quarter by implementing a service follow-up program
   - Increase service department sales by 3% per quarter, by implementing a lapsed service Inquiry program
2. Increase the quality of our service to our customers within the next 6 months by:
   - Decreasing the service request error rate by 65%
   - Increasing our Net Promoter Score by 25%
3. Increase the use of technology to effectively run our business by:
   - Launching the first release of the service and repair mobile app by the end of Q1 2019 and the second by Q2 2019
   - Performing an upgrade to the loaner car program system upgrade by the end of Q4 2019
4. Modernize our facilities by upgrading the computer hardware in the service department within the next 90 days

Step 6: Tactics
1. After service customer follow-up call program
2. Service-lapsed customer call program
3. Service & repair mobile app plan
4. Service staff training plan
5. Loaner car program system upgrade plan
6. Hardware upgrade

Step 7: Workforce
1. Service department & technology
2. Service department & outside customer service firm
3. Loaner car department & technology
4. service department
5. service department
6. Technology

Step 8: Measure & Report
1. OKRs will be compiled by the data analytics group
2. Frequency will be based on the metric collected, on the following schedule:
   - #1: Sales quarterly
   - #2: Biweekly
   - #3: Monthly
   - #4: Monthly
3. Metrics results will be posted in the TBP team war room on the fifth day of each month

Step 9: Evolve & Optimize
1. The Loaner Car program system upgrade will also require all the hardware to be upgraded throughout the dealership
2. The Loaner Car program's processes also need to be revised/modified, as the system undergoes the planned software update
3. Training will need to be developed and conducted to ensure service dept staff is up to date on the new processes

Figure 8-9. *New Horizons Service Department strategic planning canvas (large format version (https://oreil.ly/leadingLean-figs))*

Strategic Objective	Opportunity	Tactical Plan	Timeframe	Cost Estimate & Investment Strategy		
				Cost Estimate	Total	Investment Type
Increase quarter-over-quarter sales	1. Do random service follow-up customer calls	1. After Service customer follow-up call program	Next 12 months	$1.25M	$2.25M	New
	2. Perform telephone customer inquiries on lapsed service	2. Service Lapsed customer call program	Next 12 months	$1.00M		Core
Increase the quality of our service to our customers	3. Develop a Service & Repair mobile app	3. Service & Repair mobile device application	Next 6 months	$6.00M	$7.50M	New
	4. Provide training to the service staff	4. Service agent customer service training	Next 6 months	$1.50M		Enhancement
Increase the use of technology to effectively run our business	5. Upgrade loaner car program system	5. Loaner Car Program (LCP) system upgrade	Next 12 months	$5.00M	$5.00M	Enhancement
Modernize our facilities	6. Upgrade hardware throughout dealership	6. Dealership Computer hardware upgrade	Next 90 days	$2.50M	$2.50M	Enhancement
		Total Service Department Investment Allocation		$17.25M	$17.25M	

Figure 8-10. *New Horizons service department investment strategy by theme (large format version (https://oreil.ly/leadingLean-figs))*

Jim asked them to turn the page and look at the strategic roadmap (Table 8-4) that showed what they were going to accomplish in which period for the coming year.

Table 8-4. New Horizons service department 12-month strategic roadmap

Year 1: Q1	Year 1: Q2
• **Increase quarter-over-quarter sales (12 months)** **$1.25m** 1. After Service customer follow-up call program **$1.00m** 2. Service Lapsed customer call program • Modernize our facilities (90 days) **$2.5m** 6. Dealership computer hardware upgrade	• **Increase the quality of our service to our customers (6 months)** **$6.00m** 3. Service & Repair mobile device application **$1.50m** 4. Service agent customer service training
Year 1: Q3	**Year 1: Q4**
	• **Increase the use of technology to effectively run our business (12 months)** **$5.00m** 5. Loaner Car Program (LCP) System Upgrade
$4.375m/quarter Run Rate **TOTAL: $17.5m**	

Additionally, their MVP release plan (Table 8-5) detailed when the tactical plans and operational tasks would be performed, with numbering tied to the strategic objectives they had identified.

Table 8-5. New Horizons Service Department 12-month MVP release plan

Year 1:Q1 MVP Release #1	Year 1: Q2 MVP Release #2
1. After Service Customer Follow-up Call program • Write follow-up call script • Pilot follow-up call script • Revise script based on findings • Launch follow-up call program **2. Service Lapsed Customer Call program** • Write follow-up call script • Pilot follow-up call script • Revise script based on findings • Launch follow-up call program **6. Dealership Computer Hardware Upgrade** • Install new computers • Install new printers • Install new handheld devices • Configure/test hardware & network **3. Service & Repair Mobile Device Application** • Conduct TBP effort on mobile device processes • Build customer register and log-in capability • Build "Schedule an Appointment" capability • Build "Arrange for a Loaner Car" capability • Pilot/revise Service & Repair mobile device application • Launch Service & Repair mobile device application	**3. Service & Repair Mobile Device Application— (Cont'd)** • Build "Send Repair Progress" notifications • Build "Viewable Bill" capability • Build "Push Feedback Survey" capability • Build "Offer Coupons/Discounts on Next Visit" capability • Build "Push Notifications for Next Service Due" capability • Pilot/Revise Service & Repair mobile device application • Launch Service & Repair mobile device application • Solicit feedback from customers • Incorporate feedback into the mobile device app **4. Service Agent Customer Service Training** • Determine training vendor • Negotiate and sign contract • Schedule training class • Conduct training class
Year 1: Q3 MVP Release #3	Year 1: Q4 MVP Release #4
5. Loaner Car Program (LCP) System Upgrade • Install new system software • Configure new system software • Test new system software	**5. Loaner Car Program (LCP) System Upgrade— (Cont'd)** • Perform gap analysis on features & functionality • Revise/update LCP processes (if necessary) • Conduct LCP processes training (if necessary) • Launch new LCP system

With that, Jim sat back and allowed Lisa to digest what he had just presented. Nancy pointed to the graphs and charts on the wall. She reminded Lisa that they had wanted to make all this work visible to everyone in the dealership, not just the service department, for the sake of complete and total transparency and visibility.

Lisa agreed that this was excellent work and completely satisfied the deliverables for step 4. It was time to finalize their values.

Finalizing New Horizons' values

After going over all the artifacts and looking at the culture walk findings again, the team thought it necessary to make two important changes. First, they discussed "accountability" versus "empowerment," agreeing that the former meaning was embodied in the latter word, which was much more inspirational. After all, one of the main reasons for building a Lean culture is to create an empowered workforce. The team members all approved of making this change.

They also wanted to counter the misinterpretation that "No fun is to be had here!" The sales training had inadvertently communicated this, and it showed up several times in the Culture Walk Four Blocker. The team added the value of "enjoyment" (Figure 8-11) to send a message to everyone that they intended to make New Horizons a fun, exciting, innovative place.

**New Horizons
Commitment to Excellence**

OUR VALUES
Respect for People
Teamwork
Quality
Accountability
Visibility & Transparency
Continuous Evolution
Enjoyment

Figure 8-11. *New Horizons values, final draft*

Since the dealership is in a small town, Jim has always tried to make it a warm and welcoming place. He's encouraged current and potential customers to stop by any time, even just to say hi or pick up a free bottled water (offered on both the sales floor and in the Service Intake bay). This is a tradition Jim started when he opened the dealership more than 20 years ago. Jim often says that "People do business with people they know and like," and his actions have helped to foster the culture of openness, warmth, and a sense of community that Jim and the team have enjoyed over the years.

Step 5: Formalize the Actions Required to Transform Your Culture

To build a culture based on your Lean belief system that supports your values and strategic direction, you must identify the gaps where you are not yet living your culture so you can take corrective measures to bring it to life. In this step, you must accomplish the following three tasks:

1. Conduct your gap analysis by analyzing your Culture Walk Four Blocker worksheet.
2. Determine which behaviors and actions are best suited to close the gap for each observation.
3. Identify the relevant themes in order to form your kaizen teams and name the leads for each.

Conducting your gap analysis

Lisa and Nancy spent the day mapping the items on the Culture Walk Four Blocker worksheet to their newly finalized values to create the New Horizons Service Department Gap Analysis Worksheet (Figure 8-12).

The process is simple. Read each item in each block and determine which value the observation matches up with the best, from both a positive and a negative perspective. Try not to overthink this, and don't worry about duplicate entries across the stated values. Focus on picking the one that is most relevant and best represents the observation. If you feel strongly that it must appear under more than one value, go ahead and place it there. With the first observations under "Visibility & Transparency" and "Continuous Evolution," the two leaders agreed that it was important and the right thing to do to duplicate the observation concerning the staff's knowledge around the dealership's vision, mission, and value proposition, so it appears under both values. Record where the observation came from using the Observations Legend in Figure 8-12, which ensures traceability back to the Four Blocker worksheet. Understanding what types of observations you are addressing becomes very important when you set up your OKRs to measure forward progress.

Performing this mapping is a great place to start, because it identifies some of the issues that are currently causing problems. It also lets you pressure-test your values: if some observations don't fit under any of the defined values, you may have missed a pertinent value and need to rethink your list. If so, return to the previous step and discuss this situation with the team. There are no right or wrong answers. It is a matter of how you want to define your culture and what is important to your Lean enterprise.

Respect for People	Teamwork	Quality	Empowerment	Visibility & Transparency	Continuous Evolution	Enjoyment
Isolated and inaccessible leadership (IO)	Work is focused on the individual performer; the kaizen team is an island (IO)	Billing inaccuracies and incomplete work result in irate customers (EO)	Problem solving deferred to supervisor (IO)	Staff lacks knowledge around dealership's vision, mission, and values (OAO)	Staff lacks knowledge around dealership's vision, mission, and values (OAO)	Formal conversational style; casual interaction is minimal (IO)
Respect is given on formal power and position (IO)	Command-and-control leadership style; continuous feedback not supported (OAO)	Discounts given to defuse irritated customers (EO)	Staff lacks a sense of urgency and ownership (EO)		Training must be done on days off; discourages continuous learning (OAO)	Service noise level is low; Parts playing country music (IO)
Customer interactions are professional, friendly, and polite (IO)	Siloed and splintered organization; little interaction/teamwork between depts (OAO)	Irate customers venting to each other in the waiting room (EO)	No motivation to greet customers or go the "extra mile" on the customer service side (EO)	Posters denote kaizen progress, supporting visibility and transparency (WEO)	Loan department not offering/selling extended warranties (OAO)	Low job satisfaction; in their work (EO)
Customer conflict resolution is professional and thoughtful (IO)	Service department war room is Lean Central; pillar of teamwork in action (WEO)	No follow-up from sales people regarding service or customer care (OAO)	–	Certifications on the wall are old and out of date (WEO)	Inconsistent appearance of the dealership overall; outdated décor/ high tech equipment looks odd (WEO)	Dealership's tone is solemn and subdued; friendly but disengaged staff (EO)
Compensation/ rewards based on longevity, not performance (OAO)		Cluttered and disorganized service bays; no central storage for parts (WEO)	**Observations Legend** IO = Interactions EO = Emotions OAO = Organizational Aspects WEO = Work Environment		Cramped working conditions; no personal items (WEO)	Dealership doesn't convey vibrancy; bathrooms are in a state of disarray (WEO)
Bonuses are carrot-and-stick approach (OAO)		Intake area full of stains on floors and walls (WEO)			Doors are full of finger-prints; paint is rubbing off door handles (WEO)	
Pay deductions for customer discounts (OAO)						

Figure 8-12. New Horizons Service Department Culture Gap Analysis Worksheet (large format version (https://oreil.ly/leadingLean-figs))

Determining the behaviors and actions needed to close the gap

Next, Lisa and Nancy set about mapping the behaviors and actions listed in Figure 8-13 to their observations under each value to determine their options for possible corrective measures.

Again, there's nothing complicated here. Read each observation entry and assign a behavior and/or action to it, recording its identifier underneath. This time you are not limited to one potential measure. List all that apply. Understand all the options available to you so you can pick the best possible one or the most appropriate combination, based on the results you are seeking.

Behaviors (B)	Action Processes (AP)	Action Methods (AM)
B1: Enterprise Alignment	AP1: Eight Steps to a Lean Culture	AM1: Genchi Genbutsu
B2: Customer-Driven Outcomes	AP2: Lean Enterprise Strategic Planning Process	AM2: Value Stream Mapping
B3: Business-Driven Outcomes	AP3: Objectives & Key Results (OKRs)	AM3: Voice of the Customer (VoC)
B4: Strategic Planning Canvas	AP4: Conversations, Feedback, and Recognition (CFRs)	AM4: Customer Persona Analysis
B5: Investment Strategy	AP5: Toyota Production System (TPS)	AM5: Customer Experience Journey Mapping (CXJM)
B6: Strategic Roadmap	AP6: Toyota Business Practices (TBP)	AM6: Omnichannel Customer Experience Strategy (OCXS)
B7: Minimum Viable Product (MVP) Release Plan	AP7: On-the-Job Development (OJD)	AM7: Design Thinking
	AP8: Scientific Method–PDCA Cycle	AM8: Lean Startup
		AM9: Lean Six Sigma
		AM10: Agile Methods

Figure 8-13. *New Horizons possible behaviors and actions*

Don't be concerned about getting them exactly right, either. Because of the iterative and incremental nature of the PDCA cycle, if you try something and it doesn't render the results you want, you can gather feedback, analyze and learn from it, and then try again. That is the beauty of Lean: trial and error and experimentation are acceptable. Making demonstrable forward progress is better than doing nothing at all, even if you don't get it exactly right the first or second time around. Action puts your destiny squarely in your own hands, where it should be. Taking action to face the challenge head-on is the mark of a Lean leader who pursues perfection by continuously improving.

Lisa and Nancy went through all their options and determined which were most appropriate. Then they transferred the identifiers over to their Gap Analysis Worksheet. The bold notions in Figure 8-14 correspond to the Lean behaviors and actions (processes and methods) identifiers in Figure 8-13. As Figure 8-14 shows, many observations have been assigned multiple behaviors and actions or corrective measures. There are many ways to solve the issues you are facing using Lean behaviors and methods. Some will require proactive corrective measures, such as initiating kaizen teams to specifically address the problem. Others might be resolved by other initiatives currently underway. Lisa and Nancy will determine which situation holds true in the next task, as they define the behaviors and methods they will use to address these issues and problems.

The key takeaway was that they had identified real issues that were standing in the way of living their values. They could address and solve these issues as they worked toward strengthening the dealership's belief system. You can change anything if you have the motivation to do so; nothing is set in stone.

Respect for People	Teamwork	Quality	Empowerment	Visibility & Transparency	Continuous Evolution	Enjoyment
Isolated and inaccessible leadership (IO) **B1 & 3; AP4, 6, & 7; AM1**	Work is focused on the individual performer; the kaizen team is an island (IO) **B3; AP2, 3, 4, 6, & 7**	Billing inaccuracies and incomplete work result in irate customers (EO) **B2; AP2, 3, 4, & 6; AM1**	Problem solving deferred to supervisor (IO) **AP1, 2, 3, 4, & 6; AM7**	Staff lacks knowledge around dealership's vision, mission, and values (OAO) **B1, 2, 3, & 4; AP1, 3, & 4**	Staff lacks knowledge around dealership's vision, mission, and values (OAO) **B1, 2, 3, & 4; AP1, 3, & 4**	Formal conversational style; casual interaction is minimal (IO) **AP1, 3, & 4; AM1**
Respect is given on formal power and position (IO) **B1 & 3; AP1 & 7; AM1**	Command-and-control leadership style; continuous feedback not supported (OAO) **B1; AP2, 3, & 4; AM1**	Discounts given to defuse irritated customers (EO) **B2; AP2, 3, 4, & 6; AM1**	Staff lacks a sense of urgency and ownership (EO **AP1, 2, 3, 4, & 6; AM7**)		Training must be done on days off; discourages continuous learning (OAO) **AP2, 3, & 4**	Service noise level is low; parts playing country music (IO) **B4; AP2 & 6; AM1**
Customer interactions are professional, friendly, and polite (IO) **B1, 2, & 3; AP6**	Siloed and splintered organization; little interaction/teamwork between depts (OAO) **B1 & 3; AP6, AM2 & 7**	Irate customers venting to each other in the waiting room (EO) **B2, AP2, 3, 4, & 7; AM1**	No motivation to greet customers or go the "extra mile" on the customer service side (EO) **AP1, 2, 3, 4, & 6; AM7**	Posters denote kaizen progress, supporting visibility and transparency (WEO) **B1; AP2 & 6**	Loan department not offering/selling extended warranties (OAO) **B3 & 4; AP2, 3, & 6**	Low job satisfaction; in their work (EO) **B2 & 4; AP2 & 6; AM1**
Customer conflict resolution is professional and thoughtful (IO) **B1, 2, & 3; AP6**	Service department war room is Lean Central; pillar of teamwork in action (WEO) **B1, 2, & 3; AP2, 3, 4, & 6**	No follow-up from sales people regarding service or customer care (OAO) **B2 & 3; AP2, 3, 4, & 6; AM1**	-	Certifications on the wall are old and out of date (WEO) **AP2, 3, & 6**	Inconsistent appearance of the dealership overall; outdated décor/ high tech equipment looks odd (WEO) **B2 & 4; AP2 & 6; AM1**	Dealership's tone is solemn and subdued; friendly but disengaged staff (EO) **B2 & 4; AP2 & 6; AM1**
Compensation/ rewards based on longevity, not performance (OAO) **B4; AP2, 3, & 4**		Cluttered and disorganized service bays; no central storage for parts (WEO) **B3; AP2, 3, 4, & 6; AM1**	**Observations Legend** IO = Interactions EO = Emotions OAO = Organizational Aspects WEO = Work Environment		Cramped working conditions; no personal items (WEO) **B2 & 4; AP2 & 6; AM1**	Dealership doesn't convey vibrancy; bathrooms are in a state of disarray (WEO) **B2 & 4; AP2 & 6; AM1**
Bonuses are carrot-and-stick approach (OAO) **B4; AP2, 3, & 4**		Intake area full of stains on floors and walls (WEO) **AP3 & 6, AM1**			Doors are full of finger-prints; paint is rubbing off door handles (WEO) **B2 & 4; AP2 & 6; AM1**	
Pay deductions for customer discounts (OAO) **B4; AP2, 3, & 4**						

Figure 8-14. *New Horizons Service Department Culture Gap Analysis Worksheet (revised) [large format version (https://oreil.ly/leadingLean-figs)]*

Identifying your themes and kaizen teams

Now that Lisa and Nancy had completed the service department's culture gap analysis, they had all the information they needed to identify the themes they must address. They can now identify their teams and name the leads. Do not skip any of these steps. It may be tempting, but the PDCA cycle requires a good bit of planning before you can take purposeful action. Be patient to ensure you thoroughly understand the issues and problems at hand.

Using the two worksheets and chart in Figures 8-12 through 8-14, Lisa and Nancy took their last pass through the Culture Gap Analysis Worksheet (Figure 8-14). This time they were looking for major themes they could use to categorize observations. They arrived at the six themes shown in Figure 8-15. They also added which value each observation came from in blue. This ensured traceability, so that as they move forward, the teams will understand which value they are working on and how the changes they are making will affect the dealership's culture and its budding belief system and associated values.

They realized that some of the observations were already being addressed through other initiatives. They shaded these green so that the teams would not waste time on them. For example, all the items in the last column of "Brand & Reputation" were being addressed through remodeling the dealership. Some items did not require corrective action, such as the last two in the "Customer Service" column. These are actually positive results, achieved by the customer service training Lisa did last month. These improvements will need to be monitored, which can be addressed through the OKR and CFR processes, but no further action is required at this time. Now Lisa and Nancy can form the kaizen teams around these themes.

Leadership Leads: Nancy/Jim	Collaboration Leads: Lisa/Donna	Customer Service Leads: Lisa/Randy	Self-Leadership Leads: Jannie/Rick	Rewards & Recognition Leads: Nancy/Chuck	Brand & Reputation Leads: Lisa/Mary	Brand & Reputation
Isolated and inaccessible leadership (IO) B1 & 3; AP4, 6, & 7; AM1 **Respect for People**	Work is focused on the individual performer; the kaizen team is an island (IO) B3; AP2, 3, 4, 6, & 7 **Teamwork**	No follow-up from sales people regarding service or customer care (OAO) B2 & 3; AP2, 3, 4, & 6; AM1 **Quality**	Problem solving deferred to supervisor (IO) AP1, 2, 3, 4, 6; AM7 **Empowerment**	Training must be done on days off; discourages continuous learning (OAO) AP2, 3, & 4 **Continuous Evolution**	Irate customers venting to each other in the waiting room (EO) B2, AP2, 3, 4, & 7; AM1 **Quality**	Dealership doesn't convey vibrancy; bathrooms are in a state of disarray (WEO) B2 & 4; AP2 & 6; AM1 **Enjoyment**
Respect is given on formal power and position (IO) B1 & 3; AP1 & 7; AM1 **Respect for People**	Formal conversational style; casual interaction is minimal (IO) AP1, 3, & 4; AM1 **Enjoyment**	No motivation to greet customers or go the "extra mile" on the customer service side (EO) AP 1, 2, 3, 4, & 6; AM7 **Empowerment**	Staff lacks a sense of urgency and ownership (EO) AP1, 2, 3, 4, & 6; AM7 **Empowerment**	Compensation/rewards based on longevity not performance (OAO) B4; AP2, 3, & 4 **Respect for People**	Service noise level is low; Parts playing country music (IO) B4; AP2 & 6; AM1	Doors are full of fingerprints; paint is rubbing off doorhandles (WEO) B2 & 4; AP2 & 6; AM1 **Continuous Evolution**
Command-and-control leadership style; continuous feedback not supported (OAO) B1; AP2, 3, & 4; AM1 **Teamwork**	Siloed and splintered organization; little interaction/teamwork between depts (OAO) B1 & 3; AP6, AM2 & 7 **Teamwork**	Billing inaccuracies and incomplete work result in irate customers (EO) B2; AP2, 3, 4, & 6; AM1 **Quality**	Certifications on the wall are old and out of date (WEO) AP2, 3, & 6 **Visibility & Transparency**	Bonuses are carrot-and-stick approach (OAO) B4; AP2, 3, & 4 **Respect for People**	Low job satisfaction; in their work (EO) B2 & 4; AP2 & 6; AM1 **Enjoyment**	Cramped working conditions; no personal items (WEO) B2 & 4; AP2 & 6; AM1 **Continuous Evolution**
	Loan department not offering/selling extended warranties (OAO) B3 & 4; AP2, 3, & 6 **Continuous Evolution**	Discounts given to defuse irritated customers (EO) B2; AP2, 3, 4, & 6; AM1 **Quality**	Staff lacks knowledge around dealership's vision, mission, and values (OAO) B1, 2, 3, & 4; AP1, 3, & 4 **Visibility & Transparency**	Pay deductions for customer discounts (OAO) B4; AP2, 3, & 4 **Respect for People**	Dealership's tone is solemn and subdued; friendly but disengaged staff (EO) B2 & 4; AP2 & 6; AM1 **Enjoyment**	Intake area full of stains on floors and walls (WEO) AP3 & 6; AM1 **Continuous Evolution**
	Service department war room is Lean Central; pillar of teamwork in action (WEO) B1, 2, & 3; AP2, 3, 4, & 6 **Teamwork**	Customer interactions are professional, friendly, and polite (IO) B1, 2, & 3; AP6 **Respect for People**	Posters denote Kaizen progress, supporting visibility and transparency (WEO) B1; AP2 & 6 **Visibility & Transparency**			
		Customer conflict resolution is professional and thoughtful (IO) B1, 2, & 3; AP6 **Respect for People**	Staff lacks knowledge around dealership's vision, mission, and values (OAO) B1, 2, 3, & 4; AP1, 3, & 4 **Visibility & Transparency**			Cluttered and disorganized service bays; no central storage for parts (WEO) B3; AP2, 3, 4, & 6; AM1 **Quality**

Observations Legend
IO = Interactions
EO = Emotions
OAO = Organizational Aspects
WEO = Work Environment

Figure 8-15. *New Horizons Service Department Culture Gap Analysis Worksheet by theme (large format version (https://oreil.ly/leadingLean-figs))*

The observations under "Rewards & Recognition" will need to be addressed by a cross-functional team that includes Human Resources, as well as all the department heads, to ensure that any changes to the compensation and bonus system are fair and equitable across the organization. Nancy suggested that she work with Chuck to lead this team, since he heads the HR department; Jim would also be an integral part of this team. Nancy would also lead the Leadership team with Jim. Lisa decided to take the Collaboration team with Donna, the Customer Service team with Randy (one of the original kaizen team members), and the Brand & Recognition team with Mary, who heads the marketing department at the dealership.

Nancy also thought Jannie was ready to lead a team, so they assigned her the Self-Leadership team, along with Rick (also a member of the original kaizen team). In essence, the leadership paired a sensei/coach with an apprentice who could one day possibly become a sensei/coach as well. This pairing allows the dealership to develop and hone Lean leaders.

Once Jim approved the plan, Nancy communicated it via email to the entire dealership and explained the team assignments, and then she met with the team leads to launch the kaizen teams as soon as possible.

Step 6: Connect Strategy to Execution by Implementing OKRs

Strategy is the keystone of culture. It connects your belief system and values to the actions you need to accomplish as a Lean enterprise, based on the behaviors you define in your CSDM framework. As you execute your mission, you define and shape your culture by identifying what direction you want to go and how you will measure success along the way. As your strategy evolves, so too does your Lean culture.

To create a purpose-driven culture, you must align your organization from top to bottom through a set of overarching objectives defined during the development of your CSDM framework. By explicitly stating what is important to the Lean enterprise, you create your Enterprise True North, establishing a set of corporate guardrails that keep everyone on track. Side trips and detours are kept to a minimum because everyone is focused on executing on your strategic objectives. They understand what is important to the organization, and this creates a motivated workforce that collaboratively works together.

Ambiguity disappears, replaced by purpose and a keen focus on customer and business outcomes, creating perpetual forward momentum that guards against stagnation and corporate extinction. Innovation is also supported and encouraged, because your strategy is aligned with your execution engine, creating enormous competitive advantage. In the end, you have successfully created a culture that is keenly focused on continuous evolution by linking strategy to execution.

Creating a culture of perpetual forward motion

Let's turn back to the Lean enterprise strategic planning process (described in Chapter 6), shown in Figure 8-16. It all starts at the enterprise level, with senior leaders scanning and building an understanding of both their competitive environment and their customers in steps 1 and 2, and then creating three to five strategic objectives in step 3 that define what the organization seeks to accomplish in the next 12 months. In step 4, Lean leaders identify the competitive opportunities: the "how" that, if accomplished, allows them to gain and/or maintain competitive advantage. The opportunities cascade down to the tactical level in step 5, as mid-level managers develop the measurement system in conjunction with the gemba teams. The tactical managers and teams establish key results (KRs) and then toss them back to the enterprise leaders for approval and adoption.

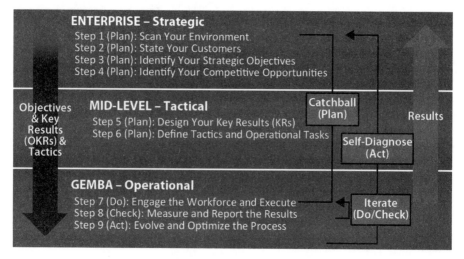

Figure 8-16. *The Lean enterprise strategic planning process*

The tactical plans and operational tasks are created in step 6, providing the mechanism that produces measurable results. When the gemba teams execute in step 7, the Lean enterprise successfully links strategy to execution and ties its beliefs and values to behaviors and actions. Results are measured and reported in step 8 on a regular cadence, which unites the entire Lean enterprise. This creates a healthy, focused, transparent, and high-performing organization with a well-defined culture that has been purposefully designed, implemented, and maintained through a structured strategic-planning and goal-setting process.

Measuring what matters using OKRs

Today, the process of setting strategic themes (determining the corporate direction) and OKRs (defining the results you want to achieve) is used by many well-known organizations, including Google, Yahoo, Intuit, and YouTube. This process originated with Peter Drucker's work in the 1960s, known as Management by Objectives (MBO), evolving into what are now called objectives and key results (OKRs), popularized by John Doerr.[5] Doerr expanded on Drucker's work by adding a component called Conversations, Feedback, and Recognition (CFRs); a mechanism designed to obtain regular feedback during scheduled check-in meetings between a leader/manager and an employee. Drucker identified these elements as being important, but Doerr codified them by adding the CFR element to the process, tying human aspects such as beliefs, values, culture, teamwork, leadership, and continuous performance management together to form a complete, closed-loop goal-setting and continuous performance management system.

Overall, both methodologies are after the same thing: establishing purpose, focus, alignment, contribution, and accountability and traceability regarding who is responsible for accomplishing the stated enterprise objectives. Setting OKRs, conducting CFR check-ins, and then executing on them are built into steps 3 through 9 of the Lean enterprise strategic planning process, as depicted in Figure 8-16. Step 9 represents adjusting and evolving the OKR process through the regular check-in process, established to measure and affirm employees' understanding of the OKRs. If a change in direction is required, the adjustment is made in real time and consistently monitored and measured.

At New Horizons, one of the strategic objectives the service department leadership set was to increase quarter-over-quarter sales. This is the "what" that sets the direction for the department. Then the OKRs combine the competitive opportunities the team identified with the measurable results they are working toward. For example:

- **Strategic Objective #1:** Increase quarter-over-quarter sales
  - **Competitive Opportunity #1:** Perform random service follow-up customer calls
    - **Key Result #1:** Increase service department sales by 2% per quarter
    - **Key Result #2:** Increase service department sales by 20% within the next 12 months

---

5 John Doerr, *Measure What Matters* (New York: Portfolio, 2018).

As you can see, these (plus the rest of the OKRs set in step 5 of Figure 8-9) are specific, measurable, and timebound, and they include hard numbers or targets. If the company increases sales by at least 2% in any given quarter by performing random service follow-up customer calls, then it has hit its target for that quarter in the service department—a measurable outcome. But to accomplish its overall objective for the next 12 months, the service department must increase overall sales by 20% in that period. Although it could meet its target during some of the quarters, the yearly goal may or may not be met. And the increase in sales is explicitly tied to performing the two competitive opportunities in this area that connect value delivery to these business outcomes.

Eureka! We've just answered the age-old question I get a lot: "How do we know if we are creating value?" It is up to senior leaders to create the conditions that enable the organization to realize and deliver value, quarter over quarter and year over year. They must first set expectations through developing strategic objectives and identifying competitive opportunities. Then, they must establish measurable performance goals that align expectations and results. This connects value to effort expended, creating a value-driven culture of achievement.

OKRs create an accountable culture through their interconnected nature. The objectives are a unifying force because it takes everyone in the organization working together to accomplish them. If one person or group does not accomplish their key results, others in the organization also run the risk of not accomplishing theirs, which may cause the entire organization to suffer the consequences. Immense peer pressure is at work—no one wants to be the one who held up the team or even the company from meeting its goals. In this manner, OKRs foster accountability and servant leadership. They inspire people to serve the greater good and accomplish the objectives while taking pride in collectively moving the Lean enterprise forward. This is how the 21st-century Lean enterprise achieves measurable and consistent success: it creates a holistic culture that works to establish and accomplish what it has committed to by throwing its energy into the pursuit of continuous operational excellence, through the consistent application of their OKR process.

Establishing OKRs at New Horizons

The process of setting OKRs at the enterprise and tactical levels, discussed in Chapter 6, is represented in steps 3 through 6 on the New Horizons strategic planning canvas (Figure 8-9), which is a simplified representation for illustrative purposes. In a Lean enterprise, each product line or department, depending on its business/operating model, creates its own OKRs that roll up to the overall enterprise's strategic objectives. At New Horizons, each department head will work with their team, and with other leaders and teams if dependencies between them are identified, to develop their OKRs. Nancy gathered her leadership team and revised their planning canvas to address only the Q1 OKRs, shown in Figure 8-17.

This canvas doesn't yet include any OKRs from the kaizen teams Nancy will lead. Those will be added once they are kicked off to address the cultural issues and problems identified at the dealership. As you can see, the OKRs in step 5 are now much more specific and address only the quarterly tactical plans and operational tasks listed in the Q1 box of the New Horizons service department MVP release plan (refer to Table 8-5). Remember, OKRs are set, monitored, and measured quarterly—the same timeframe used at both the strategic (Table 8-4) and tactical (Table 8-5) levels. Before Q2 begins, Nancy's team will meet again for the next planning cycle to figure out what can be marked complete (green), still in progress (amber), or not started (red) that was planned to start during the last quarter.

Now that Nancy has firmed up her Q1 OKRs, she's transferred them over to her quarterly OKR tracking and monitoring worksheet, depicted in Figure 8-18. This spreadsheet is a great tool for making her expectations known, holding herself and teams accountable, and communicating progress. It is crucial that you name only one person from the leadership team to be responsible for the key results you seek. You have to know who the "go to" person is for questions on progress (or lack of it) during the quarter. Often that leader will have a team to hold accountable for progress against plan as well. In this manner, the objectives cascade down through the organization, rallying the troops around a set of measurable results.

New Horizons Service Department Strategic Planning Canvas – Quarter 1

Date: 06/30/20XX
Iteration #2

Step 1: The Environment

Vision: Dedicated to customers and driven by excellence

Mission: To become the world's most renowned center for customer service in the automotive sector

Value proposition: Easy to buy and obtain service

Competitive Landscape?
We are the only dealer within a radius of 150 miles in the tristate area that sells and services this make of vehicle

Marketplace Challenges & Trends?
Another luxury vehicle competitor is building a dealership 25 miles from us, in the next town over

Step 2: Customer/Persona Identification
1. Luxury sedan owner
2. Sports coupe owner
3. SUV owner
4. Truck owner
5. Van owner

Step 3: Strategic Objectives

SO1: Increase quarter-over-quarter sales by 5%

SO2: Increase the quality of our service to our customers

SO3: Increase the use of technology to effectively run our business

SO4: Modernize our facilities

Step 4: Competitive Opportunities

CO1: Do random service follow-up customer calls

CO2: Perform telephone customer inquiries on lapsed service

CO3: Complete the Service Request Intake process kaizen efforts

CO4: Provide training to the service staff

CO5: Develop a service & repair mobile app

CO6: Upgrade loaner car program system

CO7: Upgrade hardware/décor throughout dealership

Step 5: Key Results (KRs)

SO1/CO1
a. Pilot Follow-up Call Script
b. Make 25 outbound calls/week
c. Set 5 appointments/month
d. Increase sales by 2%

SO1/CO2
a. Pilot Lapsed service Call Script
b. Make 50 outbound calls/week
c. Set 10 appts/month
d. Increase sales by 3%

SO2/CO3
a. Decrease the service Request Error rate by at least 30%
b. Increase NPS by 15%

SO2/CO4
a. Secure the training vendor
b. Complete training
c. Increase NPS by 15%

SO3/CO5
a. Complete 100% of process work
b. Launch 1st release of app

SO4/CO7
a. Complete 100% of Hardware upgrade
b. Compete 100% of Dealership redecorating

Step 6: Tactics
1. After Service Customer Follow-up Call program
2. Service Lapsed Customer Call program
3. Service & Repair Mobile App plan
4. Service Staff Training plan
5. Loaner Car Program System Upgrade plan
6. Dealership Computer Hardware Upgrade

Step 7: Workforce
1. Service Dept & Technology
2. Service Dept & Outside Customer Service firm
3. Loaner Car Dept and Technology
4. Service Dept
5. Service Dept
6. Technology

Step 8: Measure & Report
1. KPI measurements will be complied by the Data Analytics group
2. Frequency will be based on the metric collected, based on the following schedule:
   - #1: Sales quarterly
   - #2: Biweekly
   - #3: Monthly
   - #4: Monthly
3. Metrics results will be posted in the TBP team war room on the fifth day of each month

Step 9: Evolve & Optimize
1. The loaner car program system upgrade will also require all the hardware to be upgraded throughout the dealership
2. The loaner car program's processes also need to be revised/modified, as the system undergoes the planned software update
3. Training will need to be developed and conducted to ensure service Dept staff is up to date on the new processes

Figure 8-17. *New Horizons service department Quarter 1 strategic planning canvas (large format version (https://oreil.ly/leadingLean-figs))*

250

LEADING LEAN

Strategic Objective	Competitive Opportunity	Key Results	Assigned To	Mid	Status (RAG)	Final Grade	Final Status (RAG)
Increase quarter-over-quarter sales	1. Implement a service follow-up customer call program	a. Pilot follow-up call script	Gail	0%		0%	
		b. Make 25 outbound calls/week		0%		0%	
		c. Set 5 appointments per month		0%		0%	
		d. Increase sales by 2%		0%		0%	
	2. Perform telephone customer inquiries on lapsed service	a. Pilot Lapsed Service Call script	Gail	0%		0%	
		b. Make 50 outbound calls/week		0%		0%	
		c. Set 10 appointments per month		0%		0%	
		d. Set 10 appointments per month		0%		0%	
Increase the quality of our service to our customers	3. Complete the Service Request Intake process kaizen efforts	a. Decrease the Service Request Error rate by at least 30%	Jannie	0%		0%	
		b. Increase NPS by 15%		0%		0%	
	4. Provide training to the service staff	a. Secure the training vendor	Donna	0%		0%	
		b. Complete training		0%		0%	
		c. Increase NPS by 15 percent		0%		0%	
	5. Develop a Service & Repair mobile app	a. Complete 100% of process work	Rick	0%		0%	
		b. Release Service & Repair Launch 1st mobile app		0%		0%	
Increase the use of technology to effectively run our business	6. Upgrade loaner car program system	N/A	Donna	0%		0%	
Modernize our facilities	7. Upgrade hardware/décor throughout dealership	a. Complete 100% of hardware upgrade	Randy	0%		0%	
		b. Complete 100% of dealership		0%		0%	

Figure 8-18. *New Horizons service department Quarter 1 OKRs (large format version (https://oreil.ly/leadingLean-figs))*

Ensuring accountability at the gemba level

You can set OKRs at both the team and individual levels, but the deciding factor depends on what type of work the team is performing. What you are looking to foster is teamwork and collaboration. Consider whether the extra overhead of pushing OKRs down to the individual level is worth it. That is your call. In a team environment, everyone is accountable to each other for getting the work done. The team knows who isn't performing, and take it from me, this situation will not go on indefinitely. A day of reckoning will come, and you will not need to intervene. Over time, teams become self-correcting, responding and adjusting accordingly.

As you can see in Figure 8-18, each team and leader is responsible for an objective. This drives accountability, ensuring that everyone understands the objectives and measurement criteria and what is expected to be accomplished during the quarter. The teams typically meet at least once a quarter and at the end to measure progress and report final results. A typical measurement scale, such as the one used at Google and Intel,[6] consists of the following 0 to 1.0 scale:

- Red = 0.0 to 0.3 (We failed to make real progress)
- Amber = 0.4 to 0.6 (We made progress, but fell short of completion)
- Green = 0.7 to 1.0 (We delivered)

Take, for example, Rick's team objective #5: Develop a Service and Repair Mobile App. There are two key results the team is working on this quarter: (5a) complete 100% of the process work, and (5b) launch first release of the Service and Repair Mobile App. The tactical plan for this objective states that the process work will be done by the end of January, and the first measurement is scheduled for February 15. That means the team should complete this work by the mid-quarter checkpoint if they adhere to the schedule. They can register a result across this measurement scale based on progress so far. Measurement is as simple as that.

If the key result was red, scoring 0.3 or less, then Rick would need to discuss how the team is going to complete this work so that it does not jeopardize 5b., which could delay the release of the app. However, they did complete the processes for the app, so they scored it as a 1.0 (green). If at the end of Q1 the team releases the app but finishes only two of the three planned features, falling short on the Loaner Car feature, they would have to score this one a 0.6. The status must be marked as amber, and Rick and the team will need to figure

---

6 Doerr, *Measure What Matters*, 120.

out the likelihood of finishing it in the next quarter. That means the unfinished feature would have to be pushed to the Q2 release to complete the app (Table 8-5), ensuring the planned work stayed in line with actuals.

Determining the practically of developing individual OKRs

Senior leaders need to weigh out the costs and benefits of establishing OKRs with their team members. Though there is some debate as to their effectiveness within a team environment, I think there is a case to be made for setting them at this level.

Things like continuous learning and development that need objectives that must be tracked and measured are perfect for individual OKRs. Take, for example, the observation that the service technicians' certifications are not up to date. An overall service department OKR could be constructed as follows:

- **Strategic Objective #2:** Increase the quality of our service to our customers
  - **Competitive Opportunity #8 (new):** Leverage our auto manufacturer's training to offer and provide superior service to our customers
    - **Key Result #1 (new):** Maintain 100% compliance with service technician certifications each quarter
    - **Key Result #2 (new):** Maintain overall "current" certification status from the auto manufacturer over the next 12 months
  - **Assigned To:** Randy (who manages the service bay in Nancy's department)

At the individual level, each of Randy's technicians would be given a key result for Q1 of "Bring all lapsed training certifications up to date within the next 90 days." Setting this type of objective and defining the opportunity, and then establishing key results that can be tracked and measured, ensures that these crucial training classes will be taken.

Then in Q2, the individual OKR would slightly change to "Obtain/maintain all new/existing training certifications over the next 90 days." Service technicians would then be held accountable for maintaining their own certifications, existing and new. This creates accountability at the individual level for objectives and opportunities that apply to every team member.

Step 7: Conduct CFR Check-Ins to Ascertain Forward Progress

By setting OKRs and continuously measuring progress, your culture evolves in a purposeful manner, based on the objectives you set and the key results you achieve over time. It is a two-pronged approach: OKRs focus on setting priorities and communicating insights, whereas CFRs ensure these have been clearly transmitted to those responsible for achieving them. But what exactly are CFRs?

Conversations

These are held during regularly scheduled check-ins between leaders/managers and employees.

Feedback

This is information given and obtained through bidirectional communication during a formal check-in (as opposed to feedback given during genchi genbutsu) to evaluate progress against goals and discuss any necessary corrective measures.

Recognition

This is positive acknowledgment and reinforcement of an individual's contributions toward general and individual objectives.

Whereas OKRs focus on priorities, CFRs involve understanding and fulfilling basic human wants, needs, and/or desires, such as respect and recognition, encouragement, psychological and emotional comfort, support, safety, and a sense of community through affiliation. CFRs foster and evolve Lean culture by providing purpose, clarity, and feedback.

Lean leaders should hold CFR check-ins with their team members at least once a month. The following items are usually discussed:

- Progress toward existing objectives
- Priorities
- Individual key results
- Personal development items and actions
- Issues and concerns
- Adjustments
- New objectives and key results, if any
- Operational tasks, planned versus actual

Together, OKRs and CFRs replace the outdated annual performance review process with more lightweight and more adaptive quarterly goal-setting and a follow-up process that provides direct, timely, and relevant feedback. You can measure and verify that the objectives have been understood and that your workforce is headed in the right direction. If not, you can make adjustments. By leveraging collaboration and combining it with accountability, you can achieve peak performance throughout the enterprise.

By adding the concept of *pulsing*, or generating feedback through an online survey regularly administered by HR (weekly or monthly), you can quickly generate a snapshot of your current culture. Pulsing helps gauge the organization's health by pushing out a simple survey on a regular basis so that you can react to critical or negative feedback before it festers and becomes a problem.

Conducting CFRs at New Horizons

When Rick held a CFR check-in with Diane, one of the programmers on his team, it emerged that she had underestimated the work required on the service app login feature associated with objective #5 (Figure 8-18). As a result of the dealership's systems being out of date, an upgrade to Active Directory was required before she could move forward, which took more than two weeks. That caused a snowball effect with the other two planned features, and there just wasn't enough time left in the quarter to completely finish the Loaner Car feature. It was almost finished; it just lacked testing. Rich ascertained that completing the testing wouldn't slow the team down that much in Q2. This wasn't the first time the team had to deal with the dealership's old systems; Rick was thankful that Jim had finally prioritized upgrading their systems and had allocated funds to make that happen this quarter (Figure 8-10).

As a result of his conversation with Diane, Rick also spoke with the entire team around doing a systems evaluation as they undertake new projects, to determine the impact their legacy systems would have on this future work. The team brainstormed possible impacts to the features planned for the Q2 release —to address them up front, before they caused any more issues or delays with the Q2 release. In this manner, Rick's check-in with Diane allowed the team to address the issue in real time, through proactive intervention, and it was corrected before it became an even bigger issue.

Step 8: Report Progress and Make Adjustments

At the end of each quarter, all the teams hold a results meeting to report their progress. Jim decided to hold a quarterly First Monday morning key results breakfast meeting, with catered food, before the dealership opened. One by one, each team reported the progress they had made on their OKRs to the entire dealership. If an OKR was missed, the leader stated the reason, along with the adjustments necessary to complete it. The final grades were then posted in the kaizen war room, which acted as great motivation, since no one wanted to see their team's report bleeding red until the next mid-quarter results were posted. Over the next several quarters, the red turned to amber and then to green as the teams settled into the process. This was a big switch, and it took some time for everyone to find their rhythm.

As you can see, all this planning is interrelated. The strategic objectives set at the executive level are converted to competitive opportunities at the executive and tactical levels. At the tactical and gemba levels, they become tactical plans and operational tasks laid out on the strategic roadmap and MVP release plan by due date. The OKRs are set at these levels to measure yearly and quarterly results on an objective and quantitative basis. Adjustments are made through check-ins during the quarter as the work progresses. It's all driven by the organization's culture. Disciplined, successful 21st-century Lean enterprises have realized the power of this process and its effect on creating, maintaining, and sustaining culture. They operate with purpose and accountability that drives them forward to accomplish outstanding quarter-over-quarter and year-after-year systematic results.

Focusing on the Critical Need for Continuous Performance Management

Lean leadership creates a culture in which performance is measured, recognized, and rewarded continually, known as Continuous Performance Management (CPM). CPM turns a subjective process into an objective one through measurable and quantitative analysis that is fairly applied at all levels. Whereas old-fashioned annual or semi-annual performance reviews focus on past performance and results that could be six to twelve months old, CPM's timeframe is just one to three months. It is also much more forward-facing and balanced between current and past achievements, as well as future performance. This is evident in Rick's checking in with Diane: Together they were able to troubleshoot the issue and take corrective action before it was too late. Rick conveyed what he learned to the entire team, who also benefited from their conversation, applying it across the board in his area to ensure they met their Q2 OKRs. Now *that* is powerful stuff!

Understanding the Benefits of CPM

The benefits for the Lean enterprise of CPM that leverages strategic planning, OKRs, and CFRs are wide-reaching and varied. This system provides your workforce with a direct mechanism to participate actively in the achievements the company produces, which is priceless. When priorities are made clear and genuine conversations are had concerning progress, people become engaged and want to contribute continuously, and their enthusiasm becomes contagious. This forms a culture of continuous improvement and Lean thinking that propels the organization forward, creating enormous competitive advantage. Therefore, CPM is a powerful tool that creates the following benefits for the Lean enterprise:

Provides focus and commitment

Senior leaders must force themselves to prioritize, on a quarterly basis, what is important to the organization, taking the guesswork out of understanding and committing to actions. The process provides a way to decide and communicate what really matters, and to mobilize the workforce to focus and achieve results and deliver value, especially in a startup with limited resources. Being scattered across a dozen initiatives will not get you the results you want, because nothing is going to get done. As Andy Groves, former CEO of Intel, once said, "If we try to focus on everything, we focus on nothing."[7] As a Lean leader, you have to focus on the MUST dos, then commit to going after them, to truly make an impact on the Lean enterprise.

Fosters agility and alignment

CPM provides a mechanism to change direction completely in days and weeks, not months and years. If priorities change or a competitive threat arises, you can quickly rework your objectives and cascade them down to the tactical managers to set new key results, playing catchball back and forth with senior leadership, mid-level tactical managers, and the gemba teams until the OKRs are finalized and used to mobilize your workforce. Being able to press the reset button to align the Lean enterprise around new objectives quickly avoids disruption by effectively responding with speed, giving you incredible competitive advantage through nimbleness and alignment.

Encourages empowerment and ownership

Decision-making abilities will be pushed down to those who are closest to the work. When an issue arises, there is no need to go find a supervisor to analyze the situation and make a less informed decision or provide an incomplete solution. Those at the gemba are well-informed Lean leaders who understand the direction the Lean enterprise wants to move in, resulting in well-informed decisions. Everyone understands the strategic direction set by the CSDM framework and explicitly stated through the OKR system. Everyone understands who is responsible for what and the part they play in accomplishing the organization's overall objectives through team and individual ownership and accountability.

Provides transparency and visibility

Everyone understands the future the organization is trying to create through the objectives being set and how they will be accomplished. Everyone knows what everyone else is working on. There are no secrets, and

---

7 Quoted in Doerr, *Measure What Matters.*

progress is monitored and communicated every 45 days. There is no place to hide. CPM also identifies cross-functional dependencies to foster collaboration and eliminate duplication and redundancies, breaking down silos across the Lean enterprise.

Enables self-leadership, purpose, and career growth

People will discover they have a sense of purpose and the latitude to figure out how to lead themselves to success without middle management interference. What you work on becomes your responsibility, creating a sense of direction and purpose. This helps with career growth as people are challenged through continuous learning, feedback, and development.

Provides opportunities to stretch and grow

CPM encourages *moonshots*—going above and beyond what was previously thought possible. Of course, everything can't be a moonshot, but when the organization needs a way to mobilize quickly to fight off a threat, a moonshot might be exactly what is needed. Being able to change direction and be successful is an aspirational goal that any leader would love to be able to accomplish.

Allows for measurement and feedback

The CPM process ensures that objectives are quantifiable, periodically measured, and analyzed to spot trends. It also allows for timely adjustments and course corrections, when needed.

Creates a fair and unbiased rewards and recognition system

Both individual and overall enterprise performance will be accurately assessed on a regular basis. CPM then identifies the appropriate rewards and provides positive recognition to all involved. Today, people want to be acknowledged for their achievements and have their successes celebrated. Even a "Thank you!" goes a long way in encouraging positive performance that quickly becomes habitual.

Seven Things That Must Be True to Develop a Lean Culture

Through my work with Fortune 100 companies as well as with startups, I've identified seven things that must be true. These are crucial to successfully build and maintain a Lean culture.

1. Senior leadership alignment

This is probably the single most important factor when undertaking not just cultural change but any type of change initiative. Cultural change is a top-down effort. Senior leaders must first align on what needs to change, then work through the why and how. Also, they must participate in the change. Your followers are watching how you lead. If a senior leader talks a good game but does nothing to personally change or model the beliefs and values of the culture, it sends the wrong message: "Oh, that change isn't meant for me." Lean leaders are front and center, in leading the charge when it comes to culture.

2. *Visible proponents*

These are a must inside the Lean enterprise. They visibly support your cultural change efforts, from the enterprise level all the way through to the gemba teams. Change that happens with people's participation ends up being lasting and sustainable. It must be just as big a priority for the CEO and board of directors as it is for team leaders and members. Identify change champions who are responsible for encouraging and supporting actions that further support your belief system and values. These could include volunteering in community events, forming permanent departmental kaizen teams to work on continuous improvement projects, or conducting a Voice of the Customer (VoC) analysis to identify customer needs. Visible action is powerful in creating the type of culture you can be proud to be a part of.

3. *Brand alignment*

Your culture must align to your brand, customers, and employees to keep them all in sync in your marketplace. If your company's culture doesn't support customer-first behavior and actions from your employees, you are asking for problems. Remember, the world is small. It is very easy to have your "dirty laundry" go viral through poor customer experiences and low customer satisfaction. Ensure that the culture you are building is consistent with the customer and employee experiences you are trying to create.

4. *Frequent communication*

This is vital to your cultural change efforts. People do not like to be kept in the dark. They become nervous and begin to ask questions and worry about things like job security—another Lean cultural antipattern. Communicate early and often to generate buy-in and ensure everyone is well-informed and working toward the same goals. Your messaging, policies, and procedures must be consistent and not conflict with your beliefs or values. If that occurs, you will be sending mixed messages.

5. *Comprehensive application*

Make sure your cultural change efforts apply to the entire organization. No one person, department, or business unit gets a pass. Your culture must be consistent across the board. *No* exceptions. Subcultures will arise, but they must be consistent and in sync with your overall culture to ensure they do not overtake it and cause damage. Many times this is how cultures get off track over time, as top leaders move on to other positions and are replaced by others who do not have the same beliefs and values. Don't underestimate the power of one person to completely change your culture. When it comes to hiring, look for people who value the same things the company values. You'll end up with loyal employees who want to contribute to your culture.

6. Continuous reinforcement

A consist rewards and recognition program is a must. What you recognize, reward, and celebrate is what you get more of. If you want a stronger improvement culture, celebrate each aspect of your improvement efforts. Be creative to find various ways to sincerely recognize contribution. There is no one-size-fits-all approach. Success breeds success. The more you recognize contributions at every level, the more progress you will make.

7. Focus on the long game

Creating a Lean culture is a journey, not a destination. I often get asked, "How long is this going to take?" This usually comes out of at least one or two senior leaders' mouths, as we are assessing the organization's current culture. I always chuckle. My name may be Jeannie, but I do not live in a bottle, and I cannot fold my arms and blink and make your culture one that embraces Lean. I wish it were that easy, because I'd be a billionaire! Lean must evolve over time through continuous learning, feedback, and improvement with the PDCA cycle. Continuous evolution into new and better forms gets kick-started. Change becomes a behavior that is embraced and supported throughout the entire company. That is the direction you must head in, my friend. When you turn that corner and realize change is inevitable, and you harness it to your advantage by creating a culture of continuous evolution, that is when we will both know you have become a Lean leader that possesses a Lean mindset.

Conclusion

You can purposefully create and evolve your culture. It takes a lot of work, but it is crucial to your corporate survival. You must offer up your vision and define the value you want to create and deliver. That's where it all starts. It springs out of the vision you build, looking to your Enterprise True North, creating purpose, direction, and a track record of success. In the next three to five years, those who don't embrace this philosophy may very well face corporate extinction. Now is the time to step up and lead. Make your mark. Believe that, yes, you can influence your culture. Focus on achieving great things through purpose-driven behaviors. The rest will follow.

Act as a role model. Culture is to leadership as breathing is to human life. Step up and create and maintain a culture that brings your vision to life. Are you up for the challenge? I hope so. The world needs more leaders who are up to meeting this challenge.

CHAPTER 9

Becoming a Self-Led Lean Leader

Your Lean leadership journey must begin with you. Before you can even attempt to lead others, your customers, and the Lean enterprise, you must first develop the ability to lead yourself. Knowing the traits of a self-led Lean leader is one thing; embracing, embodying, and executing on them is another thing entirely. It's going to take conscious effort on your part to become a self-led Lean leader.

In this chapter, I will describe the steps you must execute to develop the skills and abilities of leading the self first, providing a starting point from which you can venture into the other dimensions of the Modern Lean Framework™. You must build a solid foundation that allows you to develop greater proficiency in all dimensions of Lean leadership.

Seven Things That Must be True to Develop Yourself into a Lean Leader

There are seven things you must do to become a self-led Lean leader.

1. *Understand that leaders are both born and made.*

   Are leaders born or made? To me, the answer is a resounding "both!" Yes, you can be born with some of the inherent traits that make you a great Lean leader, but I firmly believe that we all have some inherent leadership abilities that we can develop. Leadership, like many things, is behavioral and is therefore a learned behavior, based on the situations you encounter throughout your life.

Adversity is probably the biggest breeding ground for leadership abilities. When your convictions are tested, Lean leaders rise to the occasion. Facing "your dark night of the soul" is a character-building experience; you can come out the other side much better and more seasoned. Don't think for a minute that you are not a leader just because you don't possess the natural megawatt charisma of John F. Kennedy Jr. or the determination of Teddy Roosevelt. There are many dimensions of leadership. Figure out which ones you naturally possess and the ones you need to develop. Then build your plan and iteratively and incrementally execute on it. Like any craft, leadership requires that you practice, regardless of your natural abilities. Start where you are, but understand that you won't stay there for long when you dedicate yourself to becoming a Lean leader.

2. *Expect some degree of failure.*

This is a tough one, because the word "failure" is usually not part of the type-A overachiever's vocabulary. When you try something new, you are learning, which means there are going to be a few missteps along the way. Learning from your mistakes and making adjustments is all a part of your quest for continuous improvement. Treat the things that don't work as learning opportunities. That means analyzing the situation, discussing it with your sensei, and embracing the goodness that is inherent in this process while leaving the rest behind. Then, adjust and try again. The next time you're faced with the same challenge, you will have learned how to handle it more effectively. Life has a way of pushing the same obstacles into your path in different forms until you have successfully mastered or maneuvered around them. Facing them head-on and putting all your effort behind a successful resolution goes a long way to becoming self-led.

3. *Shift your mindset from training to developing yourself and others.*

No one can "train" leadership abilities into you in a two-day class, regardless of their training abilities. The purpose of classroom training is to create a foundation of understanding and to set the stage for development through imparting some knowledge that you will then go execute on at the gemba. Training, combined with practical application over time, helps you to develop the judgment, wisdom, and ability to truly become a Lean leader. And keep in mind that becoming one is not about your physical age, because being older doesn't always necessarily mean you are any wiser. As they say, "Practice makes perfect," and it is all about how much time and energy you are willing to invest in yourself and others.

Also, it doesn't mean you cannot lead until you become the "expert." If you wait to be deemed one, you will never get off of GO. Lean leaders face challenging situations head on and you will need both the training and on-the-job development (OJD) opportunities to foster and grow your abilities in real time.

4. *Make leadership development an objective, measurable process.*

Developing Lean leaders, like any other process, must be objective and focused on conscious effort and measurable progress. You must set your objectives, define your growth opportunities, establish your key results, and then measure and report your progress (CFRs) diligently and consistently. Take the guesswork out of what success looks like, individually and as part of the Lean enterprise. It is up to you to create a clear picture of what success looks like by clearly spelling it out in your "Personal True North" as well as in the "Enterprise True North" and system of OKRs. What constitutes personal and professional success across the Lean enterprise is not a secret understood only by the chosen few. Ambiguity is replaced by objectivity, transparency, and visibility, and no one can play favorites. Rewards and recognition are based on achieving your Lean leadership and Lean enterprise objectives.

5. *Empower others to lead.*

Leadership is a group activity, and as a Lean leader, you have a responsibility to help others become leaders. It takes a team to achieve great things —a team that is prepared and inspired to act when opportunities present themselves. It takes a team to achieve great things. One that is prepared and inspired to act when opportunities present themselves. And yes, there is both an individual, as well as enterprise nature to it. Developing yourself, as well as serving, mentoring, and teach others is all part of being a Lean leader. It is everyone's responsibility to make the organization profitable by delivering customer value; becoming a truly great Lean enterprise means developing leaders at all levels.

6. *Build a culture that encourages Lean leaders to flourish.*

A company's culture breeds its leaders, as well as attracting leaders from outside. Building a nurturing, supportive, and empowering culture that encourages Lean thinking, experimentation, learning, and continuous improvement can all start with one person modeling the Lean values, behaviors, and actions.

7. *Realize that your system of leadership at every level is a competitive advantage.*

This realization should actually become the driving force to developing yourself, as well as a network of Lean leaders that understand how to respond to disruption through innovation, which is priceless. Developing Lean leaders is not cheap, easy, or fast. Leaders are developed over time through practice and patience; an investment of time, money, and people will be required. Luckily, there is a practical nine-step system to develop Lean leaders iteratively and incrementally: the Lean Leader's Self-Development Process.

This process is the key to unlocking your leadership potential. Let's look at how it works.

Understanding the Lean Leader's Self-Development Process

Becoming a Lean leader is a lifelong journey. It requires mindful effort. First, you must understand your current state: who you are, what you are about, and the skills you currently possess. Next, you must define who you want to become, analyze the gaps, and then purposely develop yourself into a self-led Lean leader in this self-development process. Figure 9-1 outlines the nine steps.

You'll begin by understanding what type of foundation you want to build for yourself. Step 1 entails conducting a current state assessment of your belief system using Q1 of the the Leading Culture dimension of the Modern Lean Framework™ (Figure 8-2) and identifying your "Leading Self" abilities. From there, you will identify the gaps you need to address. Then in step 2, you will work through QII (Figure 8-3), which allows you to establish your purpose and identify your values, finding your "Personal True North." In steps 3 and 4, using your belief system and values as your foundation, you will define your leadership objectives and major growth opportunities to chart your self-development course over the next three to six months.

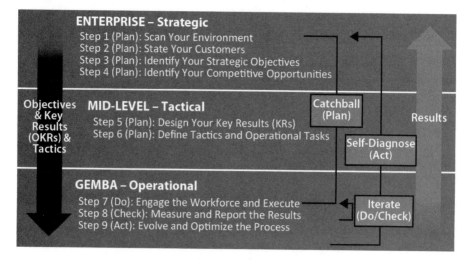

Figure 9-1. *Lean Leader's self-development process*

With these defined, you can identify your KRs and strategic, tactical, and operational behaviors in steps 5 and 6. You'll determine what actions will bring your leadership abilities to life by formalizing your tactical plan and operational tasks in step 6. Finally, you must engage and execute on your plans in step 7 and track progress in step 8, using your OKRs as guardrails as well as conducting CFR check-ins, and measure and evolve as you go, which is step 9. Again, it will be an iterative and incremental process, so don't think this is a "one-and-done thing." It will take multiple iterations, performed on a 90-day basis, to grow and evolve you into a Lean leader. Self-development and learning is a process that is not a destination, but a journey that lasts a lifetime.

Finding Your Sensei

As a Lean leader, you are not an island. You will need an objective, experienced voice to guide you. Look around your workplace and find someone who currently models these Lean leadership behaviors and characteristics. Ask them if they will guide you. If they are truly a Lean leader, they will most likely be happy to help—they are practicing servant leadership, whether they realize it or not. Part of being a Lean leader is helping others grow, learn, and achieve.

If your chosen sensei is willing to help, you might suggest that they read this book before they say yes, to understand what they are committing to, as well as to build a solid foundation for your journey. Don't get discouraged if the answer is no. Not everyone can devote adequate time to this effort, so don't take it personally. Ask again and again, if necessary, until you find your sensei. You will need an objective, questioning individual who can offer second opinions and constructive feedback.

I usually have three to five active, formal sensei/student relationships. I try not to exceed this limit, since you must be willing and able to devote the time when your students need help. Past sensei/student relationships reactivate from time to time, when a former student needs guidance. While working on this book, I got a note from a young developer I mentored a couple of years ago. When we first met, she had just joined the company; her goal was to move from an individual performer into a leadership role at the gemba level within five years. I was very proud of her when I received word that she had just achieved this goal—and I was the first person she thought to tell. The sensei/ student relationship is rewarding on both sides! No matter what your age or experience level, you have something to offer.

Life is about paying it forward. So, no matter what your age or experience level, always remember you have something to offer to others and do not discount this fact. So find that person and make the ask. Explain what you are looking for and how you would like them to help. I usually have the student set the parameters for the relationship, based on how fast they want to move.

My only caveat is that they do the work we discussed in our last meeting before they schedule another session. That puts the responsibility firmly on the student's shoulders to do the work and move the relationship forward. I, as a sensei, cannot do the work for you. This is your journey and you will need to own it.

Nine Steps to Becoming a Self-Led Lean Leader

The first step to becoming a Lean leader, with the help and guidance of your sensei, is to work through and systematically build your Lean leader's self-development canvas, just like the team did for the dealership (Figure 9-2). This canvas serves as your game plan as you move through this process, continuously updating and maintaining it during each of your self-development cycles.

The Lean Leader's Self-Development Canvas

Date:

Iteration #

Step 1: Leading Self Beliefs	Step 3: Lean Leadership Objectives	Step 5: Key Results (KRs)	Step 6: Tactics & Tasks	Step 8: Measure & Report Results	Step 2: Values & Personal True North
1. Believe, Trust, Persistence, & Tenacity: Score_____	1. xx	1. xx	1. xx	1. xx	Values:
2. Healthy Mind & Body: Score_____					
3. Handling Challenges & Bias for Action: Score_____					Vision: xx
4. Problem Solving & Decision-Making: Score_____					
5. Emotional Intelligence: Score_____					Mission: xx
6. Learning & Development: Score_____					
Step 4: Growth Opportunities			**Step 7: Engage & Execute Observations**	**Step 9: Evolve & Optimize**	Value Proposition: xx
1. xx			1. xx	1. xx	

Figure 9-2. *The Lean Leader's self-development canvas*

You will also use it during your sensei/student conversations to ensure you are keeping the important things about your self-development journey in the forefront of both yours and your sensei's minds. This, along with your strategic and Lean leadership objectives and key results (KRs), will keep you on the right path. So, let's begin by tackling Step 1.

Step 1: Assess Your Leading Self Beliefs

The first step is to develop a thorough understanding of your current belief system. Table 9-1 offers suggestions for where to look. It is broken down into six quadrants that match the traits and characteristics discussed in Chapter 3. As you work through each quadrant, you can refer to Chapter 3 as a source for additional probing questions. Remember, this assessment is for you, so be honest with yourself. What you're looking to do is identify areas that require further development.

Table 9-1. Leading Self Beliefs Assessment Six Blocker worksheet

---

Believe, Trust, Persistence & Tenacity Observations

Observe how you exhibit these qualities in yourself or when interacting with others. If no, please state why...do I:

1. Believe and trust in myself?
2. Exhibit persistence and tenacity to experiment and try new things?
3. Possess a positive attitude about failure and try to learn from it, viewing it as a learning experience?
4. Acknowledge my successes in life and give myself credit where it is due?
5. Exhibit persistence when undertaking something new?
6. Stick with things and display tenacity toward not giving up too easily when things don't go my way or exactly as I planned?
7. Practice flexibility and make course corrections as I go?

Handling Challenges & Bias for Action Observations

Observe how you exhibit these qualities in yourself or when interacting with others...do I:

1. Chart my own course and actively plan my future?
2. Not procrastinate and face challenging situations directly?
3. Understand my own reality and practice objectivity?
4. Keep a steady pace in my life and not allow myself to become unbalanced as far as work, home, play, etc.?
5. Face challenges head-on and possess a bias towards action?
6. Keep a level head, not allowing my emotions to get elevated?
7. Acknowledge the fact that I tried, no matter the outcome?
8. Welcome adversity as a way to learn and grow?
9. Display compassion in challenging situations, finding their root causes without judgment?

Emotional Intelligence Observations

Observe how you exhibit these qualities in yourself or when interacting with others. If no, please state why...do I:

1. Effectively manage my emotions, not allowing them to be over- or under exaggerated?
2. Analyze why certain emotions are elicited inside of me when it comes to situations I encounter?
3. Possess a sense of urgency to tackle difficult situations?
4. Have rational, mature, and professional conversations about the cause and effect ramifications of both my and others' behaviors when solving problems and making decisions?
5. Conduct rational evaluations of the decisions I make?
6. Apologize when I am wrong and say thank you to people when I receive their help and support?

Healthy Mind & Body Observations

Observe how you exhibit these qualities in yourself or when interacting with others. If no, please state why...do I?

1. Get enough rest most nights of the week?
2. Exercise on a regular basis?
3. Find "me time" to relax and do the things that I enjoy?
4. Seek to keep chaos and toxic people in my life to a minimum?
5. Practice self-enabling techniques and avoid self-sabotaging situations in my life?
6. Avoid playing the hero to gratify my own ego?
7. Engage in healthy conversations that do not result in drama?
8. Practice reflection and meditation to keep a clear mind?

Problem Solving & Decision Making Observations

Observe how you exhibit these qualities in yourself or when interacting with others. If no, please state why...do I?

1. Apply sound judgment and common sense when faced with a problem/decision?
2. Weigh the cause & effect relationship when I make decisions?
3. Consider how my decisions will impact the greater good from both a moral and ethical perspective?
4. Solve problems and make decisions based on facts vs emotion?
5. Apply common sense when searching for the root cause of a problem?
6. Weigh all the facts before making a decision?
7. Reflect and learn from the outcomes of my decisions?

You can easily create your own six blocker template by taking a 8.5" x 14" (legal-size) piece of paper, turning it horizontally, and dividing it evenly into six blocks. Write the titles on each and then begin to answer the questions contained in the template. It is very important that you do not use any more space than is provided in each block. This is a snapshot, not a novel. Don't worry about getting everything down on paper the first time around. What you are trying to do is identify tangible things you can focus on within a given period, usually three to six months. With each increment you will reassess yourself, because lasting change doesn't happen overnight. It's going to take multiple cycles to effect real and lasting change. Relax and enjoy the journey!

Assessing Jannie Peterson's Leading Self Beliefs

As you'll recall, Nancy served as a sensei to Jannie at New Horizons. As part of her "leading self" development process, Nancy had Jannie complete a six blocker worksheet on her own personal beliefs, shown in Table 9-2.

Table 9-2. Jannie Peterson—Leading Self Beliefs Assessment Six Blocker worksheet

---

Believe, Trust, Persistence & Tenacity Observations

Observe how you exhibit these qualities in yourself or when interacting with others. Overall, I:

1. Generally do believe and trust in myself.
2. Sometimes hesitate when I think about trying something new, due to my strong fear of failure. I know I should be more open-minded and look at it as a learning experience.
3. Do exhibit persistence when I venture out of my comfort zone and undertake something new, sticking with it to follow it through when I have the right support.
4. Need to become more flexible and learn to make course corrections when I encounter challenges. I get somewhat narrow-minded and do not adjust soon enough at times.

Handling Challenges & Bias for Action Observations

Observe how you exhibit these qualities in yourself or when interacting with others. Overall, I:

1. Feel like over the last couple of years, I've lacked direction and have been drifting to some extent. My career has stagnated, and I am reluctant to accept more responsibility at work.
2. Have allowed myself to procrastinate and do not always face challenging situations head-on.
3. Think I am objective, not overly emotional, and consider myself to have a balanced life between work, home, family, play, and social aspects.
4. Display compassion in challenging situations, always working to understand their root causes without quickly jumping to conclusions or making judgment calls.

Emotional Intelligence Observations

Observe how you exhibit these qualities in yourself or when interacting with others. Overall, I:

1. Rely on reason over emotion in dealing with difficult situations.
2. Think my sense of urgency has increased over the last six months to jump in and tackle difficult situations from a logical and rational perspective.
3. Think I conduct myself in a professional and mature manner, always being respectful in my dealings with others.
4. Am prone to admitting when I am wrong, and I probably apologize too much, even when something isn't my fault.

Healthy Mind & Body Observations

Observe how you exhibit these qualities in yourself or when interacting with others. Overall, I:

1. Am very good about taking care of myself. I usually get 7 to 8 hours of sleep at night, exercise at least 3 times a week, and I've recently adopted a gluten-free diet.
2. Enjoy reading, and I've recently started meditating in the mornings, before my first cup of coffee. My husband and I have instituted a Thursday night date night and we do Sunday evening dinners with the kids.
3. Am not interested in playing the hero and enjoy working in a team setting.
4. Keep chaos and drama to a minimum in my life.

Problem Solving & Decision Making Observations

Observe how you exhibit these qualities in yourself or when interacting with others. Overall, I:

1. Believe I am thoughtful in my decision-making and do not jump to conclusions.
2. Look for the root cause and continue to probe until I think I have identified the underlying issue or problem.
3. Have a strong moral compass and take into consideration both the moral and ethical ramifications of my decisions, by weighing out the cause and effect relationship.
4. Solve problems and make decisions based on facts, not emotions.
5. Am reflective and always try and learn from the outcomes of my decisions.

Learning & Development Observations

Observe how you exhibit these qualities in yourself or when interacting with others. Overall, I:

1. Take responsibility for my own development and believe learning is a lifelong pursuit.
2. Actively seek out and learn from those that have more experience so that I can benefit from their counsel and learn from their mistakes.
3. Give freely of my time to coach and assist others.
4. Am taking classes at the community college on leadership.
5. Have a sensei/student relationship to hep Rick develop his abilities as a Lean leader.

Nancy congratulated Jannie on completing this step. While Nancy looked it over, she asked Jannie to score her Lean self-leadership abilities using the Leading Self Beliefs Scorecard (Figure 9-3).

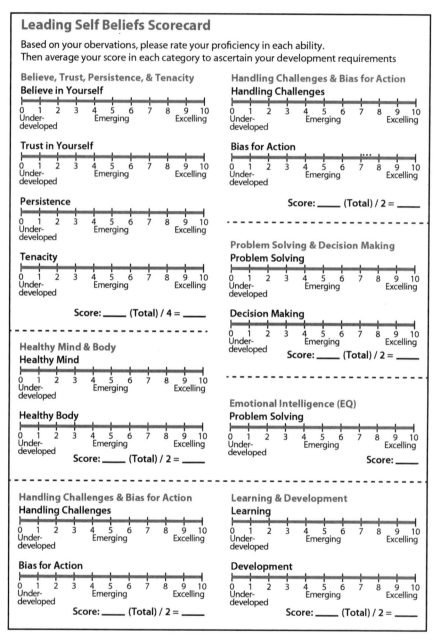

Leading Self Beliefs Scorecard

Based on your obervations, please rate your proficiency in each ability.
Then average your score in each category to ascertain your development requirements

Believe, Trust, Persistence, & Tenacity
Believe in Yourself

0 1 2 3 4 5 6 7 8 9 10
Under-developed   Emerging   Excelling

Trust in Yourself

0 1 2 3 4 5 6 7 8 9 10
Under-developed   Emerging   Excelling

Persistence

0 1 2 3 4 5 6 7 8 9 10
Under-developed   Emerging   Excelling

Tenacity

0 1 2 3 4 5 6 7 8 9 10
Under-developed   Emerging   Excelling

Score: ____ (Total) / 4 = ____

Healthy Mind & Body
Healthy Mind

0 1 2 3 4 5 6 7 8 9 10
Under-developed   Emerging   Excelling

Healthy Body

0 1 2 3 4 5 6 7 8 9 10
Under-developed   Emerging   Excelling

Score: ____ (Total) / 2 = ____

Handling Challenges & Bias for Action
Handling Challenges

0 1 2 3 4 5 6 7 8 9 10
Under-developed   Emerging   Excelling

Bias for Action

0 1 2 3 4 5 6 7 8 9 10
Under-developed   Emerging   Excelling

Score: ____ (Total) / 2 = ____

Handling Challenges & Bias for Action
Handling Challenges

0 1 2 3 4 5 6 7 8 9 10
Under-developed   Emerging   Excelling

Bias for Action

0 1 2 3 4 5 6 7 8 9 10
Under-developed   Emerging   Excelling

Score: ____ (Total) / 2 = ____

Problem Solving & Decision Making
Problem Solving

0 1 2 3 4 5 6 7 8 9 10
Under-developed   Emerging   Excelling

Decision Making

0 1 2 3 4 5 6 7 8 9 10
Under-developed   Emerging   Excelling

Score: ____ (Total) / 2 = ____

Emotional Intelligence (EQ)
Problem Solving

0 1 2 3 4 5 6 7 8 9 10
Under-developed   Emerging   Excelling

Score: ____

Learning & Development
Learning

0 1 2 3 4 5 6 7 8 9 10
Under-developed   Emerging   Excelling

Development

0 1 2 3 4 5 6 7 8 9 10
Under-developed   Emerging   Excelling

Score: ____ (Total) / 2 = ____

Figure 9-3. *Leading Self Beliefs Scorecard*

Jannie would be able to pinpoint the exact areas she needed help with.

Later that afternoon, Jannie and Nancy regrouped to go over Jannie's scorecard. Nancy was glad to see that Jannie was so enthusiastic. Jannie noted that she had been working on her "Handling Challenges & Bias for Action" skills. She said that in the past, she probably would have procrastinated, because this was hard stuff. Being objective and assessing her beliefs, skills, and abilities was eye-opening.

Nancy circled two scores on Jannie's scorecard (see Figure 9-4).

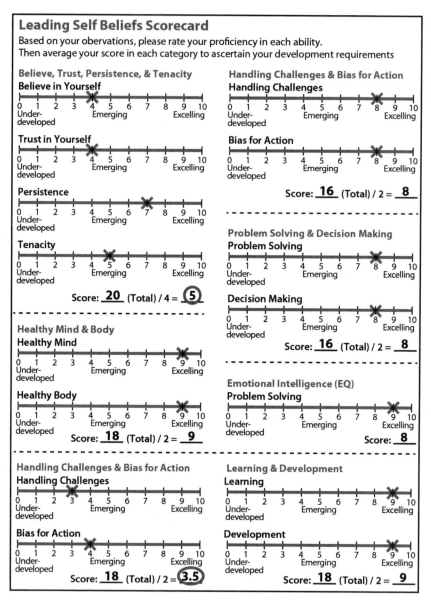

Figure 9-4. *Jannie Paterson: Leading Self Beliefs Scorecard*

Nancy agreed with Jannie's Leading Self-Observations; if they had done the exercise a few months before, she thought, Jannie probably would have scored a little lower in some of these categories.

Jannie agreed that she had been stuck in a rut. She didn't think she was up to the challenge, but Nancy helped invigorate Jannie's belief in herself and in the dealership. Yet Jannie knew she still needed more help in the areas that she and Nancy had identified. Jannie then spent a few minutes transferring her scores to her Lean leader's self-development canvas.

This process uses reflection (or *hensei*, as they call it in Japanese): you sit quietly and contemplate your abilities in each category, recording your observations. This is the qualitative portion of the assessment. Then you quantify your abilities with the scorecard, which pinpoints the most immediate areas for development. As you move forward, you can build specific development activities into your plan to strengthen your skills in these areas.

Step 2: Define Your Values and Purpose

Understanding where you want to go and how you are going to get there is fundamental to success, regardless of whether you are a Lean leader or not. Have you ever wondered why some people excel in life, while others who appear to possess an abundance of potential never quite seem to get going?

My father wanted all his children to go to college. His motivation was to ensure his girls could make it on their own in life. However, I now realize this was *his* dream and not mine, and I had adopted it over the years while I was growing up. So when it came time to enroll in college, it was a given in my mind and not a choice. Don't get me wrong—it was a great dream and motivated me to work hard. I did become self-sufficient! However, when I got out of school, I found myself a bit lost. I I had been so focused on that one goal that I really didn't see much past it. Having achieved it, "What's next?" started to creep into my mind, and panic set in. I needed something new to focus on. Getting a job would be the next logical step, but I didn't want just any job. I needed to redefine myself. How was I going to go about creating my reality as an adult?

Do those words look and sound familiar? They should, because I'm talking about vision and mission again. Your values drive behavior, which keeps you focused on your vision of who you want to become, while your mission defines how you are going to get there. In order to develop your personal vision statement (PVS) and personal mission statement (PMS), you must keep in mind the beliefs and values that drive you as a Lean leader. Both must be measurable and attainable, as well as inspiring, focused, and crystal clear, to be effective.

Building Your Personal True North

Building a "Personal True North" is a crucial step on your journey to becoming a Lean leader, one that cannot be glossed over. Like the self-assessment, this step will not be easy. It's going to take time and thoughtful effort.

The best place to start is with your personal values. What do you truly believe in? Some examples that I would use are honesty, integrity, continuous improvement, and respect for people. All of these are Lean values expressed in Quadrant II of the Leading Culture dimension of the Modern Lean Framework™ (see Figure 8-3 in Chapter 8). But this is about you. Identify three to seven values that matter the most to you. Remember, these values define who you are right now.

A simple and easy way to figure out your personal values is to ask yourself, "What is important to me?" Then brainstorm a list of values that personally resonate with you. If nothing comes to mind, you can review QII (Figure 8-3) as a starting point. Values set boundaries that keep you focused. Keep them in the forefront of your mind.

Misalignment of values causes confusion and uncertainty, because your actions will be out of sync with your servant's heart and Lean mind. Think of a time when you did something that went against your personal belief system and values. Did you feel unsettled? How did that situation turn out? When this happens, unpack it and take responsibility for what is yours. View it as a learning experience, and then move on.

Once you have defined your personal values, everything you do must fit inside these boundaries. If they do not, you are squandering your precious resources, resulting in wasted effort that will not yield the results you are looking for. With your values defined, you can now move on to developing your PVS. Who are you going to work toward becoming over the next three to six months? Ask yourself:

- What is important to me?
- Who do I want to become? What do I want to achieve?
- What motivates and inspires me to act?
- What impact do I want to have on myself? On others?

Review your answers to these questions and draft your PVS. Share it with your sensei and get feedback. Meditate and reflect on it. Rewrite it as many times as needed.

Now that you have created a vision for yourself, how are you going to make it happen? Crafting your PMS expressly states how you are going to accomplish your vision. It helps you to stay aligned with the values that are most important to you. Ask yourself the following questions:

- What do I have to do to bring my vision to life?

- What is the legacy I am trying to create for myself?
- What impact do I want to have on my work/life as a Lean leader?

Again, review your answers and create your first draft. Then share it with your sensei, meditate on it, and revise it until you are happy with it.

The last component of your Personal True North is your personal value proposition (PVP). To give your PVS context, you must now determine what your "value-add" is by executing on your mission. I am always asking my clients and colleagues:

- What outcomes are you after? Why are they important to your overall vision and mission?
- What value are you trying to create through your behaviors and actions?
- If you do these behaviors and actions, will you actually create the value you are looking for?
- What do you need to stop doing/start doing/continue to do to create value?

You'd be surprised at the reluctance I encounter when discussing the last two questions with aspiring leaders. From a Lean perspective, that is the very definition of muda (waste). It all ties back to the outcomes you are trying to achieve. Ask yourself:

- What is important to me?
- What will motivate me to act?
- What are my most pressing needs that I am trying to satisfy?
- What would be the true value I expect to create as a result of executing on my mission?
- What would I say if I had only 30 seconds to justify my value?

You guessed it: rinse and repeat as you did with your PVS and PMS. Then transfer your finished statements to Step 2 of your Lean leader's self-development canvas (Figure 9-2). These three things should not change over the next three to six months, because they represent your Personal True North. If you think a course correction is necessary, discuss it with your sensei.

Developing Jannie Peterson's True North

Jannie spent a week or so working on her initial drafts of her personal values and True North (see Figures 9-5 and 9-6).

Jannie Peterson

MY VALUES
Respect for People
Continuous Improvement
Teamwork
Quality
Mastery
Empowerment
Customer Centricity

Figure 9-5. *Jannie Peterson's values*

**Jannie Peterson
Personal True North**

VISION
To excel at being an exceptional Lean leader
who believes and trusts in herself and who is
committed to self-development, serving others,
and providing high-quality customer service

MISSION
To encourage and empower myself and others
to become the best Lean leaders possible

VALUE PROPOSITION
To courageously lead and empower myself
and others using my Lean mindset so that I face
challenges head-on, build future leaders,
and provide high-quality customer service,
all of which are achieved through my dedication
to continuous improvement, respect for people,
and commitment to teamwork

Figure 9-6. *Jannie Peterson's personal True North*

Jannie shared four values with the dealership: respect for people, teamwork, quality, and empowerment. She also added continuous improvement, customer centricity, and mastery. She chose this last value after her discussion with Nancy about believing and trusting in herself. To Jannie, that translated into empowering herself to master whatever she set out to do. Through this process, she became aware of the connection between her values and her Personal

True North. This was quite a realization: values and True North are closely interconnected. Her personal values also matched up well with the dealership's values, which is the kind of mutually beneficial relationship that creates loyalty and trust.

Jannie decided to focus her PVS on her desire to develop herself into an exceptional Lean leader who believes and trusts in her own abilities. She then used her personal mission statement to expand on the elements of encouraging both herself and others to become the best Lean leaders possible. She would do this by fulfilling her PVP, which focused on the things she needed to improve on.

She showed all of this to Nancy, who applauded her for the insights she had incorporated into her plan. Now they were ready to move on to the next step.

Step 3: Define Your Lean Leadership Objectives

Now it's time to identify strategies to grow into a self-led Lean leader. As we discussed in Chapter 6, strategic objectives are the overarching goals you want to achieve to fulfill your corporate vision. Lean leadership objectives represent the personal results you seek based on your PVP. Everything you do must track back to at least one of these objectives. Otherwise, do not waste your time and energy.

The inputs to this step are your Personal True North (PVS, PMS, and PVP) and your self-assessment scores. For Jannie, the overall value she is trying to create includes:

- Believing and trusting in herself
- Developing confidence and empowerment to face challenges
- Increasing her customer service skills
- Devoting time and energy to learning and self-development
- Developing others through mentoring and coaching

If we translate these into leadership objectives, we arrive at the following for Jannie:

1. Increase my customer service skills
2. Increase my trust in myself and face challenges
3. Dedicate time and energy to self-development and mentoring/coaching others

Having identified her objectives, Jannie is now ready to figure out the growth opportunities required to fulfill them.

Step 4: Identify Your Growth Opportunities

Like competitive opportunities for the Lean enterprise, growth opportunities for the Lean leader increase your skills and abilities and help you accomplish your objectives. A great place to look for growth opportunities is within your current organization. Jannie's dealership just spent a considerable amount of time and energy putting together its strategic planning canvas. Out of that process, she was assigned the following strategic objectives and corresponding competitive opportunities:

- **Strategic Objective #2:** Increase the quality of our service to our customers

  — **Competitive Opportunity #3:** Complete the service request intake process kaizen efforts

  — **Track:** Enterprise

  — **Role:** Team Lead

- **Strategic Objective #2:** Increase the quality of our service to our customers

  — **Competitive Opportunity #8 (NEW: From Culture Assessment):** Leverage our auto manufacturer's training to offer and provide superior service to our customers

  — **Track:** Culture: Self Leadership

  — **Role:** Lead/sensei for Randy

- **Strategic Objective #2:** Increase the quality of our service to our customers

  — **Competitive Opportunity #9 (NEW: From Culture Assessment):** Empower employees to more fully exercise their self-leadership skills and abilities

  — **Track:** Culture: Self Leadership

  — **Role:** Lead/sensei for Rick

These represent Jannie's formal goals and objectives. The first originated from the formal planning process, while the last two were generated out of the culture gap analysis. Jannie can leverage them to create her Lean leadership objectives:

- **Lean Leadership Objective #1:** Increase my customer service skills

  — **Growth Opportunity #1:** Complete the advanced customer service training course

  — **Track:** Self-Leadership Development

— **Role:** Sole Performer

- **Lean Leadership Objective #2:** Increase my ability to believe and trust in myself, facing challenges head-on
  — **Growth Opportunity #2:** Lead the Phase II Service Request Intake Process kaizen team
  — **Track:** Self-Leadership Development
  — **Role:** Team Lead

- **Lean Leadership Objective #3:** Dedicate time and energy to self-development and mentoring/coaching others
  — **Growth Opportunity #3:** Receive on-the-job development coaching/mentoring from Nancy during Phase II Service Request Intake Process project
  — **Track:** Self-Leadership Development
  — **Role:** Sole Performer
  — **Growth Opportunity #4:** Provide mentoring/coaching to Randy and Rick
  — **Track:** Self-Leadership Development
  — **Role:** Sensei to Randy and Rick

Jannie can now turn to developing her KRs accordingly.

Step 5: Develop Your Key Results (KRs)

Jannie worked on her proposed set of OKRs, shown in Figure 9-7.

Nancy thought these OKRs captured everything assigned to Jannie during the strategic planning process. The enterprise OKRs came out of the culture gap analysis conducted across the entire dealership, and Jannie captured her Lean leadership objectives and growth opportunities as well. Moreover, these OKRs looked doable within 90 days; typically, Nancy suggested people keep their OKRs to around five to seven for any given quarter, and Jannie had six.

Objective Type	Objective	Opportunity Type	Opportunity	Role	Key Results	Mid Status (RAG)	Final Grade	Final Status (RAG)
Strategic		Competitive	C3: Complete the Service Request Intake process kaizen efforts	Lead	a. Decrease the Service Request Error rate by at least 30%	0%	0%	
					b. Increase NPS by 15%	0%	0%	
Strategic	S2. Increase the quality of our service to our customers	Competitive/ Culture (Self Leadership)	C8: Leverage our auto manufacturer's training to offer and provide superior service to our customers	Lead/ sensei to Randy	a. Maintain 100% compliance with Service Technician Certifications each quarter	0%	0%	
					b. Maintain overall "Current" certification status from auto manufacturer over the next 12 mos	0%	0%	
Strategic		Competitive/ Culture (Self Leadership)	C9: Empower employees to more fully exercise their self-leadership skills and abilities	Lead/ sensei to Rick	a. Provide TBP training to all service department staff within the next 90 days to enhance problem-solving capabilities and develop a sense of urgency to solve problems/issues	0%	0%	
					b. Provide OJD to the directors inside of the dealership in the next 90 days	0%	0%	
Lean Leadership	L1: Increase my customer service skills	Growth	G1: Complete the advanced customer service training course	Sole Performer	a. Complete the course within the next 30 days	0%	0%	
Lean Leadership	L2: Increase my ability to believe and trust in myself, facing challenges head on	Growth	G2: Lead the Phase II Service Request Intake Process kaizen team	Sole Performer	b. Raise my personal NPS by 10 points in the next 90 days	0%	0%	
					a. Complete phase II within the next 90 days	0%	0%	
					b. Ensure the OKRs remain in Green status in the next 90 days	0%	0%	
Lean Leadership	L3: Dedicate time and energy to self-development and mentoring/ coaching others	Growth	G3: Receive on-the-job development coaching/ mentoring from Nancy during Phase II Service Request Intake Process project	Sensei to Rick/ Randy	a. Execute the four steps of OJD, using PDCA cycle in Q1	0%	0%	
					b. Set OKRs for each within week 1 of Q1	0%	0%	

Figure 9-7. Jannie Peterson's individual first-quarter OKRs (large format version (https://oreil.ly/leadingLean-figs))

Step 6: Define Your Tactics and Operational Tasks

Like the Lean enterprise, Lean leaders need to determine how they are going to go about accomplishing their objectives. Jannie has three objectives and four growth opportunities that tie to the dealership's overall strategic objectives, as well as her own Lean leadership objectives. Remember, Lean leaders are constantly developing both themselves and the Lean enterprise. If one is changing without the other, attrition happens, because the leader's mental dissonance must be rectified. To constantly evolve, you must develop a plan and then work your plan in conjunction with your enterprise's plan.

But how exactly will Jannie ensure her continuous evolution is aligned with that of the organization to which she is connected? The answer to that question is by developing tactical plans and operational tasks that ensure the two stay in sync. It is one thing to say you are going to set out and accomplish your objectives, however without a plan, you will most likely only get mixed results. By putting together a concrete plan with actionable operational tasks, you bring focus to your work and make it visible to your team, manager, sensei, and organization. Progress can be continuously reviewed and course corrections made in real time. "Plan your work and work your plan" is more than just a cliché: it is a Lean reality.

Jannie's tactical plans are shown in Table 9-3.

Table 9-3. Jannie Peterson's individual first-quarter tactical plans

Lean Leadership Objective #1: Increase my customer service skills
Growth Opportunity #1: Complete the advanced customer service training course
A. Complete the course within the next 30 days 1. Register for the course 2. Make travel arrangements 3. Attend the course 4. Pass final exam with a score of 80% or better 5. Present a brief summary of key points back to the service department team
B. Increase NPS by 15% 1. Execute on advanced customer service skills learned during the class 2. Perform customer verification calls one day before service appointment 3. Validate service work to be performed with customer on arrival 4. Review work performed with customer before final billing 5. Perform customer follow-up call three days after service appointment 6. Handle any disputes or unsatisfactory service issues immediately

Lean Leadership Objective #2: Increase my ability to believe and trust in myself, facing challenges head-on

Growth Opportunity #2: Lead the Phase II Service Request Intake Process kaizen team

A. Complete phase II within the next 90 days
1. Conduct TBP effort on Mobile Device processes
2. Work with the technology team to help design the app
3. Perform User Acceptance Testing
4. Perform focus group testing
5. Process any updates/revisions to the app's processes
6. Launch the app

B. Ensure the OKRs remain in Green status for the next 90 days
1. Track progress against plan closely
2. Identify any required course corrections
3. Implement course corrections; Identify/remove impediments for the team
4. Evaluate impact on schedule & OKRs
5. Measure and report progress at mid-quarter and end-of-quarter meetings

---

Lean Leadership Objective #3: Dedicate time and energy to self-development and mentoring/coaching others

Growth Opportunity #3: Receive on-the-job development coaching/mentoring from Nancy during Phase II Service Request Intake Process project

A. Execute the four steps of OJD, using PDCA cycle in Q1
1. Pick a problem with the team (Plan)
2. Divide the work among the team members (Plan)
3. Execute within the boundaries, monitor, and coach (Do)
4. Provide feedback, recognition, and reflection (Act)

Growth Opportunity #4: Provide mentoring/coaching to Randy and Rick

A. Set OKRs for each within week 1 of Q1
1. Assist in setting relevant OKRs
2. Track status and monitor progress

B. Conduct monthly CFRs with both
1. Schedule regular sessions
2. Conduct sessions
3. Provide coaching and feedback on course corrections

Nancy approved of Jannie's proposed plan, but she also stressed that there is really no right or wrong answer here. A tactical plan is really about the planning itself, which gets you working on what you set out to achieve. Writing down your plan helps you crystalize your thoughts and understand how to get results, which becomes a behavioral habit over time. As you break your work down into small pieces, you are conditioning yourself to think iteratively and incrementally, ensuring your plan is manageable. Shooting from the hip isn't the preferred method for a Lean leader.

With Nancy on board, Jannie could now move on to the next step: engage and execute.

Step 7: Engage and Execute

With the initial planning behind you, you are now ready to begin to execute on your tactical plans. This marks the beginning of your achievement cycle: the 90-day window in which you will set out to achieve your objectives and growth opportunities. This step is the "do" in the PDCA cycle. You must be diligent about recording any new observations that arise out of the execution phase. Jannie recorded two observations on her canvas as she began to engage and execute:

1. I will need a backup when I am out during training.

   She did not think about the implications of being gone for two days as she developed her plan. She'll need to update her operational tasks under "G1: Complete the advanced customer service training course" to ensure she has coverage while she is away from the dealership.

2. Since I'll be mentoring both Rick and Randy, I need to schedule time with Nancy to discuss the process.

   This is crucial, because it formalizes the process of her CFRs and OJD leadership coaching with Nancy. She'll need to add a key result under "G3: Provide mentoring/coaching to Randy and Rick."

Overall, by keeping a record of what you add and delete, on your self-development canvas (Figure 9-10), you are honing your planning skills.

Step 8: Measure and Report Results

During the execution phase, you will periodically measure the progress you are making towards your Lean leadership objectives and growth opportunities. Again, keep in mind that this is an iterative process that will repeat itself, based on either the schedule you set with your sensei or the cadence set for the entire Lean enterprise, since you have both strategic and Lean leadership objectives to accomplish in any given quarter. At this level, you are at the gemba, which means you will iterate through Steps 7 and 8 (Do/Check), in the same manner as the Lean enterprise (Figure 9-8).

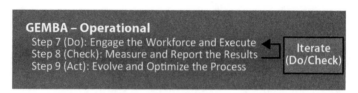

GEMBA – Operational
Step 7 (Do): Engage the Workforce and Execute
Step 8 (Check): Measure and Report the Results
Step 9 (Act): Evolve and Optimize the Process
Iterate (Do/Check)

Figure 9-8. *The gemba Do/Check iterative process*

Measuring results is a must in the Lean enterprise. Establishing measurements and then rigorously measuring, analyzing, learning, and adjusting is at the heart of the iterative Do/Check cycle, which contributes to the overall success or failure of both types of objectives.

At the end of each measurement period, as you analyze your results, course corrections and adjustments are inevitable. As at the enterprise level, the ability to change your mind and chart your course in another direction is built into Lean methods through the continuous feedback and learning cycle. As you iterate through both your strategic and Lean leadership self-development tactical plans, expect them to change and grow.

Life moves fast, and your plans can quickly become obsolete if a new competitive threat or challenge arises in your marketplace. So the Lean enterprise strategic planning process is focused on broadly figuring out what the next 12 months look like on your strategic roadmap. You then work in 90-day increments, synthesizing new information into your plans at the enterprise, tactical, and gemba levels.

The measurement and reporting frequency will depend on the OKRs being tracked, which can be on a daily and weekly basis with Lean leadership objectives and monthly or quarterly with strategic objectives. These progress checkpoints provide an opportunity to adjust. OKRs aren't static. They evolve as needed. If you're setting and forgetting your OKRs, you risk chasing objectives that are no longer relevant and possibly not even worth your time and effort. That is why it is so important to adhere to a regular CFR cadence.

Jim and his leaders set up the following measurement and reporting cadence for New Horizons:

1. Progress will be officially reported twice per quarter.
2. The first checkpoint will be 45 days after the start of the quarter.
3. The second checkpoint will be three days after the end of the quarter.
4. OKR status will be tracked using the dealership's OKR tracking template.
5. Status will be reported using the standard reporting scale in effect at that time.
6. Lean leadership self-development CFRs will be conducted weekly between the student and sensei.

Since this is Jannie's first solo attempt at leading in a Lean manner, she will start out on a weekly cadence, which can always be adjusted. It is always the student's responsibility to schedule these with their sensei. Lean leaders are self-motivated and must be thoroughly invested in their own development.

Step 9: Evolve and Optimize the Process

The last and possibly most important step is to evolve and optimize the process. This means keeping a record of revelations and changes as you move through the current execution phase. Jannie realized pretty quickly that she had not written an OKR about her sensei/student checkpoints. She recorded the missing OKR on her canvas, added it to her first quarter OKRs (Figure 9-9), and updated her tactical plans (Table 9-4).

Objective Type	Objective	Opportunity Type	Opportunity	Role	Key Results	Mid Status (RAG)	Final Grade	Final Status (RAG)
Strategic		Competitive	C3: Complete the Service Request Intake process kaizen efforts	Lead	a. Decrease the Service Request Error rate by at least 30%	0%	0%	0%
					b. Increase NPS by 15%	0%	0%	0%
Strategic	S2. Increase the quality of our service to our customers	Competitive/ Culture (Self Leadership)	C8: Leverage our auto manufacturer's training to offer and provide superior service to our customers	Lead/ sensei to Randy	a. Maintain 100% compliance with Service Technician Certifications each quarter	0%	0%	
					b. Maintain overall "Current" certification status from auto manufacturer over the next 12 mos	0%	0%	
Strategic		Competitive/ Culture (Self Leadership)	C9: Empower employees to more fully exercise their self-leadership skills and abilities	Lead/ sensei to Rick	a. Provide TBP training to all service department staff within the next 90 days to enhance problem-solving capabilities and develop a sense of urgency to solve problems/issues	0%	0%	
					b. Provide OJD to the directors inside of the dealership in the next 90 days	0%		0%
Lean Leadership	L1: Increase my customer service skills	Growth	G1: Complete the advanced customer service training course	Sole Performer	a. Complete the course within the next 30 days	0%	0%	
					b. Raise my personal NPS by 10 points in the next 90 days	0%	0%	
Lean Leadership	L2: Increase my ability to believe and trust in myself, facing challenges head-on	Growth	G2: Lead the Phase II Service Request Intake kaizen team	Sole Performer	a. Complete phase II within the next 90 days	0%	0%	
					b. Ensure the OKRs remain in Green status in the next 90 days	0%	0%	
Lean Leadership	L3: Dedicate time and energy to self-development and mentoring/ coaching others	Growth	G3: Receive on-the-job development coaching/ mentoring from Nancy during Phase II Service RequestIntake Process project	Sole Performer	a. Execute the four steps of OJD, using PDCA cycle in Q1	0%	0%	
					b. Conduct weekly sensei/student sessions with Nancy	0%	0%	
			G4: Provide mentoring/ coaching to Randy and Rick		c. Set OKRs for each within week 1 of Q1	0%	0%	

Figure 9-9. Jannie Peterson's individual first quarter OKRs (revised) [large format version (https://oreil.ly/leadingLean-figs)]

Table 9-4. Jannie Peterson's individual first-quarter tactical plans (revised)

Lean Leadership Objective #1: Increase my customer service skills

Growth Opportunity #1: Complete the advanced customer service training course

A. Complete the course within the next 30 days
1. Register for the course
2. Make travel arrangements
3. Attend the course
4. Pass final exam with a score of 80% or better
5. Present a brief summary of key points back to the service department team

B. Increase NPS by 15%
1. Execute on advanced customer service skills learned during the class
2. Perform customer verification calls one day before service appointment
3. Validate service work to be performed with customer on arrival
4. Review work performed with customer before final billing
5. Perform customer follow-up call three days after service appointment
6. Handle any disputes or unsatisfactory service issues immediately

---

Lean Leadership Objective #2: Increase my ability to believe and trust in myself, facing challenges head-on

Growth Opportunity #2: Lead the Phase II Service Request Intake Process kaizen team

A. Complete phase II within the next 90 days
1. Conduct TBP effort on Mobile Device processes
2. Work with the technology team to help design the app
3. Perform User Acceptance Testing
4. Perform focus group testing
5. Process any updates/revisions to the app's processes
6. Launch the app

B. Ensure the OKRs remain in Green status for the next 90 days
1. Track progress against plan closely
2. Identify any required course corrections
3. Implement course corrections; Identify/remove impediments for the team
4. Evaluate impact on schedule & OKRs
5. Measure and report progress at mid-quarter and end-of-quarter meetings

---

Lean Leadership Objective #3: Dedicate time and energy to self-development and mentoring/coaching others

Growth Opportunity #3: Receive on-the-job development coaching/mentoring from Nancy during Phase II Service Request Intake Process project

A. Execute the four steps of OJD, using PDCA cycle in Q1
1. Pick a problem with the team (Plan)
2. Divide the work among the team members (Plan)
3. Execute within the boundaries, monitor, and coach (Do)
4. Provide feedback, recognition, and reflection (Act)

B. Conduct weekly sensei/student sessions with Nancy
1. **Schedule regular sessions with Nancy**
2. **Conduct sessions**
3. **Implement course corrections**
4. **Provide feedback to Nancy on results**

Growth Opportunity #4: Provide mentoring/coaching to Randy and Rick

A. Set OKRs for each within week 1 of Q1
1. Assist in setting relevant OKRs
2. Track status and monitor progress

B. Conduct monthly CFRs with both
1. Schedule regular sessions
2. Conduct sessions
3. Provide coaching and feedback on course corrections

I hope I have impressed upon you that it is an outdated notion to think that once a plan is developed, it must not be changed—or worse yet, that you must get umpteen approvals to change one thing. This "old school" behavior doesn't even come close to the Lean mindset you are trying to develop. Remember, in the Toyota plant, anyone can pull the cord and stop the line when they identify something that needs to be corrected.

If you need to pull the cord and make a change, bring it to the attention of your sensei, talk through it, and immediately make any necessary course corrections. Also, remember to record the changes in step 7, detailing the catalyst for the change, as well as stating the change you made in step 9. That way you have a record of how your plan grew and evolved during the current cycle.

Summary: Jannie Peterson's Q1 Lean Leader's Self-Development Canvas

Jannie Peterson's first iteration of her Q1 Lean leader's self-development canvas (Figure 9-10) represents a major accomplishment on her road to becoming a Lean leader.

It details how she will go about achieving her leadership objectives and growth opportunities, which will be periodically refreshed and updated over the next 90 days. This canvas includes only her Lean leader self-development objectives, but she is also responsible for strategic objectives and competitive opportunities at the enterprise level. Altogether, she has four objectives and seven opportunities to accomplish her OKRs.

Jannie Peterson's Q1 Lean Leader's Self-Development Canvas

Date: 07/20/20XX
Iteration: 1

Step 1: Leading Self Beliefs

1. Believe, Trust, Persistence, & Tenacity: Score __5__
2. Healthy Mind & Body: Score __9__
3. Handling Challenges & Bias for Action: Score __3.5__
4. Problem Solving & Decision-Making: Score __8__
5. Emotional Intelligence: Score __8__
6. Learning & Development: Score __9__

Step 3: Lean Leadership Objectives

L1: Increase my customer service skills
L2: Increase my ability to believe and trust in myself and face challenges head on
L3: Dedicate time and energy to self-development and mentoring/coaching others

Step 5: Key Results (KRs)

L1/G1.a.: Complete the course within the next 30 days
L1/G1.b.: Raise my personal NPS by 10 points in the next 90 days

L2/G2.a.: Complete phase II within the next 90 days
L2/G2.b.: Ensure the OKRs remain in Green status in the next 90 days

L3/G3.a.: Execute the four steps of OJD, using PDCA cycle in Q1
L3/G3.b.: Conduct weekly Sensei/Student sessions with Nancy

L3/G4.a.: Set OKRs for each within week 1 of Q1
L3/G4.b.: Conduct monthly CFRs with both

Step 4: Growth Opportunities

G1: Complete the advanced customer service training course
G2: Lead the Phase II Service Request Intake Process Kaizen team
G3: Provide mentoring/coaching to Randy and Rick

Step 7: Engage & Execute

Observations

1. I will need to make sure I have a backup when I am out during training
2. Since I'll be mentoring both Rick and Randy, I need to ensure I schedule time with Nancy to discuss the process.

Step 6: Tactics

Please reference the following tactical plans:

1. Advanced customer service training course
2. The Phase II Service Request Intake Process Kaizen project
3. On-the-Job Development coaching/mentoring process for the Phase II Service Request Intake Process project

Step 9: Evolve & Optimize

Add the following KR to the L3G3 opportunity:

b. Conduct weekly Sensei/Student sessions with Nancy
  i. Schedule regular sessions with Nancy
  iii. Conduct sessions
  iii. Implement course corrections
  iv. Provide feedback to Nancy on results

Step: 8: Measure & Report

1. Progress will be officially reported twice per quarter.
2. The first checkpoint is 45 days after the start of qtr while the 2nd checkpoint will be held 3 days after the end of the quarter
3. OKR status will be tracked using tracking template.
4. Status will be reported using the standard reporting scale
5. Lean Leadership Self-Development CFRs will be conducted on a weekly basis between the student and Sensei

Step 2: Values & Personal True North

- Respect for People
- Continuous Improvement
- Teamwork
- Quality
- Mastery
- Empowerment
- Customer Centricity

Vision: To excel at being an exceptional Lean leader who believes and trusts in herself and who is committed to self development, serving others, and providing high quality customer service

Mission: To encourage and empower myself and others to become the best Lean leaders possible

Value Proposition: To courageously lead and empower myself and others using my Lean mindset so that I face challenges head on, and build future leaders, and provide high quality customer service, which are all achieved through my dedication to continuous improvement, respect for people, and commitment to teamwork

Figure 9-10. *Jannie Peterson's Q1 Lean leader's self-development canvas (large format version (https://oreil.ly/leadingLean-figs))*

Conclusion: Committing Yourself to the Modern Lean Leader's Way

Developing Modern Lean leaders requires a two-pronged approach: it must come from within the individual (you), and then it must be nurtured and supported in the right environment (the Lean enterprise). You must be intrinsically motivated to develop and improve yourself, while the enterprise's Modern Lean leaders must provide the conditions and opportunities to grow and evolve future Modern Lean leaders and shape the organization's vision and mission. All of the tools to accomplish both have been systematically laid out and presented in the chapters of this book, which means you have everything at your disposal to evolve into a Lean leader and create your Modern Lean enterprise.

More than anything, I hope that you now feel empowered and have a sense of urgency to take action and commit to the Modern Lean leader's Way. These are the tenets you must commit yourself to as a Modern Lean leader:

- I acknowledge that my main goal is the relentless pursuit of excellence in delivering customer, stakeholder, and company value through the creation of uninterrupted flow and the removal of waste.

- I act with a passionate servant's heart and a disruptive Modern Lean mind to lead myself, others, my customers, stakeholders, and the Lean enterprise through respect for people and continuous improvement.

- I understand that developing my Modern Lean leadership abilities is an iterative and incremental process that must be a conscious journey toward my "Personal True North."

- I possess a strong sense of urgency and a bias toward action in going right to the source of the problem to face challenges head-on.

- I commit to helping others grow and develop as Modern Lean leaders, using teamwork, effective feedback, continuous learning, and self-development.

- I follow the Lean enterprise's True North to guide me in accomplishing its vision, mission, and value proposition to always be creating and delivering customer, stakeholder, and company value.

If you would like to learn more about committing to the Modern Lean Leader's Way and joining a community of like-minded individuals and companies pursuing Modern Lean ways of leading and working, please go to *http:// ModernLeanInstitute.org* or contact us at *info@ModernLeanInsititute.org*.

I wish you all the success in the world on your journey to becoming a Modern Lean leader.

Index

Symbols
3M, 23
5 Whys, 50, 84

A
adversity, 264
agility
    CPM and, 257
    embracing, 19
    importance of, 21
    leadership challenges with, 16-19
alignment (see enterprise alignment)
Amazon, 4, 142
Apple, 17, 162, 192-194

B
bias toward action, 46-47
Blockbuster, 15, 18
BMW, 123-126, 132
    about, 123
    messaging, 124
    OCXS and, 125
brand alignment, 259
brand, creating, 132
British Petroleum (BP), 8
Buddhism, 43
business functions, 119

C
career growth, CPM and, 258
catchball, 153
centralized strategic decision-making
    (CSDM) framework, 141-161
    about, 143-145
    defining tactics/operational tasks,
        153-155
    designing key results, 152-153
    engaging workforce, 156
    executing strategy, 156
    identifying competitive opportunities,
        150
    identifying customer personas, 148
    identifying your strategic objectives,
        149
    Lean culture and, 245
    measuring/reporting results, 156
    process evolution/optimization, 157
    scanning your environment, 147
    steps to creating, 145-161
CFR (Conversations, Feedback, Recognition) check-ins, 247, 253-255
churn rate, 102
CI (continuous improvement), 30, 67
clarifying the problem, 77
CLV (customer lifetime value), 103
collaboration, innovation and, 178
command-and-control styles, 6, 17
commitment, CPM and, 257

common sense
  leading self with, 50
  leveraging for problem-solving and
    decision-making, 49
competence, conscious/unconscious, 25
competitive opportunities, identifying,
  150
conscious incompetence/competence, 25
continuous improvement (CI), 30, 67
continuous interaction of servant leadership, 59
continuous performance management
  (CPM), 256-260
corporate culture (see culture)
cost reduction focus, 9
countermeasures
  applying, 89
  developing, 87-89
  LPC and, 203
  testing, 91
CPM (continuous performance management), 256-260
CSDM framework (see centralized strategic decision-making framework)
culture
  assessing current, 220-224
  defining, 209-211
  in context of Lean enterprise, 211
  leading (see leading culture)
  Lean (see Lean culture)
  Lean enterprise, 211
  motivation and, 210
  transforming, 238-245, 238
culture clash, 226
culture walk, 220
customer acquisition, 102
customer centricity, 7
customer experience (CX), 105-107, 119
customer experience journey mapping
  (CXJM), 115-122
  benefits, 112
  defining scope and objectives, 115
  identifying customer personas, 117
  OCXS and, 132
  prioritizing/implementing improve-
    ment ideas, 122
  publishing/socializing your, 122
  research, 116

  validating, 122
  workshop for, 117-120
customer experience life cycle (CXLC)
  customer personas and, 131
  eight stages of, 106-107
customer experience strategy (CXS), 107
customer journey, 111-122
  mapping, 115-122
  role of emotions in customer experi-
    ence, 113
customer lifetime value (CLV), 103
customer outcome, 140
customer personas, 108-111
  CSDM framework, 148
  CXJM using, 117, 132
  developing relevant, 108-110
  keeping simple, 111
  Lean product canvas and, 199
customer(s), 101-135
  churn rate, 102
  customer experience, 105-107
  customer journey, 111-122
  customer lifetime value, 103
  CXJM, 115-122
  defining, 1
  delivering value to, 2-4
  disruptions through voice of, 184-186
  expectations, 119
  feedback from, 133
  goals, 119
  identifying customer personas,
    108-111
  journey (see customer journey)
  loyalty, 114
  measuring success, 102-105
  net promoter score, 104
  OCXS, 122-134
  personas, 108-111
    (see also customer personas)
  retention, 102
  role of emotions in experience of, 113
  stating, 148
  value determined by, 101
CX (see customer experience)
CXJM (see customer experience journey
  mapping)
CXLC (see customer experience life cycle)
CXS (see customer experience strategy)

cycle time, 12

D

decision-making
  common sense and, 49
  fact-based, 49
detractors, 104
developing others
  leadership challenges and, 14
  OJD for, 96-98
  self-led Lean leaders and, 264
  servant leaders' responsibility to,
    68-73
  serving while, 69-73
digitalization of products/services, 2, 137
disconnected organization, leadership
  challenges from, 11
displaying persistence and tenacity, 53
disruptions for innovation, 179-191
  economy, 181
  importance of, 179
  in customer voice, 184-186
  Lean enterprise, 183
  market/industry, 180
  political climate, 182
  technology, 181
  workforce, 182
diversity
  creativity and, 178
  The Toyota Way and, 31
  valuing, 35, 59

E

economy disruptions, 181
ego, 65
eliminating chaos, 40-42
emails, 191
emotional intelligence (EQ), 6, 52-53
emotions
  assessing, 221
  common sense and, 51
  customer experience and, 113
  facing challenges and, 48
employee-gathered data, 115
empowerment and ownership, 257
engagement, enterprise alignment and,
  138

enlightenment, 44
enterprise alignment
  engagement and, 138
  importance of, 137-139
enterprise wide, leading (see leading
  enterprise wide)
EQ (emotional intelligence), 6, 52-53

F

facing challenges, 47
fact-based decisions, 49
failure, 22
failure, tolerance for (see tolerance for
  failure)
feedback, 98, 254
Ford Production System, 26
frequent communication, 259

G

Gen Xers, 17
genchi genbutsu, 31, 156
Google, 163
growth opportunities, 282-283

H

health, mind/body, 40-46
  eliminating chaos, 40-42
  keeping healthy body, 42
  make time for yourself, 43
  understand your own reality, 43-46
hierarchical structures, 11
hierarchy of needs, 189
human thinking, innovation and, 177

I

incompetence, unconscious/conscious, 25
independent thinking, encouraging, 65
innovation
  case study, 192-194
  collaboration for, 178
  context for, 178
  disruption with, 179
  failure tolerance for, 179
  fostering, 206
  history, 176
  human thinking for, 177

iterative/incremental processes for, 178
leadership challenges and, 12
leading (see leading innovation)
moxie for, 179
qualities of, 177-179
success through, 191-194
innovative/disruptive products and services
design thinking and Lean startup cycle, 194-196
designing/building, 194-204
Lean product canvas, 197-203
New Horizons service/repair mobile device app canvas, 203
inquisitive mind, developing, 64
inside-out approach to value, 3
integrity of servant leadership, 59
interactions, assessing, 221
Internet of Things (IoT), 4, 13, 24
interview data, 114, 186, 188
investment allocation targets, 164-166
investment strategies
developing investment allocation targets, 164-166
developing successful, 162
leading enterprise wide with, 161-166
setting targets for, 163
IoT (Internet of Things), 4, 13, 24

J

journaling, 45

K

kaizen, 31
for leading others, 67
importance of, 7
Lean culture through, 224, 243-245
key results (KRs), 152-153, 283

L

leadership
challenges of (see leadership challenges)
lack of development for, 5
recognizing crisis in, 4
self-led Lean (see self-led Lean leader)

leadership challenges, 5-16
agility as, 16-19
command-and-control styles, 6
cost reduction overemphasis, 9
customer centricity and value delivery, 7
disconnected organization, 11
excessive focus on profit, 8
lack of leadership development, 5
outdated product development practices, 12
outdated workforce development/investment strategies, 14
technological advances, 13
vision/mission/value proposition transparency, 10
leading culture, 209-261
about, 36
assessing current culture, 220-224
CFR check-ins, 253-255
continuous performance management for, 256-260
culture defined, 209-211
implementing OKRs, 245-253
Lean belief system, 224-227
Lean culture, 218-256
report progress/make adjustments, 255
strategic framework creation, 231-237
transforming culture, 238-245
value identification, 227
Leading Culture dimension of the Modern Lean Framework™, 212-217
actions bringing culture to life, 217
identifying beliefs, 214
solidifying beliefs, 216
values in defining culture, 215
leading enterprise wide, 137-173
about, 36
centralized strategic decision-making for, 141-161
endgame in mind for, 140
importance of enterprise alignment, 137-139
investment strategy for, 161-166
MVP release planning, 169-170
strategic roadmap for, 166-168
leading innovation, 175-207

about, 36
continuous learning and, 206
design thinking and Lean startup
  cycle, 194-196
designing/building innovative/disrup-
  tive products, 194-204
examining sources of disruption,
  180-184
fighting off extinction through innovation, 175-179
finding disruption in the voice of your
  customer, 184-186
interative/incremental development,
  204-206
Lean product canvas, 197-203
New Horizons service and repair
  mobile device app canvas, 203
thinking with a disruptive mind,
  179-191
VoC analysis, 186-191
leading others, 57-99
  (see also servant leadership)
  about, 35
  acknowledging your responsibility to
    develop others, 68-73
  kaizen and PDCA cycle, 70
  kaizen mind for, 67
  learning to serve through TBP, 72
  learning to serve while developing oth-
    ers, 69-73
  PDCA and TBP evolution, 71
  respect and, 66
  TBP case study, 73-96
  using OJD to develop others, 96-98
leading outside in, 35, 101-135
leading self, 37-55
  about, 35
  always becoming the student, 54
  believing/trusting through self-
    development, 37-40
  common sense and, 50
  common sense for problem-solving/
    decision-making, 49
  developing a bias toward action,
    46-47
  developing a healthy mind and body,
    40-46
  displaying persistence and tenacity, 53

eliminating chaos, 40-42
emotional intelligence for, 52-53
facing challenging situations head-on,
  47
fact-based decisions, 49
make time for yourself, 43
understand your own reality, 43-46
Lean belief system, 224-227
  culture clash and, 226
  New Horizons, 226
  repetition in, 225
  tools in, 224
Lean culture
  assessing current culture, 220-224
  CFR check-ins, 253-255
  identifying themes and kaizen teams,
    243-245
  implementing OKRs, 245-253
  Lean belief system, 224-227
  report progress/make adjustments,
    255
  requirements for, 258
  self-led Lean leaders and, 265
  steps to, 218-256
  strategic framework creation, 231-237
  transforming culture, 238-245
  value identification, 227
Lean enterprise disruptions, 183
Lean leadership objectives, 281
Lean mindset, 28
Lean product canvas, 197-203
  customer/consumer identification, 199
  problem statement, 198
  product/service development, 202
  product/service roadmap, 201
  target markets, 200
  value identification, 199
Lean servant leadership, 61-66
  building tolerance for failure, 65
  defining, 58
  developing inquisitive mind, 64
  developing True North, 61
  dropping "lone ranger" act, 62
  ego/pride and, 65
  encouraging independent thinking, 65
  importance of, 60
  seeing potential in others, 63

seeing problems as opportunities to improve, 64
seeking out and providing what is needed, 64
Lean thinking, 29
live chat, 190
"lone ranger" act, 62

M

Management by Objectives (MBO), 247
market/industry disruptions, 180
"me time", 43
meditation, 44
mentors, 267
Microsoft, 17
mind, developing healthy (see health, mind/body)
minimum viable product, 196
mission
    creating, 130, 145, 147
    transparency with, 10
Modern Lean Framework™, 21-36
    21st century, 24-26
    continuous evolution, 21-23
    culture, 36
        (see also leading culture)
    dimensions of, 33-36
    enterprise wide, 36
        (see also leading enterprise wide)
    innovation, 36
        (see also leading innovation)
    leading others, 35
    leading outside in, 35, 101-135
    leading self, 35
        (see also leading self)
    Lean mindset for, 28
    Lean thinking for, 29
    Toyota and, 26-32
MTMs (moments that matter), 114
MVP release plan, 169-170
    completing, 169
    New Horizons, 170

N

needs
    fulfillment of, 189-191
    hierarchy of, 189
    prioritizing/categorizing, 188
net promoter score (NPS), 104
Netflix, 15
New Horizons car dealership case study, 73-96
    assessing leading self-beliefs, 271-277
    CFR, 255
    customer outcome and, 140
    customer personas, 109
    CXLC, 112
    gap analysis, 238
    implementing Lean culture, 227
    Lean belief system, 226
    Lean culture, 218-256
    MVP release plan, 170
    OCX mission/vision, 130
    OKRs, 249
    service department culture, 222
    service/repair mobile device app canvas, 203
    setting investment targets for, 165
    strategic framework, 232-237
    strategic planning canvas, 159
    strategic roadmap for, 167
    True North and, 279
NPS (net promoter score), 104

O

objectives and key results (OKRs), 245-253
    creating culture of forward motion, 246
    ensuring accountability, 252
    individual, 253
    measuring what matters using, 247
    New Horizons, 249
OJD (see on-the-job development)
OKRs (see objectives and key results)
omnichannel customer experience strategy (OCXS), 122-134
    brand creation, 132
    build out/revise channel, 132
    building a mindful OCXS, 126-130
    case study, 123-126
    customer feedback, 133
    defining, 123
    identifying CXLC, 131

mapping CXJMs, 132
mission/vision for, 130
personalization with, 128, 133
purchase convenience and, 128
reachability of, 127
service convenience and, 129
simplicity in, 126
steps to, 130-134
strategizing/monitoring/scaling
    throughout, 134
on-the-job development (OJD)
about, 70
case study, 86
division of work among accountable
    team members, 97
execution, 98
feedback/recognition/reflection, 98
importance of, 99
Lean culture through, 224
problem selection, 97
using OJD to develop others, 96-98
online customer reviews, 190
online/offline customer surveys and
    reviews, 189
operational tasks, defining, 153-155
organizational aspects, assessing, 222
others, leading (see leading others)
outside-in perspective to value, 3

P
passives, 104
PDCA (Plan, Do, Check, Act) cycle
clarifying the problem, 77
evolution of, 71
kaizen and, 70
key results and, 157
persistence, displaying, 53
personal mission statement (PMS), 278
Personal Value Proposition (PVP), 279
personalization, OCXS, 128, 133
personas, customer (see customer per-
    sonas)
Plan, Do, Check, Act cycle (see PDCA
    cycle)
PMS (personal mission statement), 278
political climate disruptions, 182
pride, 65

primary needs, 189
problem statement, 198
problem-solving, common sense for, 49
procrastination, 48
product development practice, outdated,
    12
product/service roadmap, 201
profit focus, 8
promoters, 104
purpose, defining, 268-281
    (see also True North)

R
reachability, OCXS, 127
recognition, 98, 254
recorded call data, 191
reflection, 98
repetition in Lean belief system, 225
respect, 31, 32
root cause analysis, 83-86

S
search data, 114
secondary needs, 189
seeing potential in others, 63
self, leading (see leading self)
self-development, 5
believing/trusting through, 37-40
continuous, 54
self-led Lean leaders and, 264
student, 68
self-leadership, CPM and, 258
self-led Lean leaders, 263-295
assessing leading self-beliefs, 269-277
building personal True North, 277
defining purpose/values, 268-281
defining tactics/operational tasks, 285
engage and execute, 287
evolving/optimizing processes,
    289-292
growth opportunities, 282-283
key results, 283
    (see also objectives and key results
    (OKRs))
leadership objectives, 281
make-or-break factor, 277
measuring/reporting results, 287

requirements for, 263-266
self-development for, 266
steps to becoming, 268-292
senior leadership alignment, 258
sensei, 267
servant leadership, 57-99
    becoming a Lean servant leader, 61-66
    characteristics, 59
    defining, 57-66
    importance of, 7, 60
    kaizen and PDCA cycle, 70
    kaizen mind for, 67
    learning to serve through TBP, 72
    origins, 58
    PDCA and TBP evolution, 71
    respecting others with, 66
    responsibility to develop others, 68-73
    serving while developing others, 69-73
    TBP case study, 73-96
    using OJD to develop others, 96-98
simplicity, OCXS, 126
SMART criteria for KRs, 152
social media, 190
Sony Walkman, 162
spirit of challenge, 30
standardizing processes, 94-96
strategic objectives
    definition, 137
    identifying, 149
strategic planning canvas, 159
strategic roadmap, 166-168
strategy, executing, 156
success measurement, 102-105
    churn rate, 102
    customer lifetime value, 103
    net promoter score, 104
survey data, 114

T

tactics, defining, 153-155
target markets, 200
targets, setting, 82, 163
Taylorism, 16
TBP (see Toyota Business Practices)
teamwork, 32, 62
technological advances, leadership challenges from, 13

technology disruptions, 181
tenacity, displaying, 53
tertiary needs, 189
tolerance for failure, 7
    building, 65
    innovation and, 179
    self-led Lean leaders and, 264
touchpoints and emotional responses, 119
Toyota
    Lean mindset and, 28
    Lean thinking, 29
    Modern Lean Framework™, 26-32
    The Toyota Way, 29-32
Toyota Business Practices (TBP)
    breaking down the problem, 78-82
    case study, 73-96
    clarifying the problem, 77
    defined, 69
    developing countermeasures, 87-89
    evolution of, 71
    innovation and, 206
    kaizen and PDCA cycle, 70
    Lean culture through, 224
    learning to serve through, 72
    monitoring results and process, 91-94
    root cause analysis, 83-86
    seeing countermeasures through, 89
    setting targets, 82
    standardizing successful processes, 94-96
Toyota Production System (TPS), 27
The Toyota Way
    continuous improvement, 30
    genchi genbutsu, 31
    kaizen, 31
    pillars of, 29-32
    respect, 32
    respect for people, 31
    spirit of challenge, 30
    teamwork, 32
TPS (Toyota Production System), 27
transforming culture, 238-245
transparency and visibility, 257
True North, 61, 172, 277
trust, 48

U

unconscious competence, 25
unconscious incompetence, 25
understanding your own reality, 43-46

V

value proposition
    Amazon and, 142
    personal, 279
    strategic objectives and, 149
    transparency with, 10
value stream, 11
value(s), 3
    (see also True North)
    defining, 3
    identifying, 199, 227
    leadership challenges, 7
    OCXS and, 131
    servant leadership and, 57
    TBP and, 72
vision
    OCX mission and, 130
    strategic planning canvas and, 145

    transparency with, 10
vision statement, 147
VoC (Voice of the Customer) analysis, 186-191
    analyzing interview transcripts for, 188
    interviews for, 186
    list sorting, 188
    need prioritizing/categorizing, 188
    needs fulfillment, 189-191
    needs hierarchy, 189
    validating findings in, 189
VoC (Voice of the Customer) program, 185

W

websites, analysis of customer behavior on, 190
work environment, assessing, 222
Work in Process (WIP), 47
workforce disruptions, 182
workshops, 119

About the Author

Jean Dahl is a collaborative, outcomes-oriented senior executive, recognized thought leader, speaker, and serial entrepreneur who is passionate about building adaptive and responsive Lean enterprises that exploit change to seize greater and greater levels of agility. She regularly consults with her clients, ranging from Lean startups to corporate giants, to bring a disruptive Lean mindset and Lean thinking to help them continuously evolve in our 21st century global economy and beyond. She is also the executive director of the Modern Lean Institute (*http://www.ModernLeanInstitute.org*), a nonprofit organization devoted to helping the world develop and build Lean leaders through a community of mentors, coaches, and senseis willing to devote their time to helping others become more effective Lean leaders in our disruptive world. Ms. Dahl is also available for corporate speaking engagements and conference keynotes. She can be contacted through the Modern Lean Institute.